T0405515

ON BALANCE

ON BALANCE

ARCHITECTURE AND VERTIGO

LUND
HUMPHRIES

DAVIDE DERIU

First published in 2023 by Lund Humphries

Lund Humphries
Huckletree Shoreditch
Alphabeta Building
18 Finsbury Square
London
EC2A 1AH

www.lundhumphries.com

ISBN: 978-1-84822-621-0

A Cataloguing-in-Publication record for this book is available from the British Library.

Cover: Causeway Bay, Hong Kong, 2014. Photograph by Tom Ryaboi.

Copy edited by Pamela Bertram
Designed by Jacqui Cornish
Proofread by Patrick Cole
Cover design by Paul Arnot
Set in Anton and Mundial
Printed in Estonia

CONTENTS

ACKNOWLEDGEMENTS

This book is the result of an extensive process of research that benefited from a range of different contributions. Over the past decade, I gathered insights into vertigo from numerous persons who generously shared ideas and experiences, helping me to discern the complexities of this phenomenon. Amidst the sheer variety of responses, one thing became clear to me: this issue resonates deeply with a good many people; and yet, it has received surprisingly scant attention within architectural culture. This realisation was a trigger that spurred me to write the book.

On Balance is an outcome of the 'Vertigo in the City' project I lead at the University of Westminster, which was prompted by a series of conversations between the sciences, arts and humanities funded by the Wellcome Trust (2014–15). I am thankful to everyone who has been involved in this collective endeavour, and in particular to Josephine Kane, John Golding and Brendan Walker who lent their knowledge and enthusiasm since its early days. My university has provided me with an academic home throughout the research: the support of the School of Architecture and Cities and the College of Design, Creative and Digital Industries allowed me to bring this project to fruition.

The visual strand of the book draws partly on research conducted at the Canadian Centre for Architecture, where I was a Mellon Fellow on the 'Architecture and/for Photography' programme (2016–17). Further, a British Academy Mid-Career Fellowship (2019–20) enabled me to carry out substantive research and to shape it into book form, as well as to curate the *Falling Away* exhibition in Ambika P3 (2021), together with Michael Mazière. My appreciation goes to everyone who contributed to this event and the related symposium, which informed the final stages of the book. Some of its contents derive from articles I previously published in *Emotion, Space and Society*, *The Journal of Architecture*, and the edited books *Dizziness – A Resource* and *Falling Away*, all of which were thoroughly revised.

Work in progress was presented at several venues, and I benefited in particular from discussions with students and colleagues at the University of Westminster, the Iuav University of Venice and the University of Applied Arts Vienna. My sincere gratitude goes to Iñaki Bergera, André Bideau, Lindsay Bremner, Amy Butt, Valeria Carullo, Maristella Casciato, Harry Charrington, Emilyn Claid, Giuseppe D'Acunto, Richard Difford, Jonathan Hale, Pan Lu, María Auxiliadora Gálvez Pérez, Angelo Maggi, Julie Marsh, Fiona McLean, Barbara Penner, Kester Rattenbury, Virginia Rammou, Michela Rosso, Swinal Samant, Andrew Smith, Douglas Spencer, Alexandra Tommasini, Stephen Walker, Christine Wall, Tom Weaver and Johan Woltjer for their support and advice at various stages of the project.

ACKNOWLEDGEMENTS

I am deeply indebted to David Cunningham, Adrian Forty and Catherine James for their thoughtful comments on the manuscript, and to Catherine Yass for sharing stimulating conversations as well as her artworks. Along the way, I have enjoyed fruitful exchanges with Ruth Anderwald and Leonhard Grond, whose precious insights have made their way into the book. My special thanks go to the ever-patient Clare Hamman for editorial assistance. The book would not have seen the light without the passion of Val Rose, who believed in its value from the start, and of the enthusiastic team at Lund Humphries who oversaw its production.

Picture search was facilitated by the support of several individuals and institutions. I would like to thank Ila Bêka and Louise Lemoine, Chen Chenchen, André Lichtenberg, Chia Ming Chen, Bradley Garrett, Charles Rice, Tom Ryaboi, Nathan Turner and Dimitri Venkov for kindly allowing me to reproduce their images in the book. In addition, I received helpful assistance from the staff at Archivio Gabriele Basilico, Claude Parent Archives, Foster + Partners, Kohn Pedersen Fox Associates, Safdie Architects, One World Observatory, Queen Elizabeth Olympic Park, and from Chris Hilton. Every effort has been made to trace the copyright holders of images included in this book. The publisher would be grateful to be notified of any errors or omissions and will amend them in future editions.

On Balance was written under difficult circumstances amid the COVID-19 pandemic. During this roller coaster of a journey I received the steadfast encouragement of family and friends, and would like to thank in particular Janaína Campoy, Josh Carney, Karine Chevalier, Eray Çayli, Kostis Kornetis, Maria Giovanna Mancini, Mauro Puddu, Annalisa Sonzogni and Asmus Trautsch for helping me to see this project through. The book is dedicated to my parents.

INTRODUCTION

We are beings of gravity.[1]

PROLOGUE

The opening shot of Alfred Hitchcock's *Vertigo* is an unrivalled image of suspense and suspension. The top rung of a fire escape ladder cuts across the frame. Two hands grip the metal bar: a man climbs onto the roof and runs past the camera trailed by policemen, the Golden Gate Bridge stretching across a dusky background. Suddenly, the last man in pursuit, detective John 'Scottie' Ferguson (played by James Stewart), slips down a roof pitch but manages to arrest his fall by clinging to the gutter. His colleague comes to the rescue, yet he too slips – and falls to his death. Aghast, Scottie stares into the abyss of the street. Somehow, he survives, yet the trauma will have a long-lasting impact on his life. The film's conceit is already evoked in the famous title sequence, designed by Saul Bass, where the titular word springs out of a woman's eye as if from a recess of her soul. That is followed by a whirl of animated spirals accompanied by Bernard Herrmann's hypnotic score, which keeps returning to its tonal centre without resolution. As a critic observed: 'The music literally induces vertigo.'[2]

Regarded as one of the greatest films of all time, and undoubtedly one of the most widely discussed by scholars and critics, Hitchcock's cliff-hanger is the cultural artefact most commonly associated with vertigo in the English-speaking world. Throughout, its twists and turns mark the story of a woman who appears to have returned *from among the dead*, as the novel that inspired the director was titled.[3] After the initial rooftop chase, a series of slippages bring Scottie and the female lead, Madeleine Elster (Kim Novak), to fall in time as well as in space – and, of course, in love too. San Francisco's hilly landscape is far more than a mere backdrop to the storyline: it functions as an analogue of the unsettling experiences that trouble the protagonists. The film conveys the feeling of vertigo in all its ambivalence; a sensation of perceptual instability that is related with a wide spectrum of emotional states, ranging from anxiety to exhilaration. Indeed, modern city life is fraught with an array of sensory stimuli that affect our sense of balance. These might be induced by fleeting aspects of the urban environment – traffic, lights, sounds – but also by more permanent features such as tall buildings, suspended structures and uneven surfaces.

Scottie's encounter with the abyss encapsulates the fear of falling from height in dramatic fashion. In *Vertigo*, episodes of dizziness are triggered by the experience of places that are bound either by thin edges (a stair handrail) or by vertical transparency (a tall apartment window). The male protagonist 'freezes' when he stares down the stairwell of a Spanish mission tower while chasing after Madeleine: he recoils in terror from the wooden handrail, powerless to impede her apparent suicide.[4] In order to conjure up the sudden feeling of light-headedness, cinematographer Robert Burks devised a dolly-zoom shot through a mock-up model that has since become known as the '*Vertigo* effect'.

The enduring power of that scene is enhanced by the fact, confirmed by neuroscience research, that climbing a tower remains the most common precipitating stimulus of height vertigo.[5] While the risk of physical harm has prompted the adoption of health and safety measures, feelings of instability are far more difficult to regulate. Indeed, our urban age is marked not only by the rise of tall structures but also by a pervasive sense of disorientation. Although verticality is an ever more conspicuous dimension of cities, however, its perceptual implications are rarely acknowledged.

Historically, the experience of heights is bound up with the advent of urban modernity, a category that has long been used to describe, often in totalising terms, a distinctly Western phenomenon that emerged in the industrial metropolises of North America and Europe. Since the construction of the first skyscrapers in the late 19th century, verticality has been a prevalent dimension of metropolitan life, as high-rise architecture gave form to a Western narrative of progress that is built upon the domination of gravity. As literary historian Paul Haacke points out, fantasies of ascension and collapse went on to permeate various strands of modernism: 'the vertical imagination of modernity has always been accompanied by a certain sense of vertigo'.[6]

Concurrently, the experience of modernity has fed a spatialised lexicon derived from the sense of balance – groundlessness, suspension, freefall – which resonates acutely today. No sooner had the new millennium begun than the tragedy of 9/11 shattered the symbols of global financial power, eclipsing with its sheer actuality the dystopian imagination of falling which had permeated the best part of the 20th century. Nonetheless, the upward growth of cities has continued apace and even intensified over recent decades. The proliferation of 'supertall' and 'megatall' buildings attests to the rise of vertical urbanism as a global paradigm, yet those summits are only the tips of an iceberg that extends to cityscapes the world over.[7]

A greater awareness of 'the remarkable verticalities of our world', to cite Stephen Graham, has emerged in recent years.[8] By heralding a vertical turn, urban scholars have brought to the fore a fundamental dimension of contemporary cities which has sparked new imaginaries as well as built environments.[9] If verticality has been recognised as a prevalent axis of urban life, however, its impact on the perception and representation of space is yet to be fully understood. How does architecture mediate our fear and desire to leave the ground? What kinds of cultural production are elicited by the dizzying rise of cities? And how do various spatial, visual and artistic practices configure the imagination of the abyss?

Vertigo offers a productive category for thinking through these questions. Reflecting on the states of suspension that characterise our urban age, this book probes how architecture is implicated in the perception of balance at a time of profound social instability. Unpacking the concept of vertigo is therefore the first step towards establishing its social and spatial significance.

MAKING SENSE OF VERTIGO

Vertigo is marked by a fundamental duality. At its simplest, it names a whirling sensation associated with a loss of equilibrium: a dizzy feeling that manifests as an illusion of movement, either of the self or of the surrounding environment. This subjective impression may be induced by physical movement as well, typically when we turn around ourselves or when external objects move rapidly around us: whether the sense of rotation is engendered by a real or an illusory motion, the resulting effect can be powerful enough to make us lose our bearings. By analogy, vertigo is also used as a metaphor to describe moral, existential, and social conditions characterised by a sense of disorientation. In its figurative meaning, then, it refers to a 'disordered state of mind, or of things, comparable to giddiness', according to the *Oxford English Dictionary*.

Etymologically the word comes from the Latin *vertere* ('to turn'), which is also the root of vertex ('the highest point' or 'the crown of the head') and the related adjective, vertical. Prior to the Latin coinage, two terms – *ilingos* and *skotodinia* – were used in Ancient Greece to describe feelings of dizziness and disorientation.[10] The former was revived in the mid-20th century by the French scholar Roger Caillois, who put forward the concept of *ilinx* to describe the feeling of excitement induced by play and games that challenge our stability.[11] It is the term vertigo, however, that proved most resilient in modern European languages. In English, it has been employed since the 15th century to describe whirling sensations, yet also general states of bewilderment or confusion. Not surprisingly, this term has enjoyed a growing popularity in modern times; as the Irish writer Richard Steele wrote in the early 1700s, 'All human life's a mere vertigo!'[12]

Hitchcock's film is a vivid reminder that sensations of swimming in the head are habitually associated with the experience of heights. Two other dictionaries offer shorthand definitions of vertigo: 'a feeling of spinning around and being unable to balance, often caused by looking down from a height' (Cambridge); and similarly: 'a loss of balance, or a feeling that things around you are spinning, often because you are in a very high place' (Macmillan). While the first parts of these entries relate to sensations that affect our sense of equilibrium, the second ones allude to their spatial contexts: more specifically, the latter ascribes vertigo to the mere fact of *being* in a high place, whereas the former implies the act of *looking down* as the precipitating cause. It is worth noting that general definitions such as these are at odds with the contemporary medical discourse, in which vertigo is 'a technical label for the symptom of perceptual disorientation, which can be due to a wide variety of causes'.[13] Within medicine, this symptom is linked with disorders of the multisensory balance system and is mostly unrelated to the experience of heights. However, the common association between vertigo and high places is not without reason.

Feelings of disorientation may be caused by a discrepancy between the sensory inputs that our body sends to our brain in order to manage posture and self-motion. As neuroscientist Thomas Brandt points out, these signals are processed by three sensory systems whose integration is essential to maintain an overall sense of balance: 'Vertigo, defined as a displeasing distortion of static gravitational orientation, or erroneous perception of either self or object motion, may [...] be induced by physiological stimulation or pathological dysfunction of any of the stabilising sensory systems: vestibular, visual, and somatosensory.'[14]

This explains why sensations of whirling may occur not only in the presence of underlying pathologies, but also as a result of external conditions that may temporarily affect anyone's equilibrium.

The most common balance disorders, such as positional vertigo and Ménière's disease, are related to impairments of the vestibular system, which is governed by the semi-circular canals of the inner ear. However, symptoms of vertigo may also involve the other sensory apparatuses that preside over our sense of equilibrium: namely the visual (optokinetic) system, which detects our changing position in space through the organs of sight; and the somatosensory system, which registers our posture and motion (proprioception or kinaesthesia) through receptors that are distributed throughout the body. Linking the spinal cord with the cerebral cortex, the central nervous system processes the signals received from these apparatuses, along with the vestibular one, in order to coordinate our balance. Whenever sensory inputs are discordant, our brain detects a danger for the unity of our body schema, hence we may feel a momentary loss of balance that manifests through sensations of whirling, swaying or tilting.

A typical scenario is the experience of high places where the information registered by our proprioceptors does not match the one apprehended by our eyes – for instance, when looking down into the distance while sensing the ground with our feet. Naturally, this kind of perceptual short circuit can lead to varying levels of disorientation, as the resulting sensations derive from a complex set of psychological as well as physiological factors that depend on specific circumstances.[15] We can, nonetheless, begin to draw a connection between the medical notion of vertigo, generically defined as an illusion of movement, and the popular association of this term with the fear of heights.

In fact, 'height vertigo' has long been used to describe physiological sensations derived from the perception of spatial depth: that is to say, the particular type of dizziness that arises when our dynamic sense of vision jars with other sensory systems. Over recent decades, this notion was superseded by a more nuanced understanding of 'visual height intolerance', the term preferred by neuroscientists to distinguish the experience of heights from what is medically considered to be *real* vertigo (a vestibular syndrome).[16] Although preliminary research suggests that about one person in three is affected by this type of intolerance, with higher levels of incidence recorded amongst females and older subjects, the modes and degrees of its manifestation are quite diverse: not only can different places cause dizziness but they can trigger varying responses in the same person over time. The fear of falling derives from a psychological response to the perception of danger that may be exacerbated by anxiety disorders, leading in extreme cases to a height-induced spatial phobia known as acrophobia.

As historian of medicine Claude Perrin observed, the concept of vertigo presents us with an enduring enigma since its meanings vary considerably between the scientific domain and everyday language.[17] Its semantics evolved until a neat distinction between literal and figurative meanings was consolidated, in the late 20th century, when an increasingly detailed taxonomy was introduced within medical discourse. Today, the continuous review of diagnostic tools renders medical terminology rapidly obsolete, making it difficult to compare definitions across time. Thus visual vertigo, of which *height* vertigo is a sub-category, has been replaced by the composite term 'Persistent Postural-Perceptual Dizziness' (PPPD or 3PD), covering a wider set of conditions manifested by similar symptoms.[18]

However, the link between vertigo and high places remains pervasive in popular culture and continues to inform artistic representations. Indeed, the figurative uses of the term alert us to the intrinsic relevance of architecture to our sense of balance, as feelings of disorientation can be triggered by objective factors such as environmental conditions, as well as by subjective ones such as pathologies and predispositions – sometimes in conjunction. And yet, this issue has long evaded architectural research.

BETWEEN THRILL AND ANXIETY

On Balance explores the relationship between architecture and vertigo from a historical-critical perspective. Considering the built environment as a field of embodied experience, it brings to light a pervasive issue that has been overlooked within the built environment professions. The seemingly obvious fact that architecture can be vertiginous is, in fact, a complex and nuanced matter that defies blanket explanations. Owing to its connection with a wide spectrum of psycho-physiological states, the perception of balance pertains to the sphere of pleasure as well as to that of anxiety. This deep-seated tension lies at the heart of the modern urban experience.

Within Western culture, the notion of vertigo has fuelled literary and philosophical narratives of modernity as a condition fraught with seemingly endless possibilities. In the early 20th century, the concept was employed to describe the 'maelstrom' of the metropolis and was appropriated by avant-garde artists who subverted the coordinates of perceptual stability in response to the rapid growth of cities. While the impulse to subjugate gravity is an inherent aspect of modern architecture, in recent decades this challenge has taken up new forms while also prompting an array of creative practices ranging from performance arts to photography and film installations. At the same time, tall structures have been rebranded as popular attractions for adventure tourism. Today, verticality is a powerful drive in the production of urban space, one that elicits a range of pleasures as well as displeasures.

While architectural researchers have long been concerned with the effects of the built environment on the human body and mind, in recent years neuroscience has informed new ways of understanding how our sensory perception is interrelated with space. Zeynep Çelik Alexander, for instance, has explored the forms of 'kinaesthetic knowing' that underpin modernist design culture by excavating the discovery of sensuous (non-discursive) modes of cognition in the mid-19th century.[19] In parallel, the field of architectural phenomenology has also been expanded through developments in neuroscientific research.[20] Harry Francis Mallgrave in particular has reappraised the cognitive engagement with space while highlighting the fundamental links between human consciousness and the sense of spatial orientation.[21] Despite a widespread concern with the experience of space, however, issues of perceptual balance have not received proper attention thus far. The reasons for this neglect are not immediately clear, although the complexity of our psycho-physiological responses to gravity may be counted as a deterrent.

If in medicine vertigo names a symptom associated with a broad aetiology, often presenting doctors with difficult diagnoses, its implications in terms of spatial experience are no less complex and diverse. The spectrum of responses to the experience of height is especially baffling, since even individuals who are accustomed to living or working at altitude can suddenly be affected by dizzy feelings. Indeed, the momentary 'freeze' which paralyses Scottie in *Vertigo* is not unknown to practitioners of extreme sports or high-rise construction workers. In her research about the industrialisation of building in post-war Britain, Christine Wall registered episodes of height vertigo that had a severe impact on workers' lives.[22] In one of her interviews, scaffolder George Garnham recollects what happened to an experienced colleague while working more than 15 metres above ground during the construction of London's Barbican Estate in 1965:

> 'I can't move, George.' He said, 'I've had it.' He said, 'I've got to get down! I've got to get down!' [...] 'Hold on a minute, Ken!' I said, 'Come on, boy!' I said, 'You've been at it long enough, you don't want this to happen.' [...] He said, 'I can't ... I can't get down, boy.' [...] and we had a hell of a job to get him below, and he never did come up no more.[23]

An analogy can be drawn between this real-life anecdote and the fictional story narrated by Hitchcock a few years earlier in *Vertigo*, whose protagonist is haunted by a height-induced trauma and retires from his job. Experiences of vertigo, therefore, throw into sharp relief an oft-neglected aspect of construction that was relevant to post-war Britain where, by the mid-1960s, one social housing block in six was over 20 storeys high. These situations, which are likely to be far more common than the scant available records, have consequences on the welfare of building labourers, adding economic casualties to the toll of injuries and deaths which continues to hit the building sector around the world.

Although the phenomenon of height vertigo has been recorded since antiquity, it became the subject of sustained neuroscience research only in the late 20th century. Concurrently, architects began to design immersive environments that staged the thrill of the abyss. This trend, driven by the imperatives of the 'experience economy', is epitomised by a brand of elevated spaces such as *skywalks*, *skybridges*, *skygardens* and *skyparks*: sundry features with the same heavenly prefix have expanded a lexicon that was dominated for over a century by a single compound word – skyscraper. Although this datum is seldom considered by architects and town planners, the built environment is involved in precipitating sensory conflicts that can impair or distort our perceptual stability. Often reduced to their functional or symbolic values, high-rise buildings play a major role in shaping the emotional landscapes of our cities.

The experience of dizzy heights reflects the precarious equilibrium of contemporary societies. Not for the first time, vertigo provides a metaphor for a moment in which the ground of individual and social lives is shaken. A critical juncture occurred in the late 1950s when a profusion of artworks and architectural projects confronted the perception of balance along with social theories concerned with the very same issue. In the last months of 1957, as Hitchcock concluded the filming of *Vertigo*, the US economy was hit by a recession that had ripple effects around the world. More recently, another moment of vertigo emerged in the second half of the 2000s, when observers strived to define a pervasive condition of insecurity that found its nadir in the global financial crisis. The spiralling effects on societies that were hit with particular severity by this downturn brought about a widespread sense of instability, a 'vertiginous life' characterised by physical as well as existential forms of disorientation.[24]

It was around this time that the sociologist Jock Young revived the metaphor of vertigo as a critical category to describe the precariousness of social life. As he observed, 'Vertigo is the malaise of late modernity: a sense of insecurity of insubstantiality [*sic*], and of uncertainty, a whiff of chaos and a fear of falling.'[25] Indeed, a generalised feeling of giddiness defines a period in which values that previously had a more solid foundation, such as social status and economic position, have become increasingly unstable. As social bonds are loosened, the structure of society is imbued with a sense of insecurity described by Young as 'late modern vertigo'.[26] Other critics have further exposed the effects of neoliberalism on social relations and identities, as an underlying sense of isolation pervades the new 'society of the precarious'.[27]

Meanwhile, the climate emergency has raised a new awareness of the planetary imbalances that define the Anthropocene. Facing the threat of ecological catastrophe, the rise of political nationalisms, mass migration and growing inequalities around the world, Bruno Latour has called for a collective response to the present state of uncertainty: 'To resist this loss of a common orientation, we shall have to *land* somewhere. So, we shall learn how to get our bearings, how to *orient* ourselves.'[28] The French philosopher argues that we need a politics of resistance underpinned by universal human values. In this pursuit of a common ground, he deploys a familiar trope: 'the sense of vertigo, almost of panic, that traverses all contemporary politics arises owing to the fact that the ground is giving way beneath everyone's feet at once, as if we are all felt attacked everywhere, in our habits and in our possessions'.[29]

The way forward to envisage a planet that can be inhabited by everyone requires, for Latour, a paradoxical concurrence: on the one hand, a deeper grounding based on a sustainable relationship with the Earth and, on the other, the integration of individuals within a global community. In order to find a place to land, however, it is necessary to share an appreciation of the common nature we have been deprived of, and to recognise how it has been colonised and dispossessed in ways that undermine the stability of life on the planet. As Latour puts it: 'The new universality consists in feeling that the ground is in the process of giving way.'[30] In other words, a consciousness of the deep imbalances that characterise our age is essential for any meaningful type of collective action aimed at reversing the status quo.

This phenomenon took up new resonance at the dawn of the 2020s, as the COVID-19 pandemic brought about a suspension of life, habits and rights amidst a sharp economic decline. *On Balance* was written at a time when the global health emergency brought large swathes of the population to a near standstill. While metaphors of groundlessness and freefall are invoked to describe these uncertain times, the common feeling of disorientation only exacerbates a pre-existing socio-economic condition. The thin veneer of stability on which neoliberal societies were treading suddenly appears to shatter, bringing about a deep rethinking of globalisation. Seldom was vertigo a more appropriate metaphor for a moment of crisis.

A HISTORY OF THE PRESENT

Against this background, the book reflects on the precarious equilibrium at the heart of contemporary cities, where the drive to conquer ever greater heights has reconfigured our perception of the abyss. It does so through a critical analysis of discourses, practices and representations that variously engage with vertigo. Traversing the visceral and metaphorical expressions of this concept, *On Balance* traces how different subjects experience, challenge and transgress tall buildings and the spaces in between. A historical genealogy is key to appraising how architecture is involved in the production of spaces that induce effects of perceptual instability. By uncovering the ideological basis of this phenomenon, the book suggests how an architectural history of the present – one that foregrounds the role of the body as an agent of social as well as individual experiences – might be written.

While interdisciplinary research is fraught with uncertainties, it can yield unexpected rewards. As Jane Rendell points out, this critical labour is a way of making relations that require a constant questioning of sources and materials before they can be brought together into new constellations.[31] Accepting to navigate uncharted waters implies the recognition of an 'other space' that lies outside the boundaries of one's own discipline: it is right at that critical edge that new theoretical and historical connections can be established. If such an approach is known to generate anxiety, this is particularly apt to the subject matter of the present book. By embracing its ambivalence, however, it might be possible to shed light on the collective as well as subjective implications of balance involved in the experience of space: a fragile condition that can only be grasped by encompassing a wide-ranging body of knowledge.

Structured in three parts, *On Balance* investigates the changing nature of how vertigo manifests in the built environment: from a historical perspective on its literal and metaphorical understanding, through the challenge staged by those looking to overcome spatial boundaries, to a critique of how vertigo has permeated architectural culture until it was commodified around the turn of the 21st century. An eclectic range of medical, philosophical, sociological, cultural, artistic and architectural positions and perspectives are explored in order to tackle this complex subject.

The opening section provides an overview of how the modern discourse on vertigo has informed the sciences, arts and humanities. Chapter 1 traces the current understanding of vertigo to the development of modern medicine in the 18th and 19th centuries, while acrophobia was identified amidst a wider psychopathology of modern space. The analysis of discourse sheds light on the cultural meanings invested in the encounter with the abyss. As vertigo came to reflect the anxiety of modern life, the cliff edge became a recurring trope in Western culture, notably in the work of philosophers such as Søren Kierkegaard, Jean-Paul Sartre and Gaston Bachelard who regarded the loss of bodily equilibrium as an allegory of human existence. Their writings are revisited alongside those of literary authors, from Edgar Allan Poe to W.G. Sebald, who evoked the anguish of falling through metaphors of vertigo.

Chapter 2 moves on to consider how visual artists represent the dizzy space of cities. It revisits the experiments of avant-garde artists of the early 20th century who reconfigured the urban as a field of dynamic vision, while also considering the work of photographers who trained their gazes on the rising American metropolis. The 'new vision' is linked with the work of contemporary visual artists, such as Gabriele Basilico and Catherine Yass, who have engaged with the conditions of vertical urbanism. Their works attest to the power of images in revealing the social, as well as spatial, dimensions of vertigo in the city.

The second part of the book shifts the attention to spatial practices predicated on the mastery of vertigo, namely climbing and wire walking. Chapter 3 focuses on the figure that arguably embodies more than any other the human quest for equilibrium – the funambulist. While 19th-century aerialists such as Charles Blondin enacted the human conquest of nature, their successors went on to challenge the heights of vertical cities. Notably, Philippe Petit built ephemeral bridges in the sky through a unique brand of high-wire performances which culminated in the 1974 coup at New York's World Trade Center: a supreme act of balance whose aura has been magnified by the collapse of the Twin Towers, wrought by the terrorist attacks of September 2001. By neutralising the dangerous effects of *ilinx*, the wire walker reclaims the space between tall buildings while embodying the human desire to inhabit the sky.

Chapter 4 examines climbing as a distinct gravity play that exposes the abyss of modern cities. The practice of mountaineering, whose heyday coincided with that of wire walking, was equally transposed to the metropolis in the 20th century. The Hollywood trope of the 'human fly' epitomised by Harold Lloyd's films illustrates the culture of verticality that emerged in the inter-war period, while the imagery of building workers at heights became integral to the representation of skyscrapers. Then, in the 1970s, skyscraper architecture became a terrain of conquest for climbers intent on transgressing the power structures it embodies, as epitomised more recently by Alain Robert's urban ascents. Further, the chapter discusses how the Urban Exploration movement has asserted the right to the vertical city, leaving in its wake a myriad of vertigo-inducing images.

The final part of the book moves into the realm of architectural culture. Chapter 5 looks at vertigo as a visceral form of amusement and examines how modern construction has been involved in fostering gravity plays that challenge the body's perceptual stability. Since mechanised thrills became regular features of amusement parks, the pursuit of *ilinx* has been a pervasive aspect of urban modernity. High-rise construction partook in the culture of gravity that permeated the long 19th century, as epitomised by pioneering structures like the Eiffel Tower and Ferris Wheel. Subsequently, amusement towers and other devices were deployed at 20th-century exhibits, paving the way for the proliferation of vertiginous attractions that have taken over architecture in recent decades. Since the turn of the millennium, urban environments have been increasingly turned into gravity playgrounds as new and existing buildings alike furnish the stages for visceral thrills.

Chapter 6 charts how different notions of balance underpinned the trajectory of modern architecture over the 20th century. It revisits the tropes of lightness and weightlessness that inspired the air-minded ethos of inter-war modernism, as daring structural acrobatics marked the emergence of a 'new monumentality'. While the impetus to lose the ground remained strong in the post-war period, alternative proposals sought to redesign the human habitat along inclined planes, with other implications of vertigo. A major shift occurred with the advent of postmodern *hyperspace*, as the American hotel atria designed by John Portman in the 1960s and 1970s heralded a brand of immersive environments. The chapter examines how this spatial mutation brought about a new architectural landscape in which the user's sense of balance was strained ever further. As the 20th century drew to a close, critics began to recognise the effects of disorientation elicited by spaces that challenge the stability of perception, hence vertigo came to the fore of architectural discourse.

Finally, Chapter 7 considers how vertigo has become an active principle in the production of space since the turn of the millennium. The design of high-rise urban observatories, in particular, signals the shift from an 'architecture of vision' (derived from the towering gaze that emerged in the 19th century) to an 'architecture of vertigo'. From exclusive infinity pools to ubiquitous glass balconies, a range of features indicate that architecture's edge has been progressively dematerialised, while further demands on perceptual stability are made by see-through platforms that arouse the thrill of vertical transparency. Examples from London, New York, Shanghai and Singapore illustrate how contemporary high-rise structures have reconfigured the abyss as a themed experience. This ongoing trend is embedded in the latest stage of consumer capitalism, whereby the manufacturing of desire multiplies the opportunities for visceral thrills: within the realm of the experience economy, architecture becomes a site for games of vertigo.

Summing up, *On Balance* argues that vertigo is not only an inherently spatialised experience, but one that is bound up with the design and representation of space. Promoting an illusory liberation from gravity, architecture contributes to exorcising the fear of falling that characterises our present condition. Seen through this critical lens, then, the built environment emerges as a contested field that is deeply implicated in our perception of balance. As vertical cities come to increasingly resemble gravity playgrounds, this book orients us through the wealth of spatial thrills, as well as anxieties, that constitute the urban age.

PART I

PICTURING VERTIGO

1

SENSING THE ABYSS

Vertigo is anguish to the extent that I am afraid not of falling over the precipice, but of throwing myself over.[1]

1 Front view of Strasbourg Cathedral, stereograph, 1902.

TROUBLES WITH HEIGHTS

At a time in which high-rise buildings reshape the skylines of cities around the world, it is easy to forget that for several centuries, church towers were the tallest human constructions. Before the Eiffel Tower dwarfed all other structures, at the dawn of the skyscraper age, the pinnacles of European cathedrals, such as those of Rouen and Cologne, were the most prominent urban landmarks. From the early 14th century onwards, Lincoln Cathedral held the record for over 200 years until its central spire collapsed. All the more remarkable is the Cathedral of Our Lady of Strasbourg, whose octagonal tower (the only one completed) reaches a height of 142 metres.[2] Notable episodes of vertigo were recorded on its spire, most famously by Johann Wolfgang von Goethe, who visited Strasbourg in 1771. At the time, Goethe was recovering from a condition that affected his balance: looking down from height made him giddy (fig.1).

The German philosopher confronted this weakness by exposing himself to its very source. He ascended the minster and stood on the open platform atop the spire several times until he overcame his fear; a vertiginous experience he likened to being lifted in the sky by a hot-air balloon. Through sheer repetition, Goethe anticipated today's behavioural therapies based on methods of habituation:

> Such troublesome and painful sensations I repeated until the impression became quite indifferent to me; and I have since then derived great advantage from this training, in mountain travels and geological studies, and on great buildings, where I have vied with the carpenters in running over the bare beams and the cornices of the edifice.[3]

In his essay 'On German Architecture', Goethe described the surprise he felt at his first encounter with Strasbourg Cathedral, whose grandeur he admired as an exemplar of the German art of construction. Contrary to misconceptions of the Gothic style, he did not find the building grotesque but full of dignity and magnificence.[4] The ascents to the spire led him to describe the edifice in a state of suspension, as though it had been a figment of the imagination.[5] Paradoxically, it was this majestic architecture that allowed him to conquer his vertigo.

The association of vertigo with the fear of heights dates back to antiquity.[6] Emotions of dread and anxiety triggered by altitude were described in the foundational text of Western medicine, the *Corpus Hippocraticum*, as well as in the canon of Ancient Chinese medicine.[7] The *Huangdi Neijing* narrates how the Yellow Emperor, or Thearch, suffered from dizziness upon climbing to an observation platform. The account of his kneeling down in order to relieve the symptoms is regarded by neuroscientists as an early recognition of the postural imbalance caused by exposure to altitudes, which is severest when standing.[8]

In modern Western culture, descriptions of height-induced vertigo and the related feelings of anxiety became common in the 18th century, when episodes were reported by authors who felt dizzy while climbing towers. Before Goethe's anecdote, the French physician and philosopher Julien Offray de La Mettrie recounted in his *Traité du vertige* (1737) an attack he had suffered on the tower of the Cathedral of Our Lady, Antwerp, whose Gothic spire reaches a height of 123 metres. In his reflexive observation, La Mettrie suggested that engrams of previous falls were responsible for his dizzy sensations: 'The fear of falling makes our imagination represent objects as they appeared to us every time we fell, that is to say turning around.'[9] Relating his experience of the tower with a disturbance of the retina, the author inferred that this type of vertigo (induced by external causes) was based on the fluidity of spirits in the human body and that its intensity would be proportional to the imagined danger. While his intuitive correlation was later disproved by science, this early treatise laid out an understanding of vertigo that was bound to have a lasting legacy.[10]

La Mettrie's work exemplifies a wealth of anecdotal evidence that is scattered across the literature of the 18th and 19th centuries, when the psycho-physiological responses to the experience of high places piqued the interest of medical writers. Another significant contribution was made by Erasmus Darwin, a polymath whose work had an influence on his grandson's theory of evolution. Darwin's *Zoonomia; or, the Laws of Organic Life* (1794) set a milestone in the history of modern medicine. This seminal treatise includes a chapter dedicated to 'the disease called vertigo or dizziness', situated between sections on other aspects of organic life such as reverie and drunkenness. Similarly to La Mettrie, Darwin considered this 'disease' an impairment of vision, or *vertigo visualis*. He explained how sight is involved in the sense of balance and noted that humans perceive their upright posture in relation to the perpendicularity of other objects. His observations of bodily movements, ranging from children spinning around to the 'swift gyrations' performed by Turkish dervishes, paved the way for scientific studies of posture and balance.[11] The experience of heights is described in a vivid passage of *Zoonomia*:

> Any one, who stands alone on the top of a high tower, if he has not been accustomed to balance himself by objects placed at such distances and

> with such inclinations, begins to stagger, and endeavours to recover himself by his muscular feelings. During this time the apparent motion of objects at a distance below him is very great, and the impressions of these apparent motions continue a little time after he has experienced them; and he is persuaded to incline the contrary way to counteract their effects; and either immediately falls, or applying his hands to the building, uses his muscular feelings to preserve his perpendicular attitude, contrary to the erroneous persuasions of his eyes.[12]

This momentary sense of instability was followed by a paralysing fear. Although Darwin's writing was caught up in the language of imagination and metaphors that preceded the rationalisation of medical discourse, his account of the high tower episode drew important connections between somatic and psychic symptoms. However, it took nearly two centuries before the phenomenon of height vertigo was scientifically investigated by neuroscientists as an instance of visual vertigo.

VERTIGO AND ACROPHOBIA

From the Renaissance onwards, medical writers ascribed the feeling of vertigo to various causes ranging from the presence of vapours in the brain to the movement of 'animal spirits in the head'.[13] The illusion of movement continued to puzzle scientists into the 19th century, when it was widely regarded as a symptom of mental health disorders and often dismissed as a mere hallucination.[14] In the early literature on phrenology, vertigo was listed among the 'diseases of the brain', and Johann Gaspar Spurzheim, for instance, described it as 'an illusory rotation of all objects around us, and of ourselves, with a fear of falling'.[15]

However, it was only in the second half of the 19th century that the physiology of the vestibular system came to be known. French otolaryngologist Prosper Ménière was the first to investigate the labyrinth of tiny organs that preside over postural equilibrium next to the organ of hearing. In 1861, Ménière found that damage to the inner ear caused it to miscommunicate with the brain, inducing a false perception of the body's posture that engenders a sensation of dizziness. A decade later, it was eventually discovered that our sense of gravity and spatial orientation is regulated by the vestibular system. Though anatomical pathology had long made it possible to dissect the organs of the inner ear, until the early 1870s the function of the semi-circular canals that meander through it had been misunderstood. As neurologist Gerald Wiest notes, the vestibular system 'was one of the first sensory systems to emerge in evolution; however, it was also the last to be discovered'.[16] Further research established the role of the central nervous system in regulating the sense of balance, paving the way for the recognition of vertigo as a neurological disorder.

The inception of vestibular science marked a breakthrough in the medical understanding of the body's sensory and motor functions. A key contribution was made by the British neurologist William Gowers, who investigated vestibular vertigo and the related diseases of the semi-circular canals. His multi-volume work, *A Manual of Diseases of the Nervous System*, published during the 1880s, refers to different impressions that were reported by patients, such as falling from heights or sinking into earth, as well as the less common sensation of rising – a sense of levity that was tentatively described as '"walking in the air"'. These conjectures indicate a persistent link between symptoms of vertigo and feelings of rising, falling and floating through space that defy the laws of gravity. At the same time, they attest to the difficulties that medical scientists still faced in their attempts to comprehend those symptoms by the late 19th century.

What became increasingly clear was that this puzzling feeling of motion was related to the perception of one's position in space. Gowers defined vertigo as 'a sense of involuntary movement' that is felt as a gyration and ascribed the defective equilibrium caused by this feeling to an impairment of the human ability to apprehend the surrounding environment:

> An exact and complete appreciation of the relation of the body to its physical surroundings is involved in the mental state that we call 'consciousness'. If that appreciation is incorrect by a false sense of movement – to that degree the sense of perfect consciousness is interfered with. Hence vertigo always involves a slight interference with consciousness.[17]

By highlighting the role of consciousness in the body's postural stability, Gowers sealed the modern definition of vertigo as a symptom rather than a disease, marking a difference from popular terms such as giddiness and dizziness. His separation between 'subjective' and 'objective' types of vertigo helped to refine the diagnostic approaches. A clear-cut distinction between inner and outer realities reflected the dualism of modern Western science that was later problematised by psychoanalysis through a more nuanced cognizance of body–mind relations. In parallel, psychologists began to link the effects of vertigo-related syndromes with the emotions of fear and anxiety that were experienced by subjects with an impaired sense of balance.

Phobic reactions to altitudes began to be detected in the late 19th century by the Italian psychiatrist Andrea Verga, who coined the term acrophobia (from the Greek *akros*, 'highest', and *phobia*, 'fear') to define this psychopathological aversion to high places: an irrational fear that severely affected him. In an article published in 1888, Verga described in detail his inability to climb a ladder without having heart palpitations, a morbid anxiety that seized him at the slightest sight of someone leaning over a window or balcony.[18] Climbing a tower was a source of major discomfort, regardless of the actual danger of falling:

> When I have reached the top of a tower or a belfry, I always prudently stand in the centre, and I do not attempt to look down, for it seems to me that I must be hurled into the abyss that is gaping for me below; and what is very curious is that whilst I am ascending a tower or a belfry, I experience a painful sensation, just as if my belly was being dragged out of me, and no argumentation by myself or by others, as to the solidity of the edifice, and my personal safety, succeeds in quieting me.[19]

While Verga related his fear to the instinct of self-preservation, he still admitted to feeling 'ashamed' of a weakness that inhibited him from enjoying many places and sights. His disclosure was published at a time when a number of new phobias were being diagnosed. These psychological diseases were entwined with the emergence of the modern metropolis and the new modes of experience that were brought along by dense crowds, mechanised transport and spaces of unprecedented scale.[20]

The architectural historian Anthony Vidler has pointed out that spatial phobias began to be identified in the 1870s as pervasive aspects of big city life: 'doctors were at once reflecting and countering an emerging and generalized fear of metropolis'.[21] Of particular consequence was the notion of agoraphobia, coined in 1871 by the German psychiatrist Carl Friedrich Otto Westphal to describe the terror of crossing streets, parks and squares that he frequently diagnosed amongst city dwellers. A year before, the Viennese neurologist Moritz Benedikt had used the word *Platzschwindel* (vertigo in a square or public place) for a similar feeling of anxiety, often accompanied by dizziness and disorientation, that seized upon growing numbers of people.[22] This condition was the subject of heated debate amongst German-speaking scientists who came up with various concepts such as *Platzangst* and *Platzfurcht* – respectively 'fear' and 'dread' of open places. Although this terminology was short-lived, as Vidler notes, it demonstrates a sustained attempt to claim the new anxiety disorders away from the vertigo syndromes that were investigated within vestibular medicine.

Sensations of dizziness were associated with a widening range of pathologies towards the end of the 19th century. In Paris, the neurologist Jean-Martin Charcot drew significant links between agoraphobia and claustrophobia through his pioneering research on hysteria at the Salpêtrière Hospital. Training under Charcot's supervision, a young Sigmund Freud made his first references to vertigo (*Schwindel*) as a symptom of anxiety neurosis – a topic he returned to over and over throughout his career.[23] Freud's approach to anxiety significantly evolved from the 1890s to the 1930s as he attached an ever-greater role to the psyche in his observation of neurotic cases.[24]

Freud regarded vertigo as one of the primary manifestations of anxiety, which initially he attributed to different causes: he interpreted the fear of windows felt by some of his patients, for instance, alternatively as a symptom of sexual anxiety or as a height-induced trait revealing a destructive drive.[25] Studying agoraphobia led him to consider it an anxiety hysteria along with other phobias that were based on the perception of imaginary dangers. An important shift occurred in the mid-1910s, when Freud set about examining the affective states associated with anxiety. It was at that moment that vertigo was linked with phobic neurotic anxiety: once a psychic component was recognised, its symptoms began to be treated with psychoanalysis.[26] This chain of discoveries allowed Freud to establish that anxiety was a signal of danger registered by human consciousness. He concluded that vertigo was a psychic defence mechanism through which the unconscious sought to avoid the discharge of energy accumulated in the central nervous system.

While vertigo was regarded as a symptom of spatial diseases related to life in the modern metropolis, acrophobia received comparatively minor attention. Vidler refers to the pervasive fear of falling that was registered in the medical discourse of the late 19th century, hinting at the experience of towers and moving trains; yet the phobia of high places occupies a marginal place in his psychopathology of urban space. Its discovery within psychiatry, as we have seen, was separate from the medical research on vertigo that became increasingly focused on vestibular disorders. Although the term acrophobia was not recognised within neuroscience for several decades (there is no mention of it, for example, in the 1907 edition of Gowers's *Manual*), the connotation of height vertigo as a pathological fear of falling makes it especially relevant to the experience of urban modernity. Verga's observations on high places were recorded at a critical juncture in the history of Western architecture when the Eiffel Tower was under construction and two years after the Home Insurance Building in Chicago, completed in 1885, heralded the skyscraper age. Acrophobia named a condition that was going to become increasingly widespread with the rise of vertical cities, although it remained couched in ignorance and prejudice for a very long time.[27]

ON A CLIFF EDGE

Well before the skyscraper age, allegories of the cliff edge had inspired writers and philosophers concerned with the disquiet of modern life. Western authors began drawing links between the sensation of vertigo and the related emotions of fear, anxiety and anguish in the mid-19th century. As Joyce Davidson points out: 'Vertigo has provided a favourite metaphor in existential accounts of *Angst*.'[28] In the wake of the first Industrial Revolution, several writers reflected on the heady heights of modernity, transposing the concept of vertigo from the sphere of bodily experience to the realm of moral life. Hence, the precipice became a cultural topos with the power to elicit a metaphysical form of vertigo; that is, as suggested by psychoanalyst Danielle Quinodoz, a state of consciousness that is provoked 'by confronting the great existential questions: life, death, infinity, eternity, the sense of one's own being or nothingness, the feeling of emptiness'.[29]

Anxiety became the subject of philosophical enquiry well before it was linked with spatial phobias and other mental disorders. A notable case is Søren Kierkegaard's 1844 treatise, *The Concept of Anxiety*, which sought to revive the principles of Christian theology.[30] The Danish philosopher distinguished a subjective type of anxiety, the turmoil arising from individual circumstances, from an objective variety which stemmed from the original sin and the consequent loss of innocence. The former defined a selfish disposition exacerbated by industrial modernity with its prospect of seemingly infinite possibilities. Hence, feelings of anxiety derived from the endless freedom that attracted and disoriented people at once. This state of disquiet was likened to the act of looking into an abyss:

> Anxiety may be compared with dizziness. He whose eye happens to look down the yawning abyss becomes dizzy. But what is the reason for this? It is just as much in his own eye as in the abyss, for suppose he had not looked down. Hence, anxiety is the dizziness of freedom, which emerges when the spirit

> wants to posit the synthesis and freedom looks down into its own possibility, laying hold of finiteness to support itself. Freedom succumbs to dizziness.[31]

Half a century after Erasmus Darwin had related vertigo to the physiology of vision, Kierkegaard considered the moral implications of looking down from height. Accordingly, embracing the virtue of finiteness would lead on the path in religious faith, which offered an antidote to the anxiety that sank the modern soul beneath the weight of unlimited potentialities. A healthy dose of anxiety could save an individual from the danger of moral falling and its extreme consequence – suicide.[32] The dizzying precipice conjured up, allegorically, an angst that must be controlled in order to eschew its vicious effects.

By associating anxiety with dizziness, Kierkegaard relied on the image of the abyss to evoke a state of moral confusion. Around the same time, this trope inspired Romantic writers. At the outset of his short story, 'The Imp of the Perverse' (published the year after *The Concept of Anxiety*), Edgar Allan Poe discussed the self-destructive impulse that is inherent in human nature, anticipating a theme that would become central to modern psychoanalysis. Here the dizzy sensations induced by the proximity of a cliff edge serve to introduce the desire to jump into the void, whose pulling force exerts a vicious attraction:

> We stand upon the brink of a precipice. We peer into the abyss – we grow sick and dizzy. Our first impulse is to shrink from the danger. Unaccountably we remain. By slow degrees our sickness, and dizziness, and horror, become merged in a cloud of unnameable feeling. [...] And because our reason violently deters us from the brink, *therefore*, do we the more impetuously approach it. There is no passion in nature so demoniacally impatient, as that of him, who shuddering upon the edge of a precipice, thus meditates a plunge.[33]

The notion of vertigo, whose semantic field encompasses a darkening of the mind, is a plausible term for the 'cloud of unnameable feeling' that Poe was at pains to define. Predating Freud's theories of the unconscious and death drive, this passage captures the aesthetic sensibility which ran against the grain of Enlightenment ideas on self-preservation.

The impulse aroused by the sight of the abyss continued to stir up literary and philosophical representations. In Thomas Hardy's 1873 novel, *A Pair of Blue Eyes*, one of the characters (Henry Knight) falls off a cliff while contemplating an ocean liner that is passing by: while he clings on to a rock, a fossil embedded in the

2 Cataract Canyon, looking down from cliff near junction of Grand and Green, 1871.

stone confronts him from the depths of its geological era.[34] Here the Romantic trope of the abyss evokes a tension between nature and culture, embodied by the Londoner who has slipped over the edge. The Western imagination of the abyss had recently been expanded by the topographical and geological surveys of American canyons, such as the expedition led by John Wesley Powell through the valley of the Colorado River (fig.2).

Whilst, over the 19th century, the precipice was associated with the might of nature, the scene of vertigo was to be replaced by architecture as the modern city became the stage for a new type of sublime. The industrial metropolis harboured a process of creative destruction that reconfigured the coordinates of everyday life. Several critics have commented on the pervasive sense of instability that became associated with this historical shift, a condition that was summed up by Michel Foucault: 'Modernity is often characterized in terms of consciousness of the discontinuity of time: a break with tradition, a feeling of novelty, a vertigo in the face of the passing moment.'[35]

ANGUISH OF FALLING

While the most diverse aspects of modernity were captured by poets and artists, the sense of anxiety that weighed on industrial societies formed a persistent object of philosophical enquiry into the 20th century. The concept of vertigo resurfaced in Jean-Paul Sartre's *Being and Nothingness*, published in the midst of the Second World War.[36] Sartre argued that nothingness was a form of being rather than its mere negation, since it was experienced in very concrete ways by human consciousness. Drawing on Kierkegaard's notion of anxiety, he set it apart from the concept of fear: while the latter derived from the presence of external beings, for Sartre, the former originated in one's inner self: 'Most of the time dangerous or threatening situations present themselves in facets; they will be apprehended through a feeling of fear or of anguish according to whether we envisage the situation as acting on the man or the man as acting on the situation.'[37]

In order to visualise this distinction, the philosopher evoked the vertiginous feeling that arises from the act of walking on a cliff edge. The anguish provoked by such a dangerous circumstance was put down to the imagined agency of throwing oneself off the edge, which transcends the mere possibility of falling. Fear is the initial reaction to the danger that presents itself to our consciousness when we become aware of the yawning abyss. According to Sartre, we overcome its dizzying effect by internalising the range of possibilities that lie ahead of us:

> Vertigo announces itself through fear; I am on a narrow path – without a guard-rail – which goes along a precipice. The precipice presents itself to me as *to be avoided*; it represents a danger of death. At the same time I conceive of a certain number of causes, originating in universal determinism, which can transform that threat of death into reality; I can slip on a stone and fall into the abyss; the crumbling earth of the path can give way under my steps. [...] At this moment *fear* appears.[38]

Our mindfulness of the potential consequences helps us to overcome this emotion. However, we soon realise that another course of action, to throw oneself over the precipice, is equally possible.[39] Here, Sartre echoed the anxiety of possibilities that Kierkegaard had put forward a century earlier. Whilst the latter essentially reduced the experience of the precipice to the act of looking down, however, Sartre pictured a more dynamic scene in which the subject becomes aware of the impending danger to slip and fall. Crucially, fear turns into anguish when we realise that our future being will be different from the present one, hence we cannot exclude that other actions will take place in the mode of not-being. This tension makes us dizzy as we realise that our next steps will depend on the conduct of a self which is not there yet, nor can its actions be foreseen: 'Vertigo appears as the apprehension of this dependence. I approach the precipice, and my scrutiny is searching for myself in my very depths.'[40]

Through this moving description, Sartre effectively redefined the fear of falling as a distinct form of anguish. Seen as an existential lapse into the realm of nothingness, height-induced vertigo transcends the level of bodily experience and arouses the consciousness of our being that asserts its will to live. Unlike the consciousness invoked by 19th-century neurologists such as Gowers, who was primarily concerned with the processing of sensory inputs by the human brain, Sartre referred to a mental state that operates at a deeper existential level. Meanwhile, as the philosopher conjured up the anguish of human existence, a moral and material abyss was opened by war.

Vertigo became a recurring trope of Western culture in the post-war period, as writers and artists sought to process the trauma of mass destruction. Hitchcock's masterpiece encapsulates the growing interest in issues of balance that emerged in the 1950s, when the concept of vertigo was charged with renewed allegorical meanings. The screenplay was adapted by Alec Coppel and Samuel Taylor from the novel *The Living and the Dead*, jointly authored by the prolific crime writers Pierre Boileau and Thomas Narcejac, which initially appeared in French as *D'entre les morts* (1954). Unlike its adaptation, the book is set in wartime France and the conflict provides the background for the story. The main character (Roger Flavières) is ashamed of his fear of falling and his stigma exposes the deeper instability of modern bourgeois society: 'The truth was that they were all like him, Flavières, trembling on the edge of a slope at the bottom of which was the abyss.'[41] The protagonist's moral plight was a means of addressing the widespread sense of disorientation that characterised a generation ravaged by the enigma of its own survival, a condition the poet W.H. Auden had poignantly named 'the age of anxiety'.[42]

Towards the end of the novel, Flavières admits to feeling lost when Madeleine walks out of their liaison, and his feeling is described in giddy terms: 'With that thought, Flavières's head began to swim, and he was assailed by a horrible feeling of emptiness, an emptiness like space itself, limitless, unceasing, and without reprieve.'[43] Space here is represented as void: a sense of loss threatens to pull the subject into a bottomless fall, akin to the abyss that terrifies the acrophobe. Above and beyond its storyline, *The Living and the Dead* reflects a moment of disquiet in which post-war societies were reckoning with the devastation wrought by the second worldwide conflict in the space of three decades.

PSYCHOLOGY OF GRAVITY

While vertigo became a metaphor of modern existence, the tower was elevated to a literary and philosophical trope signifying the anguish of falling. A key figure in this respect is Gaston Bachelard, whose research into the poetic imagination was of great influence on Sartre, among others. After dealing with lightness in *Air and Dreams*, Bachelard investigated the psychology of gravity that stood in dialectical relation with it: *Earth and Reveries of Will* was the final instalment of his phenomenology of the elements.[44] One of its main ideas is that rising and falling are inextricably bound up in the human imagination. Bachelard considered verticality in perceptual rather than geometrical terms as a double movement that can stretch our dynamic imagination upward or downward, and indeed, in both directions at once.

Central to this theory was a frightening episode the philosopher had suffered at the age of 20, when he climbed up the lantern of Strasbourg Cathedral. This memory was far more than a passing anecdote as it allowed him to discuss the impact that an imaginary fall can exert on the mind. A pithy remark summed it up: 'It is not rare, in effect, for an entire life to be affected by a single episode of vertigo.'[45] Citing the illustrious precedent of Goethe, who had climbed the same tower in the early 1770s to overcome his aversion to heights, Bachelard had an altogether more daunting recollection. Unlike smaller towers he had ascended before, this climb led to an '*inhumanly abrupt*' event that left him with a lasting trauma.[46] Having walked the staircase up to the octagonal spire, he was unexpectedly faced with the abyss:

> Following the guide up the stone stairs, visitors are protected at first on their right by a line of delicate columns, but *suddenly*, very near the summit, this perforated lacework comes to an end. To the right, there is nothing but empty air, a great void extending over the rooftops. The stairway turns so narrowly that soon visitors are left alone, out of sight of the guide. Life depends on their hold upon the railing.[47]

Here is one of the most dramatic accounts of height vertigo written by any philosopher, one in which physical balance is elevated to a matter of life and death. Whereas La Mettrie had recalled his spell of dizziness atop Antwerp's cathedral in order to corroborate the physiology of vertigo, Bachelard summoned up his own memory to highlight its psychological aspects. This episode has lost none of its evocative power since it refers to a situation that still resonates with readers on the spectrum of visual height intolerance. According to neuroscientists, the act of climbing a tower is still 'the first and most common precipitating stimulus' of height-induced vertigo, followed by other activities that sufferers are most averse to, such as 'climbing up a ladder, hiking, walking over a bridge, or looking out of higher buildings'.[48]

Back in the 1940s, however, Bachelard relied on his own experience to appraise its psycho-physiological impact of climbing a tower, and compounded his recollection of the Strasbourg episode with reflections on its consequences:

> Going up and coming down: twice, the experience of absolute vertigo lasting but a few minutes; and the mind is marked for life [...] Never again was I to enjoy mountains and towers! The *engram* of an immense fall is within me. When this memory comes back to me, when this image comes to life again at night and even in my waking dreams, an indescribable malaise fills my deepest being. I suffered in writing these lines, and in recopying them I suffer again, as from a fresh and all too real adventure.[49]

Despite Bachelard's efforts to banish this moment from consciousness, its reminiscence haunted him with 'noxious and cruel' images.[50] By the time of his ascent, in 1904 or 1905, the Eiffel Tower stood at over twice the height of Strasbourg Cathedral, yet the episode was triggered not so much by sheer altitude as by the lack of protective barriers, which prompted him to muse on the French word *garde-fou*: 'Guard-rails protect us against that most basic, that most commonplace madness, the kind that can come over us as we cross a bridge, or pause at the top of a flight of stairs.'[51] This mundane architectural element has in fact a vital function that impinges upon the psychology of gravity: it constitutes a perceptual as well as material threshold that defends us from the threat of the void – yet also shields us from its lure. With nothing but a thin railing as protection, the lantern of Strasbourg Cathedral became for Bachelard an architectural equivalent of the Sartrean precipice.

After that episode, the fantasy of falling from a high place haunted Bachelard's dreams and prevented him from going up again, anywhere. Its recollection, over four decades later, led him to foray into the biographies of other writers who disclosed a variety of troubles with heights. If Alexandre Dumas was reportedly so tormented by vertigo that he lost his balance whenever his body was suspended above the ground, Henrich Steffens (a Romantic poet and philosopher who is credited with having influenced Kierkegaard) related his sensations of falling to a deeper existential angst: 'For him, that dizzy feeling [*le vertige*] was experienced as a sudden attack of loneliness. People thus afflicted are beyond salvation; no helping hand can stay their fall. Poor victims, struck with dizziness [*vertige*] in the fundamental sense, they feel *alone* to the bottom of their beings. They are falling alive.'[52] By conflating loneliness with vertigo, Bachelard implicitly aligned the inner quest for stability with the loss of bodily balance induced by the encounter with the abyss. While this analogy between physical and moral falls echoes Kierkegaard's and Sartre's writings, his emphasis on poetic reverie marks it out from them.

Meanwhile, medical scientists paid increasing attention to the systematic occurrences of dizziness, hence 'true' vertigo came to define the symptoms of vestibular problems.[53] After the Second World War, scientific research led to the recognition that the sense of balance relied in fundamental ways on the embodied experience of space. As one author put it succinctly: 'Dizziness means a disturbed sense of relationship to space.'[54] While symptoms of dizziness and vertigo were increasingly treated as disorders of the balance system, their broad aetiology called for the diagnostic skills of multiple specialists from neuroscience and psychology as well as otolaryngology. At the same time as the concept of vertigo was redefined within clinical practice, it took on greater significance as a metaphor in art and culture.

THE TOWERING GAZE

If vertigo is an inherently spatialised phenomenon, the tower is its prime architectural scene. We have seen how, in 20th-century phenomenology, it replaced the cliff edge as a trigger of perceptual disorientation. In the 1960s, under the influence of structuralism, various cultural theorists foregrounded the visual possibilities opened up by high vantage points over the corporeal sensations they gave rise to. Interestingly, the notion of vertigo is conspicuous for its absence from the main texts that defined the critical discourse on the perception of the city from above over the second half of the last century.

Roland Barthes steered away from it in his famous 'Eiffel Tower' essay, wherein he used the term 'architectures of vision' (*architectures de la vue*) to describe the engineering marvel that turned the 'fantasy of a panoramic vision' into material reality.[55] As the advent of balloon flights opened up a new field of vision, the Tower par excellence gave material form to an aerial imagination which had hitherto been the province of artists and writers; it was popularised by Victor Hugo's novel, *Notre-Dame de Paris*, with its sweeping bird's-eye view of the French capital. For Barthes, the Tower epitomised the rise of a new form of perception that made it possible to comprehend the structure of the metropolis at a glance. By positing the city as an unfolding text to be read and deciphered, his argument privileged the power of intellection over the experience of space.

A similar tendency to reduce high-rise architecture to a vantage point characterises Michel de Certeau's oft-quoted account of Manhattan from atop the World Trade Center. Although de Certeau refers to the 'voluptuous pleasure' of seeing the city as a whole (a phrase that suggests a sense of dizzying exhilaration), the experience he recounts is effectively reduced to a purely visual act.[56] The observation deck becomes the platform from which a *dieu voyeur* observes the city like a picture and lays claim over it. The ensuing 'fiction of knowledge', concludes de Certeau, 'is related to this lust to be a viewpoint and nothing more'.[57]

Underlying this critique was a religious conception of the gaze which the French philosopher, an eclectic Jesuit scholar, had derived from a humanistic tradition dating back to the Renaissance. For him, the Twin Towers occupied a position of power that desecrated the hallowed view from the sky represented in the Christian tradition by an all-seeing divinity – an iconography dear to the Jesuits. Both his and Barthes's texts emphasise, from different angles, the symbolic function of the tower within modern structures of power and knowledge.

De Certeau's critique of the totalising gaze appeared in his seminal book, *The Practice of Everyday Life*, which became widely influential through its English edition published in 1984. That was also the year when Milan Kundera's philosophical novel, *The Unbearable Lightness of Being*, appeared in French and English translations. This age-defining book tackles the dialectic of lightness and heaviness in political as well as existential terms against the background of 20th-century Czech history.[58] All throughout, Kundera refers to vertigo as a means of questioning the moral dilemmas faced by the protagonists during the Prague Spring of 1968 and its violent repression. The main female character, Tereza, is beset by unrelenting bouts of vertigo as she is constantly torn between the desire to elevate her existence and an 'insuperable longing to fall'. Reflecting on this tension, the author offered a literary definition that is reminiscent of Sartre: 'What is vertigo? Fear of falling? Then why do we feel it even when the observation tower comes equipped with a sturdy handrail? No, vertigo is something other than the fear of falling. It is the voice of the emptiness below us which tempts and lures us, it is the desire to fall, against which, terrified, we defend ourselves.'[59]

Exploring the conundrums of life and politics under the Cold War, Kundera alluded to the impulse that is known in French as *l'appel du vide* (the call of the void). This ineffable desire has fascinated a number of artists and writers, and in recent times has attracted growing interest from scholars in different areas, from cultural history to the science of human emotions. Contrary to prior assumptions, psychologists have suggested that the so-called 'high place phenomenon' does not relate to suicidal instincts but is linked to the spectrum of anxiety sensitivity.[60] Accordingly, subjects with affective disorders would be more likely to misinterpret the safety signal that is perceived when facing the potential fall from a high place as an urge to jump. The command to pull back from the edge would therefore respond to a self-defence mechanism rather than to a subconscious desire to leap: 'experiencing this phenomenon may have the counter-intuitive effect of affirming one's will to live'.[61]

Kundera's reference to vertigo had no scientific claim, yet it resonated with established allegorical meanings. In line with a genealogy of literary and philosophical works that preceded it, *The Unbearable Lightness of Being* manifests the anxiety of falling as a political as well as personal dilemma underlying the protagonists' lives. In parallel, a widespread sense of instability was detected in the West as neoliberal politics held sway on both sides of the Atlantic. Towards the end of the 1980s, the American author Barbara Ehrenreich reflected on the shift from the liberal and optimist outlook of the 1960s towards a more conservative and cynical one. The latter coincided with a new self-consciousness of the professional middle class: as this social group took up a moral and political role as 'an elite *above* others', it became anxious about its capital based on skills and knowledge rather than on solid wealth.[62] Under pressure to renew their undependable assets from one generation to the next, middle-class families were affected by a pervasive feeling of insecurity: 'Even the affluence that is so often the goal of all this striving becomes a threat, for it holds out the possibility of hedonism and self-indulgence. Whether the middle class looks down toward the realm of less, or up toward the realm of more, there is the fear, always, of falling.'[63]

This is further evidence of how tropes of gravity resurfaced in different guises over the 20th century. As this 'age of extremes' drew to a close, the concept of vertigo was mobilised by different authors who strived to capture the increasing disjunction between the self and the social world. This tendency is exemplified by the work of W.G. Sebald, whose prose fiction weaves together history, memoir, fiction and travel writing into composite narratives that transcend conventional genres. The German author brought a pervasive sense of melancholy to bear on his reflections about war and the Holocaust. Paul Auster aptly remarked: 'The beautiful thing about Sebald's writing is that it keeps us in a state of permanent disequilibrium.'[64]

This peculiar condition is vividly expressed in the sui generis novel, *Vertigo*, where the narrator conveys his mental confusion through a blend of impressions, memories and historical facts woven into a series of wanderings across places and times. It has been noted that the original title (*Schwindel. Gefühle*) is a play on the German word *Schwindelgefühle*, which in its composite form means dizzy feelings or dizziness.[65] As a separate word, however, *Schwindel* signifies lie and deception as well as vertigo – a dual meaning that chimes with the illusory sensation of whirling. A section of the book revolves around a trip to Italy in which the author fell into an acute state of depression that bordered on despair. While roaming the streets of Milan, the narrator decided to climb the spires of the Gothic cathedral and the ensuing experience revealed a loss of stability:

> I was unable even to determine whether I was in the land of the living or already in another place. Nor did this lapse in memory improve in the slightest after I climbed to the topmost gallery of the cathedral and from there, beset by recurring fits of vertigo, gazed out upon the dusky, hazy panorama of a city now altogether alien to me.[66]

A feeling of disorientation had been afflicting the protagonist well before he set out to gaze at the panorama, yet his bodily experience precipitated that feeling in a visceral way. The subsequent description from the Duomo's viewing gallery has all the hallmarks of height vertigo; it evokes a distorted reality in the vein of an expressionist tableau, tinged with the shades of confusion that have long been associated with this concept:

> A menacing reflection of the darkness spreading within me loomed up in the west where an immense bank of cloud covered half the sky and cast its shadow on the seemingly endless sea of houses. A stiff wind came up, and I had to brace myself so that I could look down to where the people were crossing the piazza, their bodies inclined forwards at an odd angle, as though they were hastening towards their doom.[67]

Recalling the real-life circumstances in which he nearly fell off the edge, Sebald summoned up atmospheric elements in order to convey the incongruity between his inner state and the surrounding environment, a mismatch that is suddenly and dramatically brought to light by a gust of wind. In his analysis of Sebald's work, cultural geographer John Wylie comments apropos of this bird's-eye view that 'such vertiginous perspectives are a metaphor through which different voices express the uneasy feeling of temporal dislocation'.[68] Similarly to various precedents in 20th-century culture, ranging from Hitchcock to Kundera, here the existential significance of vertigo derives from an unsettled experience of time as well as space.

There are traces of the sublime in Sebald's landscapes, yet his imagery is also pervaded by the uncanny. Intriguingly, Wylie interprets his work through the lens of Jacques Derrida's 'spectral logic', whereby the relationship between self and place is not one of dwelling but one of haunting: the ghostly presence unsettles not only the order of life and death but also that of past and present through the very act of its return.[69] Taking this argument forward, we might regard the tower as an architectural revenant, a recurring site of vertigo that comes back, over and over again, to haunt the Western cultural imagination.

A distinct manifestation can be found in science fiction, wherein high-rise structures were recurring tropes throughout the 20th century. As Amy Butt notes, vertigo became a widespread theme in the 'new wave' of this genre, as the ethos of high-rise social housing made way for a growing sense of failure – particularly in the US and UK.[70] In novels of the 1970s, such as Robert Silverberg's *The World Inside* and J.G. Ballard's *High Rise*, tower blocks harbour the protagonists' inner lives and thereby allow the authors to formulate their critiques of vertical habitats. The characterisation of the apartment block as an architectural cliff, in *High Rise*, echoes the analogy with natural landscapes that runs through this chapter, with the significant difference that Ballard employed it to describe a primordial condition in which city dwellers regress to a pre-civilised form of life. His subsequent works never ceased to portray the urban middle class in a state of suspension, ever torn between a longing for stability and the anxiety of collapse. Meanwhile, the vertical city continues to play a symbolic role in science fiction literature, as the genre reasserts the imaginative freedom that historically characterised it.[71]

By awakening our imagination of the abyss, writers and philosophers prompt us to reconsider the experience of dissociation and disorientation that is a pervasive aspect of urban life. Their works question the mismatch between inner and external space that lies at the heart of vertigo. This concept has been invoked time and time again since the 19th century to describe various states of existential, subjective and social instability. Today, it continues to exert a powerful hold on the imagination, particularly at a time when individuals and whole societies feel increasingly deprived of their foundations.

2

DIZZY VISIONS

Blinded by the light, overwhelmed by the noise and vitality of the city, I was overcome with vertigo. My head began to spin.[1]

3 László Moholy-Nagy, view from the Pont Transbordeur, Marseille, 1929.

MODERN EXPERIMENTS

In 2007, the Museum of Modern Art of Bologna hosted an exhibition, *Vertigo*, which revisited a century of artistic production 'from Futurism to the web'. The title evoked the vortex of relations between the contemporary art world and new forms of communication that reshaped visual culture at the turn of the millennium. As explained by the curator, Germano Celant, the advent of new media, technologies and practices had brought about a hybrid cultural sphere in which traditional boundaries were increasingly blurred. The fluid contamination of languages produced by ceaseless flows of images and open systems of production and reproduction undermined the old hierarchies, paving the way for 'a complete democratisation' of art.[2] Market values were gradually dissolving, with bewildering effects, the ideal sphere in which the art system had long cultivated its autonomy. In this respect, the *Vertigo* exhibition harked back to another critical juncture, in the early 20th century, when the art world had been radically transformed.

Arguably, there is a further way in which contemporary visual culture stands in a dialectical relation with the modernist avant-gardes. While the latter saw a burgeoning of experiments in film and photography that shocked the viewers into novel forms of perception, recent decades have witnessed the rise of a new image culture along with a revival of the urban environment as a field of visual experiments. This nexus comes to life in the work of several artists that represent architecture as a site of dizzy experience, casting it alternatively as the subject of camera-based observations or as a viewing platform onto the city – in some cases, both at once. While tropes of gravity have informed a number of visual and performance artworks since the 1960s, this chapter focuses on a specific strand of photography and film that summons up the visceral dimension of high-rise environments.[3] It probes how selected artists have contributed to shape our imagination of verticality, making visible the social as well as spatial conditions embodied by architecture at a time of intense urban transformation.

In order to establish a genealogy of this phenomenon we should return to the moment of its emergence, in inter-war Europe, where the modern metropolis became a laboratory for avant-garde artists associated with the 'new vision' (*Neues Sehen*). Iron structures such as Berlin's Radio Tower, Marseille's Transporter Bridge and the Eiffel Tower offered unequalled platforms from which the surrounding cityscapes, as well as those engineering marvels themselves, could be framed (fig.3). Albeit with different aesthetic sensibilities, photographers as diverse as László Moholy-Nagy, Germaine Krull and André Kertész shared an impetus to reconfigure the built environment from uncustomary perspectives.[4] Their visual language was favoured by the advent of hand-held cameras with fast lenses in the 1920s, but also by the parallel boom of illustrated magazines. Meanwhile, eminent architects and critics, including Erich Mendelsohn and Sigfried Giedion, embraced that medium to illustrate their own publications with pictures taken from elevated viewpoints (see Chapter 6).

In Soviet Russia, Aleksander Rodchenko and fellow Constructivists framed their subjects from oblique vantage points as a means of challenging the canon of bourgeois representation. Rodchenko's slanted views of Moscow, shot between the late 1920s and the early 1930s, were among the radical visual experiments of the revolutionary period, when photography became an instrument of socialist art.[5] Against this background, artists of the October Group set about exploring the dynamic aspects of city life. Chief amongst them, Rodchenko maintained that multiple snapshots should be taken from viewpoints most appropriate to each subject, and partial views then be recombined in order to attain a deeper understanding of reality. In a provocative article, he urged his followers to reorient their cameras: 'Photograph from all viewpoints except "from the belly button," until they all become acceptable. The most interesting viewpoints today are "from above down" and "from below up," and we should work at them.'[6] This intimation to frame the world from unconventional points of view was, in all but name, the manifesto of a new photography that drew impetus from the conditions of a rapidly industrialising and urbanising country.

Oblique angles became the signifiers of a modern way of seeing, as the simple act of tilting the camera aimed to shake off the burden of pictorial representation. As noted by the critic Peter Galassi, this framing technique led to a variety of photographic effects: 'The oblique [perspective] can disengage the viewer from the scene, rendering it as a pattern of unfamiliar forms, unburdened of their worldly association. Or it can aggressively implicate the viewer in the scene, evoking a vertiginous plunge into an all too palpable space.'[7] Rodchenko was a master of the vertiginous plunge. This radical mode of vision came to a head in the early 1930s, when he documented the 'new Moscow' under construction. Diagonal compositions allowed him to transfigure ordinary scenes into highly dynamic views, as the visual field of the city appeared to be spinning before the viewer's eyes. In effect, Rodchenko's work marked the climax of an avant-garde movement whose vision of revolution was predicated on a revolution of vision.

Similar techniques became popular in avant-garde cinema, notably within the film-making collective known as *Kinoks* ('cinema eyes'). In the 1929 experimental film, *Man with a Movie Camera*, the group's figurehead Dziga Vertov (né David Abelevich Kaufman) conveyed the pace and space of modern life through a montage of shots filmed in different Soviet cities. This take on the 'city symphony' genre displayed a sweeping range of views that were taken from elevators, cars and trams, as well as from static platforms offering new perspectives. Edited in a fast tempo by Elisaveta Svilova, the film brings together fragments of a visual kaleidoscope set in motion by the encounter between the movie camera and its ever-shifting subjects. Its protagonist climbs on bridges, pylons and rooftops in order to reach vantage points that allow him to frame dynamic urban scenes. Along with Rodchenko and other Soviet artists, Vertov took on urban heights as a means of framing places and patterns from above (a vertiginous reference was implicit in his artist name, which translates as 'spinning top'). Their experiments are typical examples of the aesthetic of defamiliarisation (*ostranenie*) theorised by the critic Viktor Shklovsky, which aimed at making the everyday strange and unfamiliar. Taming vertigo, then, was key to disclosing a world of unbound visual possibilities.

Original research was also conducted within other avant-garde movements such as Italian Futurism. On the eve of the First World War, Anton Giulio Bragaglia pioneered the technique of photodynamism, which consisted of recording the successive positions of a moving subject on a single image. His 1913 essay, *Fotodinamismo futurista*, established a new visual paradigm that was to have a vast influence on 20th-century photography. If the experiments with chronophotography conducted by Étienne-Jules Marey had broken down the successive position of a moving body on a single strip of film, thus anticipating the development of cinematography, Bragaglia's technique strove to capture the essence of movement itself.

The vitality of this new imagery was augmented, and even authenticated, by its ability to evoke dizzying sensations. As Bragaglia explained: 'The fact that our evocations appear vertiginous and confusing at first sight, demonstrates how movement exists in our work.'[8] By throwing the viewer's perception out of kilter, photodynamism was deemed to enhance the creative potential of the medium: 'we are studying the trajectory, the synthesis of action, that which exerts a fascination over our senses, the vertiginous lyrical expression of life, the lively invoker of the magnificent dynamic feeling with which the universe incessantly vibrates'.[9]

These ideas went on to inspire inter-war artists such as Fedele Azari, Tullio Crali and Guglielmo Sansoni (aka Tato) to paint dynamic landscapes from the air. In 1929, their endeavours prompted a group of artists headed by Filippo Tommaso Marinetti to publish the Manifesto of Aeropainting, which laid the foundation for a new aerial aesthetic. Consequently, Azari and others developed the method of aerophotography in an attempt to represent the changing states of mind provoked by the experience of flight. By triggering the shutter while nose diving, these pilots-cum-photographers produced dizzying pictures of cities which brought Bragaglia's research to fruition, yielding motion blur effects that resemble those produced by zooming techniques. Even ancient sites such as the ruins of the Roman Forum became the subject of dynamic compositions. As aerial photography rapidly broadened the horizon of urban visuality, the *vue en plongée* (a French term derived from the language of cinema) became part of an expanded imagery of the modern city that aimed to radically modernise the habits of perception.

ANGELS AND AVIATORS

Photographers played a significant role in depicting the rise of the American metropolis. In his 1924 book on architecture and civilisation, *Sticks and Stones*, Lewis Mumford railed against his fellow critics who sang the praise of skyscrapers. If those buildings had become symbols of modern civilisation, he argued, that was an achievement driven by economic rather than humanistic values: the business districts of American downtowns were increasingly driven by the pursuit of 'pure mechanical form'.[10] Replicating a building type that was applied to ever more functions, the ubiquitous office towers were deemed to have deprived cities of their human scale. They constituted, in Mumford's words, 'one of the greatest mechanical achievements in a thoroughly dehumanized civilization'.[11] For him, vertical architecture was a mere technical process detached from the reality of everyday life. Yet, even on a stark observer like Mumford, as later on Le Corbusier, skyscrapers exerted a mix of repulsion and fascination.[12]

The reproduction of photographs in newspapers and magazines was an integral part of that skyscraper boom. Mumford protested that tall buildings were often depicted in the press from elevated viewpoints which transcended the perception of street walkers: 'In short', he quipped, 'it is an architecture, not for men, but for angels and aviators!'[13] While those colossal edifices were expressions of the machine age, they commanded a superhuman gaze to view them. Over the 1920s, aerial photographs became a popular form of illustration and significantly expanded the field of urban visuality. As modern architecture became bound up with the mass media, this encounter had specific connotations in the vertical metropolis: photographers who documented the rise of skyscrapers became the chroniclers of a historic shift that entailed not only modern construction techniques but a new perception of space as well.

Mumford's critique was formulated amidst the creative destruction that transformed Manhattan in the early part of the 20th century.[14] With the architecture of skyscrapers coming into full swing, photographers sought out elevated vantage points to frame the metropolis. A significant figure was Alvin Langdon Coburn, who trained his camera on the urban landscape after a trip to the American West during which he had contemplated the depths of the Grand Canyon. His 1913 exhibition, *New York from Its Pinnacles*, included a much-celebrated picture taken from the observation deck of the Metropolitan Life Tower the previous year, 'The Octopus', which set a milestone in the photography of the modern city. This view of Madison Square Park, where the footpaths mark a pattern of lines criss-crossing in the snow, reflects not only Coburn's pictorialist aesthetic but also, importantly, 'a new alienated urban experience' that found expression in the detached vantage point.[15] As several critics have noted, the elongated shadow cast over the park alludes to the anxiety of modern urban life. New York's early skyscrapers acted at once as viewing platforms and viewed objects, anticipating a trope that was to recur in the inter-war period when the vertical growth of the city reached epic proportions.

In the hands of Lewis Hine, the camera became a tool of social critique at a time of rapid urban growth: 'interpretive photography' were the words he stamped on the back of his prints. The famous shots of the Empire State Building under construction, in the early 1930s, form an extraordinary social portrayal of the vertical city (fig.4). By framing the views over Manhattan that were opened up by the tallest building in the world (a record the Empire would retain for over four decades), in effect Hine represented the vertiginous space of the metropolis. Through this series of images, popularised by the photobook *Men at Work* (1932), ironworkers balancing themselves on metal posts, girders and wires compelled viewers to experience the cityscape in a vicarious state of suspension. These portraits have been recognised as allegories of an industrial society that the photographer was consciously involved in, as he shared with his subjects the dangers of operating at exceptional heights.[16]

4 Lewis Wickes Hine, 'Jumping the derrick' (worker on a scaffold), Empire State Building, New York, *c*.1930.

Despite Hine's empathy with his subjects, or perhaps because of it, the Empire series has inevitably raised questions about the role of images that turn manual labour into spectacle.[17] The representation of 'sky walkers' in inter-war publications and newsreels contributed to shape a heroic narrative of the vertical city resting on a vigorous male body at ease in high places and seemingly immune to the threat of vertigo. As the race to the sky went on, the imagery of men at work fuelled a rhetoric of the American metropolis as a site of superhuman power. This narrative was fraught with misconceptions surrounding the Native American workers from southern New England who, since the 1880s, had supplied the main labour force for the construction of skyscrapers and bridges.

The Mohawk (as Europeans called the Iroquois tribe of Kanien'kéha:ka) began their involvement with railroad bridges in Canada, where they demonstrated uncommon agility working at heights that often troubled their French colleagues. Construction became a source of sustenance for many indigenous families and was handed down from one generation to the next: the pride of doing what others could not contributed to forge a spirit of ethnic identity. When the skyscraper age eventually took off, films and publications fostered the popular credence that so-called 'cowboys of the skies' were immune to height vertigo. The myth of the fearless Mohawks obscured the fact that walking on narrow beams, often battered by winds and without safety measures, is a source of danger for anyone. As David Weitzman points out, their fear of heights was assimilated and channelled into a form of respect for gravity and alertness to its consequences, which in turn led ironworkers to test their endurance through ever higher tasks.[18] A connector interviewed by Weitzman gives the main point: '"I found the work was thrilling, dangerous, but very rewarding personally. There are many moments when you have to overcome your fears, and in doing so you rise to an emotional plateau. Then you go on to the next challenge, looking for the next high."'[19] While ironworkers performed hazardous tasks that resulted in accidents and casualties, their superior ability to cope with heights was not due to an immunity to vertigo, but rather to a process of habituation.

Prior to Hine's work on the Empire, Margaret Bourke-White had documented the making of the Chrysler Building. Having set up her studio inside one of the steel gargoyles, between 1929 and 1930 she depicted the urban scenery that fascinated her while recording the rising construction. Bourke-White, who became an accomplished aerial photographer working with the U.S. Army Air Corps in the Second World War, was never afraid of heights: in fact, she believed to have a 'God-given sense of balance'.[20] In her autobiography she recalls the advice received from welders and riveters on the Chrysler Building site about how to stand for hours on open scaffolds: 'when you are working at 800 feet above the ground, make believe that you are 8 feet above the ground, make believe that you are 8 feet up and relax, take it easy. The problems are really exactly the same'.[21] This advice resonated with Bourke-White's childhood memories of walking to school 'on the thin edges of fences'. Amongst the photographers who pictured the rising metropolis, she is perhaps the one who came closest to embodying the positions of angels and aviators evoked by Mumford.

However, it was Berenice Abbott's documentation of New York throughout the 1930s that revealed the vertical cityscape as an apotheosis of corporate architecture. In her acclaimed photo-book, *Changing New York* (1939), the writer Elizabeth McClausland likened Abbott's shots of Wall Street from on high to pictures of natural landscapes: 'In the roof's eye view of the financial district, serrated roof-lines create a pattern like that of the West's vast canyons, in which soil erosion has carved out abstract sculptures of earth and stone.'[22] Those plunging perspectives gave prominence to the gigantism of New York's architecture while exposing the depths of urban space. In its dual function of visual subject and viewing platform, the skyscraper came to embody a brand of modernity that was quintessentially American: 'this modernity', historian David Nye observes, 'emphasized how the businessman's gaze dominated the new man-made landscape'.[23]

Nye describes the turmoil provoked by the age of skyscrapers in terms of 'technological sublime'. Modern towers epitomised the triumph over nature alongside the suspension bridges that spanned the waterways of American cities.[24] Not only did they reshape the metropolitan skylines with their vertical geometries, they also embodied the power position of the corporations that ruled over the economy: 'If the skyline suggested the creation of an artificial nature, the Olympian gaze from atop a pinnacle of commerce suggested subjugation as the obverse side of mastery.'[25] The towering gaze embodied by the skyscraper was inseparable from the sense of fear and anxiety provoked by the experience of heights: 'As in the natural sublime, there was an element of terror in looking at the city from a high place, gazing down a sheer wall.'[26]

By embodying that dominant vantage point, Abbott revealed the contrast between the rampant high-rise construction and the vernacular buildings and street trades that were dwarfed by them. The new urban order is vividly expressed in the plunging views of Wall Street taken from high-rise office blocks. In these now-classic photographs, such as the roof's-eye view from the Irving Trust Building, the oblique composition accentuates the vertiginous effects of the plunging shot: a feeling enhanced by the receding edge in the foreground, from which the viewer's gaze slides into the street down below (fig.5). Such a contrast redoubles the shock of realising how the city's material and social fabric was rapidly changing.[27]

Abbott had come in contact with artists of the European avant-garde milieu while living in Paris and Berlin during the 1920s and become so fascinated with the work of Eugène Atget that, after his death, she carried his archive of prints and negatives with her when she returned to America. Her survey of New York's streets and buildings, funded by the Federal Art Project, attests to the power of photography to expose the bewildering pace of change. Being afraid of heights, Abbott refrained from leaning over tall window ledges, yet managed to hold her bulky apparatus in the threshold space between inside and outside. Her shots from on high convey a mix of daring and hesitation, as though the camera acted as a shield between the photographer and the abyss. In keeping with her desire to give expression to every subject, those roof's-eye views may be regarded not only as depictions of buildings and canyons but as attempts to capture the visceral feelings elicited by their new vantage points. These images convey like few others the vertigo of the metropolis: that ineffable yet all-pervasive sensation which bears on the experience of time as well as of space.

5 Berenice Abbott, Wall Street from roof of Irving Trust Co. Building, New York, 1938.

THE FALLING GAZE

As the field of aerial vision was expanded through ever more advanced technologies over the second half of the 20th century, the photography of cities from tall buildings lost the powerful impact of its heyday, yet never disappeared. Between the late 2000s and the early 2010s, as vertical urbanisation grew rapidly around the world, several photographers set out to represent cityscapes in ways that harked back to the 'new vision' of the inter-war period. The destabilising effects of looking down from on high are explored by Navid Baraty in the *Intersection* project, in which plunging shots emphasise the spatial depth of New York's canyons. As the internet became awash with pictures shot by amateurs leaning over high-rises, Baraty's bird's-eye views echo the quest for abstract patterns that animated 20th-century avant-garde photographers (plate 1).

Nor was this revival an American prerogative. The downward view from heights reflected the spread of vertical urbanisation. André Lichtenberg's *Vertigo* series (2008) is a set of vertical photographs taken from One Canada Square in London's Canary Wharf (the UK's tallest building at the time) which employ a long depth of field to plunge the viewer's gaze into the urban abyss. As in some of Abbott's photographs of 1930s' New York, the simultaneous perception of the skyscraper's facade receding from the foreground, and of the street in the background, conjures up a sensation of perceptual instability that is akin to dizziness (plate 2). With all their differences, both Lichtenberg's and Baraty's works signal alternate ways of engaging with urban verticality. Taking on skyscrapers as architectural subjects and viewing platforms at once, their photographs expose the dizzying spaces of contemporary cities.

The intrinsic link between verticality and vertigo was made explicit by the photographer Gabriele Basilico, who, after studying architecture, developed a distinct method for measuring space with the camera.[28] Over a prolific career that spanned the 1970s to the 2010s, Basilico observed cities as entities in continuous transformation. Similar to Abbott's approach, his research began as a catalogue of buildings and developed into an analysis of urban environments nourished by a slow and contemplative gaze. Despite being a convinced horizontalist, renowned for his black-and-white shots from street level, in the latter part of his life the photographer embraced the downward view as a central motif.

A pivotal moment was the solo exhibition *Verticale*, held in Turin in 2007, which brought together a selection of Basilico's photographs taken in cities as diverse as Barcelona, Monaco and San Francisco. It was a conscious attempt to revive the *vue en plongée* by echoing the giddy-making works of the early 20th century. However, Basilico's approach to verticality transcended the technical definition of plumb view and referred, more broadly, to a 'dynamic attitude of the gaze' that allowed the photographer to picture the abyss below.[29] It was this attitude that prompted him to excavate in different cities the layers of spatial depth that are visible from on high. Verticality, therefore, was not reduced to a geometric quality of architecture (the perpendicular dimension of structures against the horizontal plane), but rather, interpreted as a critical way of seeing.

The title of the Turin exhibition signified for Basilico a distinctive mode of urban observation: 'The attraction towards a vanishing point that makes one's gaze fall downwards and, with a near sense of vertigo, brings closer the movement and flows that occur between the city's full and empty [spaces].'[30]

This artistic research culminated in a project that Basilico carried out in Moscow with the architect Umberto Zanetti, which led to the 2008 photobook *Mosca Verticale* (translated into English as *Vertiginous Moscow*).[31] The title's adaptation highlights the sense of perceptual disorientation underlying this particular work. Its structuring devices are the seven monumental towers erected at Stalin's behest, between the late 1940s and the mid-1950s, in order to enhance the city's architectural profile. In line with the master plan approved by Stalin himself in 1935, the so-called 'Seven Sisters' were intended to harmonise with the historical fabric, crowning the vast redevelopment that transformed the Soviet capital. This was in contrast to the skyscrapers that defined New York's skyline, whose dark canyons were seen by the Soviet authorities as a symbol of capitalist greed. Hence, the chosen term for the new high-rise buildings (*vysotnye zdaniya*), was at variance with the word skyscraper, which 'came to be seen as impregnated with Americanism'.[32]

Built in the socialist classicist style that became the trademark of post-war architecture in the USSR, they were designed to be the smaller siblings of the Palace of the Soviets, the colossal project which, at over 400 metres, would have surpassed in size any other construction in the world. Although the latter was never achieved, the monumental towers that were erected redefined Moscow's skyline, providing a web of orientation points that unified the centre of the city with its edges.[33] In the historian Karl Schlögel's words: 'They stand in exposed, dominating positions, just as castles were formerly built on strategically advantageous sites.'[34] As a consequence, these landmarks provided Basilico with a series of privileged observation points to apprehend the scale of Moscow's post-Communist transition.

The visual contents of *Vertiginous Moscow* are characterised by an alternation between monochrome photographs of the towers taken from street level and colour views from their summits, combining high-angle shots with panoramic ones. Throughout the book, abrupt variations of perspective, tone and focal length reposition the viewer vis-à-vis the subject. The angles of vision are constantly shifting as straight shots are interspersed with oblique ones, creating an effect of visual disorientation. This seemingly jumbled structure in fact reproduces, dialectically, the dual nature of the towers: at once monumental architectures and vantage points. By framing the city as a landscape, Basilico established a distance that would allow him to recombine, in 'stereoscopic' fashion, his memories of the former Communist city with impressions of its changed fabric. Upon re-visiting Moscow, he was struck by the intensity of the traffic and by the signs of fast-growing yet blatantly uneven wealth. The foci of the project were partly chosen in recognition of their enduring prominence, but, over and above, they responded to visual motives:

> I also chose the towers because the most important thing they gave me was a 360° vantage point of the entire capital that would enable me both to document the city and to capture the alluring sense of mental and physical vertigo, as well as the visual dynamic that is all too easily attributed to artists of the Revolution like Alexander Rodchenko.[35]

Adopting this attitude, *Vertiginous Moscow* invites us to gaze upward as well as downward, a double movement that is central to the psychology of gravity. The tilted camera angles are an explicit tribute to the New Vision: 'A reference and also a homage to the memory of the *vue en plongée* that, from the Bauhaus experiments through to the 1930s, was an aesthetic and symbolic code of modernity as well as an original visual interpretation of space.'[36] Today, the towers house public institutions such as the Ministry of Foreign Affairs along with various offices, hotels and apartment blocks. The most compelling section of the photobook regards Moscow State University (MGU), the imposing architectural complex that offers exceptional vantage points over the city from Lenin Hills (fig.6 and plate 3). Crowned by the tallest tower (at 240 metres in height), it partly made up for the loss of verticality caused by the aborted centrepiece of the scheme.[37]

In a tutorial published in *Abitare*, Basilico himself described the feelings inspired by that vantage: 'When you reach the topmost point of a skyscraper like the MGU university tower in Moscow and look down on the surrounding city, you experience two things: vertigo/instability, and a desire to contemplate.'[38] The sequence of images of and from the main university building unfolds as though from a banking aircraft that gradually steadies its flight, an impression that is heightened by the close-up views of turrets in the foreground. In the closing pictures, the straightened horizon line restores a sense of balance after a destabilising journey.

Searching the landscape for spatial relations, Basilico investigated the city's change while also alluding to its possible futures. While capturing the

6 Gabriele Basilico, view of Moscow State University complex, 2007–2008.

transformation of the post-Soviet capital, *Vertiginous Moscow* evokes its vertical growth impending in the background, where the International Business Centre looms with its cluster of skyscrapers. This high-rise district (also known as Moscow City) is an index of the corporate verticality that has reshaped the city's skyline in the early 21st century. Basilico's project manifests a dynamic attitude that was honed through conscious and controlled operations. By letting his gaze fall from Moscow's towers, he represented the visceral sensation of height vertigo: the perceptual tension between a static, grounded body and the shock imagination of a sudden freefall that is induced by looking down a sheer drop. The falling gaze was about to become, in different guises, a popular means of exploring the space of vertical cities and their pace of change.

MOVING IMAGES

While photographers have been exploring a variety of oblique and vertical perspectives on cities, video and film artists have developed in parallel new ways of representing our bewildering urban condition. A case in point is Tom Wolseley's essay film, *Vertical Horizons: In the Shadow of The Shard* (2017), which puts forward a critique of neoliberal development by focusing on the mixed-use skyscraper designed by Renzo Piano Building Workshop and formerly known as London Bridge Tower: Europe's tallest building until it was overtaken by the high-rises of Moscow City. Placed at varying distances from The Shard, the camera moves in circles that encompass the surrounding landscapes while the voice-over narrative blends personal and political reflections. Through slow circular motions, the film engenders a cumulative effect of displacement in the viewer. Rather than adopting dizzy-making shots, Wolseley opted instead to conjure the transformation of the city through a series of pans across London's 'vertical horizons', meditating on the politics of urban growth and its socio-economic implications.

In other cases, the rotation of the camera allows film makers to reproduce a feeling of disorientation that is akin to vertigo. This technique is used to powerful effect in another essay film, *Many Undulating Things* (2019), whereby Bo Wang and Pan Lu expose the power structures underlying the urban development of Hong Kong. A queasy-making scene is shot in the courtyard of the first social housing estate built in the metropolitan area: pointing upward, the camera slowly pivots around the vertical space framed by the complex, with the sky as its backdrop, while the narrator declares his troubles with balance. This shot reminds us that height-induced vertigo may be elicited by looking up as well as down: for height perception is a case of distance perception, which in the absence of nearby reference points in space may impair our sense of balance and induce a behaviour of 'depth avoidance'. While this behaviour is driven by an instinctual response to avert the danger of falling down, our visual apparatus processes distance in a similar way when we look up, which explains why many people are troubled by the sight of tall buildings from below.

In Hong Kong, which contains some of the most densely populated places in the world, the upward perspective from housing courtyards is often bound on all sides by high-rise blocks. This unique urban landscape has sparked off representations such as *Vertical Horizons*, a photobook by Romain

Jacquet-Lagreze whose images invite our gaze to fall up, as it were, into the portion of sky framed by the buildings.[39] While this point of view tends to aestheticise the geometric patterns of architecture, however, the dizziness conveyed by the upward shot in *Many Undulating Things* reinforces a critique of speculative development. Throughout the film, the voice-over guides us through a multitude of spaces ranging from the container port, where workers assist the crane-lifting operations, to the ubiquitous escalators that traverse interior and exterior spaces alike. Thereby, the film sheds light on the often invisible processes that underlie the production of space in this 'city without ground'.[40] Hong Kong emerges as a place in a state of precarious balance.

Other tendencies can be detected in mainland China, where the process of vertical urbanisation marked the country's emergence as a global economic superpower. A 2017 video installation by the artist Chen Chenchen, *The Mercy of Not Killing*, makes reference to the cliff-hanger trope of Hollywood cinema. It features a group of men hanging on the edge of a concrete water tower, framed by a drone camera that revolves around the scene in circular movements (plate 4). While the spiralling motion enhances the sense of vertigo, a 'making of' video shows the men being held fast by an invisible wire in the style of action movies. Chen's overt intention was to highlight a universal spirit of compassion, a sentiment that may also be detected in the dramatic opening sequence of Hitchcock's *Vertigo*.

The encircling of the tower from the air is reminiscent of Steve McQueen's short film, *Static* (2009), shot from a helicopter that hovers over the Statue of Liberty in New York, scrutinising it from different angles. If McQueen's work addresses issues of freedom, surveillance and control in the context of American history, Chen's video implicitly evokes the state of suspension in which the lives of many workers are precariously held. In the gallery setting, viewers are invited to identify with the aerial gaze by stepping on a raised platform that simulates the top of the tower, watching the video at their feet.[41]

This work has drawn comparisons with the plight of Chinese workers who stage life-threatening performances on rooftops in protest against harsh labour conditions. As Margaret Hillenbrand notes: 'In suicide shows, that place of exile is metaphorized as the looming freefall on the brink of which the protestor teeters in full view of impromptu audiences on the street below.'[42] Building rooftops provide places of escape in which lives at the margins of society can be made visible, not only to direct bystanders but to viewers on social media. *The Mercy of Not Killing* draws implicit attention to these events;

yet, for Hillenbrand, it effectively denies the workers' right to assert their own performative space by parodying them in an art installation. Nonetheless, Chen's piece testifies to the power of a visual trope that is brought to bear on the socio-spatial disorientations of our epoch.

Adapting framing techniques that have long belonged to cinema's stock-in-trade, contemporary image makers have resorted to radical effects such as overturning the camera (or the picture itself) in order to summon up vertiginous sensations. This aesthetic of inversion is deployed by Dimitri Venkov in the short film *The Hymns of Muscovy* (2018), which transports the spectator on a slow-motion ride through the Russian capital, or rather to its fictionalised alter ego renamed after the medieval Principality that preceded the Tsardom. The cityscape is shown upside-down, giving viewers the impression of flying through visionary landscapes as though in a sci-fi movie. Here Stalin's high-rises feature amongst a sequence of historical and contemporary buildings that appear to be suspended over the sky. In a journey through architectural styles, the camera glides smoothly past industrial constructions, office towers and apartment blocks, cruising all the way to Moscow City. The business district appears through a veil of mist, evoking a dreamlike vision from another world. Having reached its final destination, the camera pans vertically across the skyscraper cluster, pulling our gaze down into the sky deep below (plate 5).

By turning architecture on its head, *The Hymns of Muscovy* confounds our perception in a strangely familiar way, for the view of the city is not merely tilted off the vertical axis but completely overturned. The result is a mirror image that resembles a landscape reflected off the surface of water. Here the dynamic attitude requires spectators to let their gaze fall downwards. However, this visual effect should not be reduced to a mere formal experiment. The process of inversion embodies Venkov's sense of alienation in a city where social life seemed to be losing its grounding. His film, then, may be regarded as an allegory of the condition of instability into which the capital, and the wider country, was falling ever more deeply while its architectural pinnacles reached new heights. This reflective nostalgia is all the more poignant in light of the totalitarian drift that swept over Russia, culminating in the military invasion of Ukraine in February 2022.

Broadly speaking, the visual artworks examined in this section resonate with the perception of falling that, as the artist and theorist Hito Steyerl has pointed out, permeates contemporary visual culture: 'Traditional modes of seeing and feeling are shattered. Any sense of balance is disrupted. Perspectives are twisted and multiplied. New types of visuality arise. [. . .] Grappling with crumbling futures that propel us backwards onto an agonizing present, we may realize that the place we are falling toward is no longer grounded, nor is it stable.'[43] Steyerl critiques the idea of a safe and stable ground as a modern construct that originated in the Renaissance with the advent of linear perspective, establishing a scopic regime that has been overcome by groundless forms of perception. Embracing a space of representation defined by the freefall, rather than by a reassuring yet illusory ground, she suggests, is a frightening yet also liberatory gesture.

ART OF VERTIGO

Among the artists who have more consistently deployed the camera in order to destabilise the viewer's perception of architecture is Catherine Yass, whose film installations might be regarded as a veritable 'art of vertigo'.[44] Yass's concern with buildings emerged in the 1990s amid a broader turn to site specificity in art practice; then, in the noughties, verticality became a focus of her work. By depicting structures in a state of abandonment, demolition or transformation, her film installations have since exposed architecture as an embodiment of ideology.

Yass's 2002 piece, *Descent*, provides an unsettling glimpse of high-rise construction in London's Canary Wharf. The viewer's gaze glides vertically along the skeleton of a tower in slow motion: only when the fog dissipates, and surrounding buildings enter the frame, do we realise that the camera (lodged in a crane) is moving down and not up as it seemed. Michael Newman aptly noted that the picture is arrested before touching the ground, as often happens in dreams of falling.[45] *Descent* evokes a wake-up call from the dream of an upside-down world. By reversing the upward direction of the corporate city, this work reveals a deeper political motive: the sky-bound process of construction is turned on itself as the gaze is slowly grounded. Here the high-rise business district, symbol of the economic deregulation that marked the Thatcher years, reawakens our ancestral imagination of the abyss – that bottomless place which opens up when the ground underneath our feet slips away (fig.7).

In his psychology of gravity, Bachelard considered ascent and descent in dialectical terms: 'Verticality is so impressionable a human dimension that it

7 Frame from *Descent*, film installation, 2002.

occasionally permits an image to be elongated, stretching it in two directions at once, both upwards and downwards.'[46] This double movement is central to *Descent*. As a building crane pulls our gaze along the vertical axis, confounding our notions of lightness and heaviness, our perception of time, too, becomes elastic. An unnatural slowness pervades the film since the implied fall, which would only last a few dramatic seconds in real time, is protracted over eight long minutes. The sense of dislocation makes you interrogate when, as well as where, the scene is taking place; for the construction site bears archaeological and futuristic semblances at once. In this respect, *Descent* evokes the biblical Tower of Babel and its failed dream to conquer the sky, a hubristic tale that is bound to resurface with the boom of vertical urbanism.

Yass's subsequent films sustain her critique of verticality as a prominent, and highly problematic, aspect of urban development. If *Descent* was based on a technique of inversion, other works conjure a sense of vertigo through camera movements as well as rotations of the image. Prompted by the refurbishment of London's Broadcasting House, *Flight* (also made in 2002) was shot from a miniature helicopter flying around the building's roof, leading to a visual experiment in 'the kinetics of vertigo'.[47] This approach was further developed in *Lighthouse* (2011), which is centred on a decommissioned structure standing on a concrete platform, uninhabited, five miles off England's southeast coast. The precarious state of the Royal Sovereign Lighthouse raises questions about our ambivalent relationship with modernity and its material structures. Hovering over the concrete tower and panning across its surface from different angles, the camera's eye draws attention to a conceptually slippery material that has historically been endowed with symbolic and political meanings.[48] The state of suspension in which the subject is caught as it awaits demolition is depicted in vertiginous fashion, giving expression to the artist's concern with 'the spatial dimension of time'.[49]

A poignant sense of loss also pervades *Royal London* (2018), shot in an 18th-century public hospital undergoing partial demolition. Capturing the building in a state of ruination, here Yass evokes the threatened collapse of a public health service that epitomised the welfare state. The camera turns and tilts queasily through multiple revolutions in rapid sequence until it looks up through an aperture where debris falls towards the lens. The cinematic metaphor is emphasised by implicit references to Hitchcock's *Vertigo*, not only in the stairwell but also in the burial shots, which call to mind Scottie's nightmare of falling into the grave. In *Royal London* the sense of dizziness transcends the experiential level to suggest a spiral of social disintegration.

Yass's art of vertigo reaches its climax in *Last Stand* (2019), which focuses on a building site in Nine Elms, a former industrial site that was turned into the largest regeneration zone in Europe – or, according to a critic, a 'forest of towers [. . .] devoid of the most basic social facilities'.[50] The film sets off with the camera tracking up on a crane along a concrete frame under construction: blue numbers are etched on each floor, punctuating the ascent like giant elevator buttons. At the summit stands the artist herself, on a metal scaffold, surrounded by iron reinforcement rods jutting out of the concrete. Perched atop the unfinished structure, Yass takes a stand against the vertical growth that has been reshaping London's landscape. The construction site here embodies the stealthy yet relentless triumph of neoliberalism, whose ascendancy relies upon the compliance of subjects-entrepreneurs to perpetuate its values (fig.8).

The camera, mounted on a crane as in *Descent*, moves in circles around the artist's unwavering body and shows the urban environment that is rising all around. Multiple rotations elicit the frenetic growth of a city driven by

8 Frame from *Last Stand*, film installation by Catherine Yass, 2019.

corporate offices and luxury apartment blocks. Turning the gaze of power on itself, the artist's body becomes a living measure of the scale of construction. In fact, *Last Stand* conflates three intertwined forms of vertigo: the vicarious sensation that is felt by identifying with the artist; the visual disorientation caused by the revolving camera movements; and the dizzy pace and scale of development. The combined effect of these aspects, from the experiential to the conceptual, induces a profound sense of dislocation. In Yass's film, the act of standing at the summit of a tall structure is antithetical to the notion of *living on the edge* that pervades our performance society.

In 2002 the illusionist David Blaine performed a dramatic stunt in New York by standing on a 30-metre-high pillar for a day and a half before he jumped to safety in front of a spectating crowd. The performance, titled *Vertigo*, was an act of extreme physical endurance which resonated, unmistakeably, with the traumatic events that had shaken that city the previous year. In *Last Stand*, rather than thrilling the viewer with a sensational feat, Yass embodies an altogether different resolution as she bears witness to a landscape that is changing out of proportion under the force of a rampant property market. Her show of defiance lays bare the tension between the impulse to conquer the sky and the spectre of an imminent downfall, evoking once again the hubris of sky-bound construction. This work prompts us to apprehend vertigo in all its ambivalence: an inebriating feeling of liberation but also, at the same time, a worrying symptom of instability.

A distinct sense of vertigo pervades the architectural film installations that Yass has made since the noughties. Architecture is depicted in a state of suspension between the desire of elevation and the fear of falling, thereby highlighting the precariousness of our social fabric. Not by chance has Yass's work been associated with those art practices that embrace dizziness as a method, seeking out 'the creative and generative potential of this in-between state'.[51] Bringing this attitude to bear on architecture, her films subvert the stability of the ground and explore the capacity of this medium to create new types of visuality. Thereby, they exemplify a direction of visual art which, as Steyerl suggests, enacts the experience of falling by aesthetic means.

In different ways, the artworks and projects discussed in this chapter suggest that architecture is implicated at various levels in the experience of vertigo. While this phenomenon is usually associated with a psycho-physiological sensation, one that can be triggered by the experience of tall structures, the sense of perceptual disorientation applies just as powerfully to our response to the social and political conditions in which we live. Much as contemporary writers and philosophers have employed the concept of vertigo in metaphorical ways, artists have been variously interpreting architecture as an ungrounded field. If these works make you dizzy, they also make you alert to the contradictions that are inscribed in the built environment.

Plate 1 Navid Baraty, photograph from the *Intersection* series, New York, 2012.

Plate 2 André Lichtenberg, 'North Side' from *Vertigo* series, 2008.

Plate 3 Gabriele Basilico, view of/from Moscow State University, 2007–2008.

ABOVE
RIGHT

Plate 4 Frame from *The Mercy of Not Killing*, video installation by Chen Chenchen, China, 2017.

Plate 5 Frame from *The Hymns of Muscovy* (dir. Dimitri Venkov, Russia, 2018).

RIGHT, TOP

Plate 6 Philippe Petit walks on a wire between the Twin Towers of the World Trade Center, New York, 7 August 1974.

RIGHT, BOTTOM

Plate 7 Nik Wallenda walks on a wire at Marina City, Chicago, 3 November 2014.

Plate 8 Catherine Yass, *High Wire*, four-screen film installation exhibited in Ambika P3, London, 2021.

VUE DE L'ENFER PRÈS DE LA MONTAGNE DE L'OISEAU ET DU GLACIER DE RHINWALD.

Publié par Louis Bleuler à Schaffhouse en Suisse

LEFT

Plate 9 Johann Ludwig Bleuler, 'View of hell near the Mountain of the Bird and the Rhinewald glacier', aquatint, 1836 or after.

RIGHT

Plate 10 Greenpeace activists climb The Shard as part of the 'Save the Arctic' campaign, London, 11 July 2013.

Plate 11 Alain Robert scales the Ariane Tower at La Défense, Paris, 8 October 2009.

Plate 12 A now-demolished gas holder in Wood Green, part of the industrial heritage of East London, 2014.

JOBOX

Plate 13 Tom Ryaboi, 'Highlife', Toronto, 2014.

Plate 14 Caspar David Friedrich, *Wanderer above the Sea of Fog*, 1818.

PART II

TAMING VERTIGO

3

WIRE WALKING IN THE CITY

Tell me, am I wrong to mock vertigo from summit to abyss, to reveal the world as I see it?[1]

9 'Il volo del turco': man walking a tightrope between St Mark's campanile and a mooring pad in Venice, woodcut, 16th century.

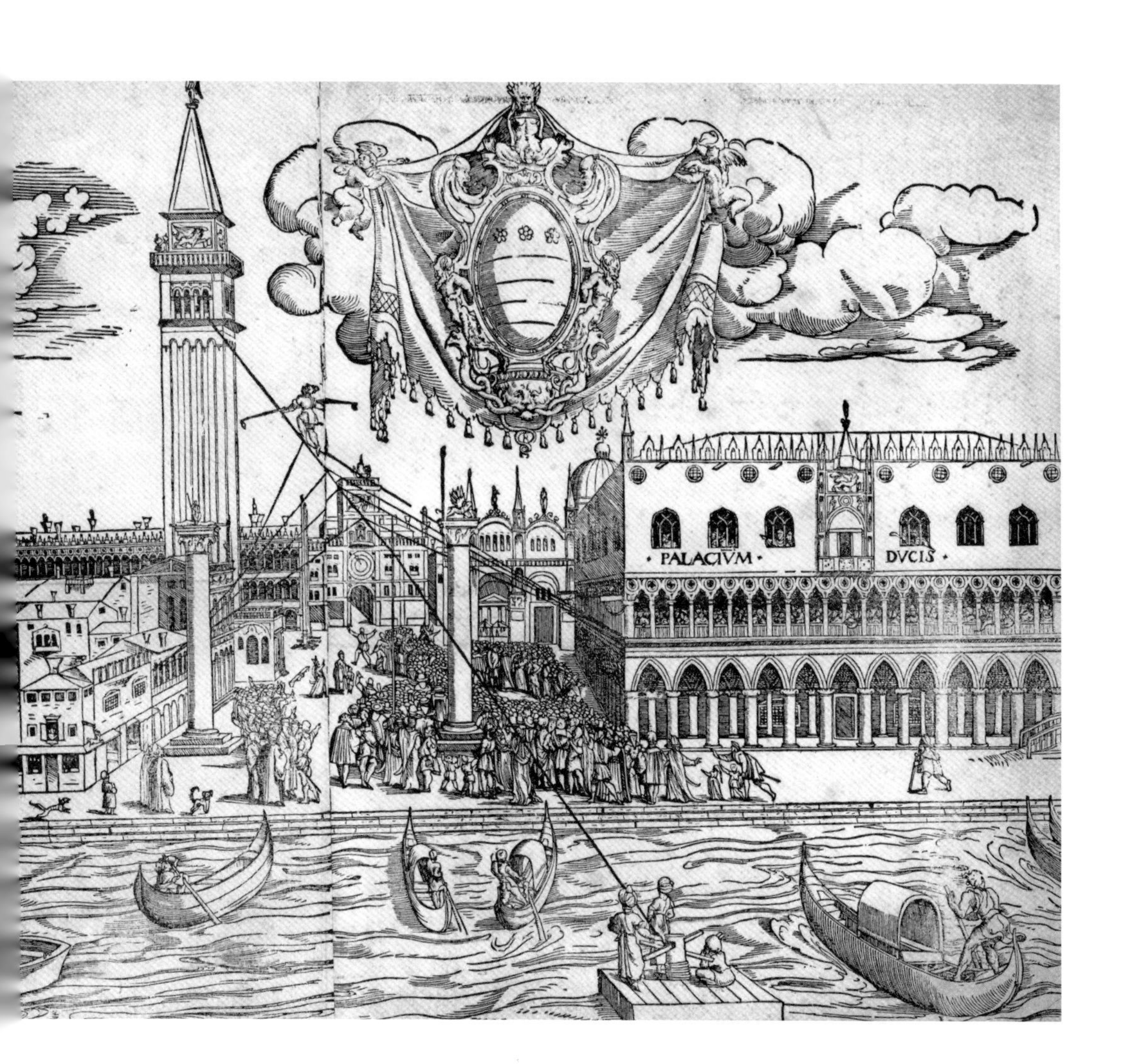
PALACIVM DVCIS

THE PLAY OF BALANCE

It is hard to find a figure that encapsulates the pursuit of balance more vividly than the funambulist. Tightrope walking – also known in the past as rope dancing – evokes a liberation from gravity that sums up the human longing for weightlessness. In his seminal 1958 book, *Man, Play and Games*, Roger Caillois singled out this practice as an exemplar of equilibrium. Exploring the structures of human play, Caillois adopted the Greek word for whirlpool, *ilinx* (from which derives *ilingos*, vertigo) to denote the pursuit of visceral thrills that are akin to an eddy or vortex. His research developed on the premise laid out two decades before by the Dutch historian Johan Huizinga, whose *Homo Ludens* had provided the first systematic enquiry into the play element in Western culture.[2] Under *ilinx*, Caillois subsumed a whole typology of 'vertigo games' which Huizinga had overlooked because of their alleged lack of cultural significance.

The French author laid emphasis on those forms of play that induce a state of transport in their players, an abandonment that derives pleasure from the momentary loss of balance: 'In all cases, it is a question of surrendering to a kind of spasm, seizure, or shock which destroys reality with sovereign brusqueness.'[3] Games of *ilinx* include activities that alter our perceptual stability through bodily movement (for example, dance) or mechanically induced speed (for example, fast cars or roller coasters), but also through the agency of substances that alter our consciousness (for example, alcohol or drugs). Caillois aligned these with the spontaneous dimension of play, the visceral impulse towards disorder and chaos. Yet, at the same time, he recognised that games of *ilinx* may also belong to the sphere of rationality, the opposite tendency governed by rule, technique and discipline:

> The desire to overcome an obstacle can only emerge to combat vertigo and prevent it from becoming transformed into disorder or panic. It is, therefore, training in self-control, an arduous effort to preserve calm and equilibrium. Far from being compatible with *ilinx*, it provides the discipline needed to neutralize the dangerous effects of *ilinx*, as in mountain climbing or tightrope walking.[4]

This passage encapsulates the ambivalent nature of *ilinx*, which relates to the instinctual pursuit of vertigo but also, by extension, to those practices that aspire to subdue it. For Caillois, the funambulist embodies this trait of *homo ludens* in its purest form: 'On the high wire, the very heart of prowess and the only aim is to master vertigo. The game consists expressly in moving through space as if the void were not fascinating, and as if no danger were involved.'[5] Real hazards, however, are never banished from this realm of play.

The tightrope art, which dates back to Ancient Greece, flourished in Europe during the Middle Ages as a form of private entertainment for the upper classes. Early forays into public places were recorded in Venice in the middle of the 16th century, when the spectacle of the 'Flying Turk' became part of the carnival celebrations (fig.9). The rite was inaugurated by a young acrobat who walked on a rope stretched between a boat moored in the lagoon and the bell tower in St Mark's Square, embodying the fraught relationship between the Republic of Venice ('La Serenissima') and the Ottoman Empire. As the theatre scholar Erith Jaffe-Berg notes, 'the performer accentuates the implicit boundary between water and land and between the northeastern Mediterranean (Turkey) and the north-central Mediterranean (Venice). The Turco is literally on a boundary symbolized by the rope and by the fact he hovers over both terra firma and water.'[6] The ritual, which in different guises continues to this date, drew attention to the architectural landmark that towered above the city, casting its symbolic power over the fluid space of exchanges across the sea. Thereby, St Mark's Campanile became the focal point of a performance that turned funambulism into a public spectacle.

For a long time, urban acrobatics continued to be associated with the licentious morals of street life. A turning point was marked in the late 18th century by the emergence of the modern circus, which channelled the growing desire for sensory engagement amid a wider reorganisation of leisure in Europe.[7] With its medley of acrobats, jugglers and clowns, the travelling circus represented a microcosm in which the orderly rules of urban life were subverted. In turn, this alternate world captured the imagination of modern artists who regarded the audacity and creativity of circus performers as a means of rising above the oppressive social conditions. Jean Starobinski has pointed out that 19th-century French painters and writers, from Edgar Degas to Théodore de Banville, identified their poetic activities with the prowess of the acrobat-clown, whose dangerous art was elevated to an allegory of freedom.[8] If the clown always 'comes out of another space', showing up against a gaping void, the aerialist performs risky manoeuvres over a terrifying abyss.[9]

10 'Descent of Madame Saqui surrounded by Fireworks', aquatint, 1822.

The tightrope walker enacts a symbolic conquest of space by reaching the end of the line.

While this practice flourished in the circus, during the 19th century it found new stages in the open air. The funambulist took a firm hold on the Western imagination as urban crowds were enchanted by spectacular rope-walking feats. A pioneer of this art was Marguerite-Antoinette Lalanne, better known as Madame Saqui, who became a celebrity in the early 1800s owing to her flamboyant theatrics enhanced by risqué costumes (fig.10). She burst to prominence through a sensational walk performed at Tivoli Gardens, in Paris, for a public celebration that included pantomimes and firework displays. The collective euphoria that marked the scene, drawing a thundering applause, was later recounted by Saqui's biographer: 'We squeeze on the embankment, anxiously waiting; all Paris is there, all eyes are fixated on the rope.'[10] Besides her legendary Parisian acts, which included rope-walking through fireworks across the Seine, the funambulist graced spectators at London's Vauxhall Gardens and other amusement parks. Saqui was among the acrobats who let the art of funambulism prosper outside the confines of the circus, establishing her own theatre in Paris at a time when growing urban populations created a new demand for public entertainment.

DANGEROUS CROSSINGS

In the wake of the first Industrial Revolution, the tightrope came to epitomise the human drive to conquer nature amid the relentless progress of technology. Transfixing the public with its unique blend of prowess and grace, this art peaked in the middle of the 19th century amidst an array of entertainments that thrived on the dangers of falling. Hemp ropes were replaced by metal wires, made first of copper then steel, allowing stunts to be carried out at ever greater heights over natural gorges and rivers as well as urban squares and parks. Balancing on the narrowest edges, aerialists had to confront the lure of the void and withstand the threat of the elements. Their ability to fight off height vertigo was key to their awe-inspiring performances.

The rise to prominence of these public spectacles is bound up with the aesthetics of the sublime. In thrall to the spectacle of nature, Romantic writers of the early 19th century embraced the giddy states of consciousness provoked by the sight of the abyss. In Percy Shelley's *Mont Blanc* poem, for instance, an ecstatic vision of the Alps epitomises the overbearing power of nature:

> Thou art pervaded with that ceaseless motion,
> Thou art the path of that unresting sound –
> Dizzy Ravine! and when I gaze on thee
> I seem as in a trance sublime and strange[11]

Previously, Immanuel Kant had described how natural landscapes had the power of destabilising the human senses and, consequently, of elevating the spirit. In his *Critique of Judgment*, he deployed the category of 'dynamically sublime' to describe an aesthetic experience that was akin to an inner vibration: 'a rapid alternation of repulsion from, and attraction to, one and the same object'.[12] The realisation of human impotence in front of nature was the prelude to a moment of recognition in which reason would transcend physical obstacles and thereby assert its superiority. With reference to natural formations such as rocks, volcanoes and waterfalls, Kant wrote:

> Compared to the might of any of these, our ability to resist becomes an insignificant trifle. Yet the sight of them becomes all the more attractive the more fearful it is, provided we are in a safe place. And we like to call

> these objects sublime because they raise the soul's fortitude above its usual middle range and allow us to discover in ourselves an ability to resist which is of a quite different kind, and which gives us the courage [to believe] that we could be a match for nature's seeming omnipotence.[13]

The caveat was essential since, for Kant, the aesthetic contemplation of landscapes was emboldened by the safety of a sheltered place. This idea was in turn derived from Edmund Burke's mid-18th-century conception of the sublime, which laid the foundation for the subsequent appraisal by the German philosopher. As Burke observed, 'When danger or pain press too nearly, they are incapable of giving any delight, and are simply terrible; but at certain distances, and with certain modifications, they may be, and they are, delightful, as we every day experience.'[14] A century on, amid the technological onslaught of the industrial era, the might of nature was challenged by a host of performers who defied the force of gravity. Modern practices like parachuting and high diving brought about a new imagination of heights and lent celebrity status to their practitioners. So pervasive was the imperative to master the force of nature that the 19th century has been dubbed 'the gravity century'.[15]

In the mid-1800s, wire walking became one of the most popular forms of spectacle in the West. The climax was on 20 June 1859, when the French celebrity funambulist Jean-François Gravelet, better known as the Great Blondin, crossed Niagara Falls with the aid of a balancing pole on a cable rigged nearly 50 metres above the water (fig.11). In the process, Blondin traversed the invisible border between the United States and Canada, a frontier that was loaded with meanings including symbolic references to the American history of slavery.[16] The event reportedly attracted circa 25,000 spectators amassed at various points on terra firma, on scaffolds and along the suspension bridge that spanned over 250 metres across the Niagara River. By a historical coincidence, the bridge, engineered by John Augustus Roebling and built between 1851 and 1855 using his innovative method (ropes attached to the main cables and spun on pulleys), became the viewing platform for that sensational wire-walking act. Crowds of onlookers lined the roadway on the lower deck and spilled into the upper railroad track as well. Blondin's performance had enormous resonance around the world and was hailed as one of the greatest human achievements of all times. Taking place a year after the opening of the first transatlantic telegraph and in the midst of the Colorado Gold Rush, it embodied the affirmation of human willpower over nature.

11 Charles Blondin's rope ascension over the Niagara River, *c.*1859. Stereograph by George Barker.

Blondin stunned crowds at Niagara over two consecutive years, accomplishing ever more challenging stunts that became legendary, such as walking blindfolded, on stilts, and carrying his manager on a rope. During a European tour, in 1861, he performed across the transept of the Crystal Palace in Sydenham, where the iron-and-glass structure had been re-erected after the Great Exhibition. The funambulist exalted the vast interior space with arresting feats that included somersaults on stilts, thus transposing the gravity challenge to the temple of modern construction. His contemporary biographer, George Linnaeus Banks, expressed admiration for this event and wondered about the perspective from up high:

> It would be almost impossible to witness anything so strangely interesting as this performance. There is a sort of fascination, at least for some people, in looking down from a great height. From the topmost gallery the descent must have been terrific, and what then was it likely to be when seen from the rope itself? One can hardly help shuddering at the very thought of it, especially when the impression is fresh upon the mind of 'fantastic tricks' which the audacious acrobat played over the yawning abyss. 'Twas a sight never to be forgotten.[17]

Not everyone was equally impressed though. While the drive to impose an order on nature was a defining trait of the Industrial Revolution, the sight of a man risking life and limb on a rope raised eyebrows. In Britain, *The London Review* played down the wire walker's prowess and criticised the furore over a spectacle that many people purportedly attended in the hope of witnessing an accident:

> The mere act of walking or dancing on a tight rope is one that, however hard we might find it ourselves, evidently presents no difficulty whatever to those who are early trained to it. Again, the capability of looking down from all heights with equal indifference, is a faculty which no sailor, no bricklayer finds any difficulty in acquiring, and which inhabitants of mountainous districts possess, if we may say so, by nature.[18]

12 Charles Blondin at Shoreditch, engraving by Gustave Doré from *London, a pilgrimage* (1872).

This commentary belied a moralist strand of Victorian culture, coupled with an unscientific understanding of height vertigo at a time when the tallest buildings were still medieval church spires. Yet, the figure of the funambulist had a unique ability to capture the imagination that came to fruition over the second half of the gravity century. In 1872, an engraving of Blondin performing in a Shoreditch theatre featured in *London, a pilgrimage*, the acclaimed book by Gustave Doré and Blanchard Jerrold (fig.12). This flawed yet popular representation of the imperial capital, which was serialised before it appeared in book form, attests to the vogue of a performance art that was chosen to illustrate 'London at play'.

Above and beyond the heroics of individual performers, the modern zeitgeist endowed the tightrope with allegorical meanings.[19] In the prologue of Friedrich Nietzsche's *Thus Spoke Zarathustra*, the eponymous prophet harangues a crowd assembled in a market square where a rope is hanging between two towers: 'Man is a rope stretched between animal and overman – a rope over an abyss', he says to deaf ears.[20] An aerialist then begins to walk over the square with the aid of a balancing pole, only to be chased by a malign jester who crushes him to the ground. Zarathustra consoles the dying man by praising his attempt at the 'dangerous crossing' – a graphic image of the Nietzschean will to power. Commenting on this text, Steven Connor has aptly observed: 'The tightrope walker enacts the tense passage between worlds.'[21] The funambulist pushes the boundaries of human ability through a balancing act that brings onlookers to ponder the fine line between places, countries, conditions – and, ultimately, between life and death.

In the late 19th century this art witnessed its golden age through a spate of performers who sought to emulate Blondin's heroics, some of them taking up his name as well. They included a popular Spanish funambulist called Arsens

13 Maria Spelterini crossing St Aubin's harbour on a tightrope, from *L'Univers illustré* (1873).

Blondin and the English acrobat Selina Young, whose stage name (Paulina Violante) was changed to 'the female Blondin' in 1861 after her namesake's London shows. In the same year Young, who had performed at the Crystal Palace before the Great Blondin himself, crossed the Thames on a rope, establishing a type of urban performance in which the wire formed a tenuous and temporary bridge across a waterway.

Several other women threaded on Madame Saqui's steps to attain the status of gravity heroes. A special place was held by the Italian Maria Spelterini, who was the first woman to walk on a wire across the Niagara Falls. She also crossed the Moskva River in Moscow and the Neva in St Petersburg, reinforcing the significance of wire walking as a means of connecting places. Spelterini's performances, which included a stunt at St Aubin's harbour on the island of Jersey (fig.13), drew ecstatic reactions from commentators who praised her ability to walk 'at vertiginous speed' as well as blindfolded and with her feet wrapped in baskets: 'if her exercises no longer inspire dread', wrote a journalist, 'they seduce at least for the grace and perfection with which they are executed, and which cannot be surpassed'.[22]

The appeal of funambulism gradually diminished as new spectacles took centre stage. All endeavours to rival Blondin's formidable stunts were seen as less of an achievement, hence the 'noble gravity daredevil' began a retreat to the circus.[23] Meanwhile, the modern metropolis was shaping into a place of artificial mountains and canyons as the advent of steel-frame construction, coupled with the invention of the elevator, ushered in the skyscraper era. While high-rise buildings provided a glaring expression of modern technology, the birth of aviation fulfilled the dream of flying after a century in which gravity had been defied through a host of inventions and practices. Gradually, the drawing power of funambulism wore out, yet this ancient art was kept alive by myriads of lesser-known performers over the 20th century. In the aftermath of the Second World War, troupes of young acrobats performed on the wire over the rubbles of German cities, embodying a collective desire for balance and stability: the very act of looking up and contemplating a new rise was a cause for solace after the trauma of mass destruction.[24]

EPHEMERAL BRIDGES

An outstanding figure was Karl Wallenda, an acrobat hailing from a German circus family who had moved to the United States in the 1920s and led his own progeny to legendary status: The Flying Wallendas. In the 1960s, he performed a series of 'skywalks' across natural gorges in a bid to revive the feats accomplished by his famed French precursor a century earlier. Wallenda's final walk took place in 1978, when he fell to his death during a publicity stunt on a wire battered by heavy winds between two hotel buildings in San Juan, Puerto Rico. According to Garrett Soden, the dramatic event ended the epoch of 'gravity heroics' epitomised by the wire walker.[25] Although Wallenda went down as the 'last of the circus's "great" gravity performers', his demise did not spell the end of funambulism.[26] On the contrary, it might be argued that a new phase had already begun. In the early 1970s, Philippe Petit reinvented this practice on the wane by elevating it to an urban art, one in which the city was no longer a mere background but an integral element of the performance.

By transposing the theatrics of rope walking to the depths of urban space Petit crafted a unique brand of funambulism. His walks on the high wire derived from a combination of self-taught street art and poetic reverie that he described as 'writing in the sky'. The first public forays, at Notre Dame Cathedral in Paris (1971) and Sydney Harbour Bridge (1973), were early attempts to create 'ephemeral bridges' across landmarks. These illicit stunts, which were invariably attended by the local police, reached a pinnacle in the high-wire walk between the Twin Towers of the World Trade Center in New York. For a brief moment, on the morning of 7 August 1974, Petit inhabited the abyss of Lower Manhattan by walking back and forth between the tallest paired buildings in the world at over 400 metres high.

This supreme act of balance shifted the perception of the towers from the vertical axis, associated with surveillance and control, to the horizontal axis of everyday life. On the wire, Petit performed his favourite routines such as the act of carrying the balancing pole on one shoulder to mime a homeward-bound worker. By trespassing the airspace between the skyscrapers, he highlighted the power structures that rule over, and effectively produce, the city's vertical dimension. Everything came to a standstill when Petit accomplished what was later described as 'the ultimate urban subversion of modern times'.[27] The apparent mismatch between his fragile body on the wire and the immensity of vertical space that he traversed was in itself a dizzying sight to behold, one that unsettled the conventional narratives of scale based on the miniature and the gigantic.[28]

Several commentators have noted that Petit's high-wire walk somehow managed to humanise the towers.[29] His performance bridged the gap between the human scale and gigantism of corporate skyscrapers. From the beginning, the public perception of the World Trade Center was at odds with the humanistic beliefs of its architect, Minoru Yamasaki, who had drawn inspiration from St Mark's Square in Venice for his idea of a central plaza surrounded by towers – an urbanistic model that, with hindsight, made an unwitting reference to the history of funambulism. The scheme integrated on the same site private companies and public agencies involved in global trade so as to provide, in the architect's words, 'a physical expression of the universal effort of men to seek and achieve world peace'.[30] Nonetheless, the high-rise complex came to embody the dominion of financial capital, whose towering symbols Petit confronted with his own body. While reclaiming the vertical space of the metropolis, in effect, he reinvented the tradition of rope walking for the urban age.

Following the Twin Towers coup, Petit was invited to perform in cities around the world. He developed a series of theatrical performances that climaxed in 1994, when he staged an elaborate walk on an inclined wire, in Frankfurt, as part of the celebrations for the city's 1,200th anniversary. Designed as a journey through the city's history, the performance was witnessed by half a million people on site and broadcast live on television. The Frankfurt act prompted Kurt Wurmli, an artistic consultant and technical supervisor on Petit's performances, to call for theatrical high-wire walks to be recognised as total artworks (*Gesamtkunstwerk*).[31]

Two decades after his master stroke, Petit's art of writing in the sky had gained wide public acclaim and was complemented by writings on paper. His main book, *On the High Wire* (1985), was translated into English by Paul Auster, who coincidentally happened to be in Paris at the time of the Notre Dame stunt.[32] After befriending the funambulist in New York, Auster became a champion of his work and called for wire walking to be taken seriously as an art form on account of its unique aesthetic force:

> The high-wire walker's job is to create a sensation of limitless freedom. [. . .] No art, it seems to me, so clearly emphasizes the deep aesthetic impulse inside us all. Each time we see a man walk on the wire, a part of us is up there with him. Unlike performances in the other arts, the experience of the high wire is direct, unmediated, simple, and it requires no explanation whatsoever. The art is the thing itself, a life in its most naked delineation.[33]

In the aftermath of the 9/11 attacks, the aura of Petit's Twin Towers walk was amplified by a poignant sense of nostalgia. His own narrative of the events inspired a wealth of popular representations and contributed to the making of a modern myth.[34] In his memoir, *To Reach the Clouds*, Petit tells the story of the 1974 coup as a tribute to 'his' towers.[35] Later republished as *Man on Wire*, the book became the subject of an acclaimed documentary of the same title, directed by James Marsh, which was marketed with the tagline: '1974. 1350 feet up. The artistic crime of the century.' The idea that Petit executed his plan like a heist is central to the storyline: both book and film portray a rebellious young man, unafraid to trespass in order to realise his dream after meticulous preparations with a band of accomplices.[36] His ultimate violation, however, was against the law of gravity.

A key to the success of *Man on Wire* was the funambulist's capacity to neutralise the effects of vertigo and, thereby, to avert the angst that is provoked by the encounter with the abyss. Infiltrating the World Trade Center was essential to realise the artistic crime, yet the most significant space that was encroached upon was the dizzying void between the skyscrapers. As Petit himself declared in an interview: 'I rarely looked at the towers. I looked at the negative space that the towers had engendered, and I thought – somebody has to trespass, you know, in that negative space.'[37] His goal was to conquer the airspace defined by the architectural complex where nobody had ever set foot. To walk between two towers a quarter of a mile high, where not even helicopters were allowed to fly, was an extreme act of defiance that draws parallels with Blondin's crossing of Niagara Falls. While the latter had overcome gravity at a site in which it was spectacularly manifested by nature, Petit took the challenge to the vertical city. Throwing an ephemeral bridge across the Twin Towers, he revealed the human-made abyss in all its vertiginous depth.

A metal wire rigged between two buildings may not have been what the German philosopher Georg Simmel envisaged when he described the bridge as the archetype of 'the will to connection'.[38] Nonetheless, Petit's walk distilled the human disposition to create paths: to cite Simmel, 'the bridge symbolizes the extension of our volitional sphere over space'.[39] Not only do bridges connect what is separate (or, rather, what we perceive to be separate); crucially, they also make that connection visible. To consider the high wire an ephemeral bridge, therefore, means to recognise the gesture that underpins the very act of joining places. While suspended structures have symbolic as well as practical values by virtue of their resistance to gravity, the wire has a distinct imaginative agency in that it provides the funambulist with the thinnest support required for an act of balance. In the Twin Towers walk, Petit succeeded in mastering vertigo, appearing to onlookers as if he were walking in mid-air (plate 6).

BEYOND EQUILIBRIUM

If Petit's coup has become a paragon of human balance, this is largely due to its post-9/11 revival. *To Reach the Clouds* describes the process of familiarisation that allowed its author to overpower the adverse effects of vertigo by making acquaintance with the scene. Disguised as an architectural journalist, at one point he obtained permission to interview the builders on the roof of the South Tower under construction. On that occasion, the head of the World Trade

Center reportedly brought up the myth of the 'fearless Mohawks' and told him: '"They're famous for their absence of vertigo, you know."'[40] That comment, which would have been commonplace at the time, prompted Petit to draw an analogy between the coup plotters and the ironworkers 'who assemble steel at dizzying heights'.[41] Neither they nor wire walkers are naturally shielded from the paralysing effects of altitude: however skilled, they need to develop ways of coping with vertigo.

When Petit had an opportunity to explore the South Tower's rooftop, during a reconnaissance mission, he resisted the temptation to let his gaze plunge: 'Then I lean over the edge [...] so I can look straight down. I do not. [...] I had not dared to reach the ledge, had not risked looking down. It was enough to look across.'[42] The day after, he made his way up one more time: 'Again, I consider climbing down to the lower edge, where the sheer aluminum cliff initiates its vertiginous descent. Yesterday I dared not. Today I must. [...] It cannot be done all at once. To overpower vertigo – the keeper of the abyss – one must tame it, cautiously.'[43] Confronting what Petit called the 'almighty void' posed a stern challenge even to the meticulously trained performer: 'Ah, yes, my mind registers, far, far down, the ground, the streets – but my eyes refuse. Yet I breathe in voluptuously the unknown that eddies below. I keep fighting.'[44]

Even when the coup was staged, Petit's struggle was not over until he stepped on the wire and commenced his walk from the South Tower to its northern twin. The initial moments were fraught with hesitation and it was only after completing the first crossing that he fully overcame his fear. As he finally looked down, the void was no longer a source of anxiety but of blissful pleasure:

> As I move along the edge [...], I can't resist the visual dive: I glide in, feel the width of the abyss, I slide down and taste its depth, with delight I brush by the marble plaza at street level, then I hurtle back up along the silver facades onto the dazzling surprise of my sight landing exactly where it started.[45]

Soon he was off again, drawn by the irresistible call of the wire. As Petit's steps became easier, he could embrace the view in a state of serene control, sit on the wire, and salute the city: '*I stare proudly at the unfathomable canyon, my empire.*'[46] Once the abyss had been conquered, Petit reached an exhilarating sense of freedom that he conveyed to the spectators who stared up from the street. That emotionally charged moment is the fulcrum of Colum McCann's novel, *Let the Great World Spin*, which from the opening pages dwells on the collective feeling that united onlookers in front of the unexpected. The walk is described at length, midway through the book, in a passage that marks a watershed between what happened before and after: 'The core reason for it all was beauty. Walking was a divine delight. Everything was rewritten when he was up in the air. New things were possible with the human form. It went beyond equilibrium.'[47]

McCann's account is one of several that praise Petit's performance. However, the notion of beauty does not quite capture the overwhelming impact of the event on those who witnessed it, and in different ways on those who have since experienced it through representations. According to Steven Miller, the uncanny sense of balance achieved by that act transcends the domain of beauty: 'It is unassimilable, overwhelming, and transformative.'[48] Not only were the lives of all protagonists forever marked by it; so too was the image of the towers in the lives of New Yorkers, and in some way the image of the city, tout court.

A more suitable category to describe Petit's artistic crime may be that of sublime. Transposing this aesthetic experience from the realm of nature to the urban environment, it might be argued that the walk brought out the verticality of the metropolis through a mixture of terror and fascination. Gliding along the wire, the funambulist drew attention to the 'almighty void' between the towers and thereby transfigured the artificial canyon into a human landscape. This balancing act, however, was not immune to the effects of height vertigo.

Petit's case attests to the conundrum that besets even the most skilful of aerialists. Indeed, the fact that high-wire walking is considered the epitome of acrophilia may falsely suggest that aerialists are somehow unaffected by sensations of height dizziness and by related emotions of fear or anxiety.[49] In fact, similarly to other high-altitude workers, gravity performers need to pre-empt those reactions through a process of habituation. As Thomas Brandt explains, '[h]abituation to height vertigo may occur through repeated exposure, as is observed in steeplejacks, roof-workers, and tight-rope artists, who achieve a remarkable degree of postural balance with seeming insensitivity to height'.[50] Back in the 1980s, when neuroscience researchers were making strides to understand this phenomenon, Petit gave an account of the peculiar tension felt by funambulists in his pocket treatise, *On the High Wire*. The incipit of the final chapter, titled 'Fear', sums up the pressure that needs to be withstood when facing the abyss without safety harnesses:

> A void like that is terrifying. Prisoner of a morsel of space, you will struggle desperately against occult elements: the absence of matter, the smell of balance, vertigo from all sides, and the dark desire to return to the ground, even to fall. This dizziness is the drama of high-wire walking, but that is not what I am afraid of.[51]

The passage confirms the importance of cultivating discipline and self-control in order to impede a loss of balance and its potential consequences. In his study of play and games, Caillois noted that mental strength, coupled with methodical training, is an essential condition to achieve the body's stability on a high wire. Unperturbed by the call of the void, funambulists achieve a superior control over the pull of gravity that allows them to quell the fear of falling and inspire awe: 'The tightrope walker only succeeds if he is hypnotized by the rope', writes Caillois, 'the acrobat only if he is sure enough of himself to rely upon vertigo instead of trying to resist it. Vertigo is an integral part of nature, and one controls it only in obeying it.'[52] These words sum up Petit's capacity to attain a degree of bodily equilibrium on the wire that requires an equal level of inner balance.

In psychoanalytic terms, the ability to de-idealise the obstacles that arise from one's own limits is what allows gravity performers to keep vertigo at bay. For Danielle Quinodoz, 'they design their game very carefully instead of seeking illusory magical victories likely to let them down; they aim for triumphs that are both spectacular and attainable: that is, brilliant but in no way magical'.[53] In the Twin Towers coup, the intent of accomplishing a seemingly impossible feat was realised through careful preparation as Petit managed to compensate for the drive to omnipotence with a grounded awareness of his limitations. If he appeared to Auster 'as if suspended magically in space', this was not the result of illusory tricks but of preparation and composure.[54] Indeed, the arrangements that allowed Petit to overpower vertigo in such extreme conditions take up a substantial part of the story narrated in his memoir and subsequent adaptations.

In the aftermath of 9/11, the Twin Towers act revived the cultural significance of the funambulist as an allegory of balance, as if keeping that moment alive could counter the trauma of the fall.[55] In this respect, Auster's comment about the 'unmediated' experience of funambulism may have captured the aura of that gesture, yet did not anticipate the subsequent value it would gain through media representations. In the field of performance studies, Chloe Johnston has noted that *Man on Wire* contributed to inscribe the event in the collective memory of the Twin Towers, in New York and beyond. With hindsight, the fact that Petit did *not* fall provides a symbolic, and emotionally charged, counterpoint to the towers' collapse: 'It is us that keep Petit in the air and the story in the collective consciousness. It satisfies a need to remember a site of tragedy, to wonder at human accomplishment. Perhaps by catching Petit, who never fell, we reclaim a space whose meaning changed irrevocably in the years since he walked in the sky.'[56]

The coup has been mythicised in Robert Zemeckis's blockbuster film, *The Walk* (2015), which casts Petit as an incarnation of the American dream. In this adaptation, released in both 2D and 3D, the high-wire performance was recreated in a computer-generated model of Manhattan's cityscape: Joseph Gordon-Levitt's steps (the lead actor who was trained by Petit himself to walk on a low wire) were composited with those of an acting funambulist. The climactic sequence unfolds through a series of vertiginous shots that turn the wire walker's point of view into an immersive cinematic experience. By striving to simulate his perception of the abyss, the film transfigures the balancing act and effectively obliterates its imaginative élan.[57] The gamut of visual effects for which the film has been celebrated result in a hyper-realistic picture that, as a critic observed, 'reduces – or, rather, inflates – the walk from sensation to sensationalism'.[58]

This inflation was echoed by a publicity campaign that advertised the film's high-tech wizardry with the slogan: 'Experience the impossible'. Not only was the aura of the performance devalued by an orgy of digital simulation, but its subject, too, was transformed in the process. It is as though the dynamic imagination embodied by Petit's attempt to reach the clouds had been lost to a simulacrum powered by cloud computing. While Petit himself regarded his writing in the sky to be a distinct art form, his coup was inexorably drawn in the realm of media spectacle: a transformative act fictionalised into a superhuman feat.[59] This modern mythology suggests that the status of wire walking has been gradually shifting from a performance art to a visual simulacrum. Even though the funambulist continues to stage the passage between worlds, it has crossed from the realm of poetic imagination, in which vertigo is evoked and provisionally tamed, to a simulacrum in which the keeper of the abyss is vanquished by digital means.

In conjunction with the launch of *The Walk* in Australian cinemas, in 2015, a new feature was added to the Skydeck of Melbourne's Eureka Tower, where a glass box projects out of the skyscraper and hangs over the void at 285 metres above the ground. The attraction, called 'the Edge', consisted of a green screen set that gave visitors the illusion of crossing a wire suspended over the city. Branded as The Walk Experience, the high-tech gimmick was advertised with the slogan, 'Take vertigo to the next level at Eureka Skydeck!' After Petit's act of transgression was fictionalised as a 3D simulacrum, the publicity stunt took the process of simulation one step further by commodifying the encounter with the abyss as a themed experience. This ephemeral attraction signals a wider shift whereby the longing for weightlessness personified by the funambulist is appropriated by an entertainment industry that sells the illusion of experiencing the impossible. The 'sensation of limitless freedom' invoked by Auster, therefore, gives way to the imperatives of a modern liquid society in which ever more exclusive experiences claim to liberate the individual from the constraints of gravity.

MEDIA SPECTACLE AND ART

In the early 21st century, funambulism has been reconfigured in the realm of media spectacle, as typified by the high-wire walks of Nik Wallenda (the great-grandson of Karl Wallenda). After a string of widely reported stunts at natural sites such as Niagara Falls and the Grand Canyon, Wallenda staged an urban performance at Chicago's Marina City in 2014. The chosen location occupies a special place in the history of post-war architecture. Built in the 1960s to Bertrand Goldberg's design, Marina City set up a model of mixed-use urban regeneration through a planning process that involved labour unions working with the developers and other stakeholders in an attempt to create an integrated community. Despite a series of financial and management problems, the complex has been associated with the social mobility of blue-collar workers: today, it is widely held as an icon of American brutalism.[60]

Wallenda's performance consisted of two consecutive walks: the first across the Chicago River, ascending an incline of 19 degrees between Marina Tower West and the Leo Burnett Building; and the second, blindfolded, between the two Marina City towers (plate 7). These twin buildings, whose rugged cylindrical volumes with curved balconies have been likened to corncobs, comprise of apartments and offices stacked above a multi-storey car park. Owing to the arrangement of buildings around a civic plaza, the complex was hailed as 'a new concept of urban life' when it was built. The public space inspired by European squares had influenced Yamasaki's master plan for the World Trade Center; hence, somewhat ironically, an invisible thread connects Wallenda's performance with Petit's coup. Yet, the two events could not be further apart: whereas the latter drew its aura from a unique combination of mastery and surprise, the former was carefully staged for the cameras as well as for hundreds of people watching on site.

The Marina City stunt, which was telecast on the Discovery Channel (*Skyscraper Live with Nik Wallenda*), ended with the wire walker's triumphal landing on a roof deck. Online viewers had a choice of six cameras to follow 'Nik's progress' from varying distances and angles, including one strapped to his body for point-of-view shots. The programme exemplifies a brand of televised events that arouse the fears and thrills caused by the experience of high places. These dramatised media spectacles have a bearing on the perception of verticality, insofar as they cast the city as a theatre for gravity plays that challenge, vicariously, the spectator's sense of balance. In turn, they reflect a culture of hyper-visibility in which all distance is eliminated, everything is accessible at a fingertip, and any presence of negativity is erased.[61]

The multiple points of view enact a media environment in which visual contents are customised, yet, at the same time, shielded from uncomfortable sights (the *Skyscraper Live* streaming was delayed by ten seconds so that it could be interrupted in the event of an accident). Deprived of its aspects of mystery and secrecy, the performance loses its imaginative power as its aura is irretrievably dissipated on the screen. With reference to Kant's notion of sublime, we might argue that the screen itself becomes the ultimate safe place from which the abyss can be contemplated. Framed and mediated by a technical apparatus, the balancing act is choreographed as a record-breaking feat. Miller draws a useful distinction between these terms apropos of funambulism:

> A feat demonstrates what a person can do; it is the tour de force of a person whose identity lies in his own abilities; it reveals that – now and forever – he is who he is. An act, on the other hand, is defined by its transformative force. [. . .] Whereas the accomplishment of a great feat confirms the performer's advertised identity, the act leaves nothing, beginning with the actor, as it was before.[62]

This transformative agency is what separates balancing acts such as Petit's early high-wire walks from the feats of gravity performers intent above all on demonstrating their skills. To some extent, Wallenda's performances hark back to the 19th-century heyday of funambulism, when Blondin and other aerialists stunned large crowds with ever more sensational acrobatics. As demonstrated by the success of the Marina City event, onlookers continue to be mesmerised by such gravity-defying stunts. In the age of media spectacle, however, the tightrope is aligned with an extreme sport culture that favours the achievement of new records over the value of aesthetic reflection. Inevitably, new modes of spectatorship have a bearing on the impact of a performance art that, historically, has allegorised the precariousness of human existence. Within the realm of representation its imaginative power has not been entirely lost though.

A counterpoint may be found in *High Wire*, a 2008 multi-channel installation by Catherine Yass which depicts high-rise architecture as a place fraught with vertigo (plate 8). The work focuses on Red Road Flats, Glasgow, an ill-fated housing complex that has since been demolished. When inaugurated, in 1971, the estate was the tallest social housing project in Europe and was hailed as a modern solution to the city's slums. Over time, the place became increasingly segregated and blighted by neglect and crime: so much so that, by the turn of the 21st century, it had come to epitomise the foundering of housing policies in Britain. In marked contrast with the fate of Chicago's Marina City, Red Road turned out to be a short-lived experiment of residential architecture, echoing the downfall of the Pruitt-Igoe housing complex in St. Louis, Missouri (demolished in successive phases between 1972 and 1976). After decades of social anomie, the Glasgow estate was torn down, despite a local campaign to prevent its clearance.

Demolition plans were afoot when Yass set her sights on the estate. Working with the tightrope artist Didier Pasquette, an apprentice of Petit's, she staged a high-wire walk between two of the 31-storey-high towers and filmed it from different points of view (one of the cameras being mounted on the funambulist's helmet). The event was intended to symbolise the experience of vertical housing and its underlying tension between the dream of conquering the sky and the fear of falling. However, the performance was hindered by heavy winds and, unexpectedly, Pasquette had to step back to safety part-way through it (fig.14). By conceding to the force of nature, he came to embody an architectural ambition that was about to collapse. As art

14 Frame from *High Wire*, film installation by Catherine Yass, 2008.

historian Catherine James observes, 'The funambulist's aborted performance symbolizes the failed integrations of body and space attempted by urban planners. By transferring a circus act to a housing estate, [Yass] kindles a playful dreaming about space to challenge architecture's core functions of stability and shelter.'[63]

While Pasquette showed dexterity on the wire, he also exposed the human fragility in the face of heights, an anti-Icarus who renounced an aerial fantasy to preserve his life. His backward walk recognised the impossibility of the task, as if the void could not be bridged and the estate had to be left to its destiny. This dramatic twist endowed the artwork with a life-affirming gesture that reverberated through the place, lending fresh significance to the subject of funambulism. Connor draws out its significance in terms of dwelling: 'The wire-walker of *High Wire* represents a new kind of allegory for us, one that bears, appropriately enough for a work that has a residential complex as its setting, on the question of accommodation, of where we are to reside and the kinds of living it may be possible for us to make there.'[64]

Today Red Road Flats is regarded as a failed experiment of social housing, a tale of rise and fall that is poignantly evoked in *High Wire*. By destabilising the viewer through multiple camera viewpoints, the installation conjures up a mismatch between inner feelings and outer reality that is akin to feelings of vertigo. Exhibited in Glasgow in the same year that *Man on Wire* was released, this work brings out the funambulist's imaginative power in a different yet somewhat complementary way: although Pasquette was unable to cross the void, his aborted attempt fixed an indelible image of Red Road that is no less poignant than Petit's Twin Towers act. Indeed, stills from *High Wire* have since been used to illustrate the estate in the press, a testament to the artist's and aerialist's joined abilities to capture the tension of that place. While funambulism is increasingly normalised within the realm of media spectacle, it continues to embody our incessant quest for balance and to provoke reflections on the dizzy spaces of cities through artistic representations as well as live performances.

4

URBAN ASCENTS

. . . climbing reveals space.[1]

15 Frame from *Feet First* (dir. Clyde A. Bruckman, USA, 1930), The Harold Lloyd Corporation.

I.N. VAN NUYS BLDG.
I.N. VAN NUYS
BUILDING

HEADS FOR HEIGHTS

In his aforementioned study of play and games, Roger Caillois states that climbing epitomises, along with tightrope walking, the desire to tame vertigo (*ilinx*). Modern practices of urban climbing descend from the passion for mountaineering that spread across Europe in the wake of the Industrial Revolution. While the Alps had been crossed since Hannibal's epic campaign in the Second Punic War (218 BCE), then sporadically during the Middle Ages, mountain peaks did not provide a stimulus for discovery until the mid-18th century when the encyclopaedic spirit of the Enlightenment prompted Swiss naturalists, led by Horace-Bénédict de Saussure, to carry out scientific expeditions to remote glaciers. Then, in the 19th century, mountaineering grew into an increasingly popular activity. The hazards involved in those early expeditions were depicted by artists such as Johann Ludwig Bleuler, whose topographical views of the Alps accentuated the abyss formed by rocks and crevasses. One of them represents an ascent of the Rhinewald glacier amid a vertiginous landscape that is likened in the caption to a 'view of hell' (plate 9).

The English attraction to the Alps manifested itself from the early 19th century through a wealth of cultural artefacts ranging from the reconstruction of a Swiss chalet complete with alpine scenery in Regent's Park, London, to the locations of Mary Shelley's *Frankenstein*. As Jim Ring notes, the English took upon themselves the historical mission to civilise the Alps.[2] The golden age of alpinism climaxed in the late 1850s, when Victorian climbers scaled some of the highest peaks such as the Wetterhorn and the Matterhorn. Founded in London in 1857, the first Alpine Club counted among its members John Ruskin, who greatly contributed to fostering an aesthetic appreciation of landscapes. Worried about the numerous reports of accidents, Ruskin was among the 'indoor gentlemen' who preferred to contemplate mountains from afar.[3] He deplored that by the 1880s, alpine tourism had become a mass phenomenon.

The heyday of mountain climbing coincided with that of wire walking, with which it shared the impetus to conquer nature by overcoming the force of gravity. From the perspective of psychoanalysis, these two practices have been considered among the 'dangerous games with vertigo' performed by athletes, acrobats and altitude seekers that embody the quest of equilibrium.[4] It should not be surprising, then, if both found new locations in the skyscraper age. Just as alpine crests exerted a powerful attraction over the early mountaineers, so did the steel-and-glass cliffs of the 20th century galvanise height practitioners who, from the 1970s onwards, took on vertical cities.

Yet the practice of scaling buildings has a longer history that originates, at far lower altitudes, in fin-de-siècle England. This activity, also known as 'buildering' and 'stegophily', was popularised by Geoffrey Winthrop Young, a mountaineer-cum-poet who championed the art of climbing on walls and roofs. As a student of classics at Cambridge, Young elected the historical town as his field of expeditions. In *The Roof-Climber's Guide to Trinity*, a parody of Victorian alpine guides published in 1899, he described in colourful prose the challenges arising from the popularity of mountains:

> In these athletic days of rapid devolution to the Simian practices of our ancestors, climbing of all kinds is naturally assuming an ever more prominent position. Since the supply of unconquered Alps is limited and the dangers of nature's monumental exercise-ground are yearly increased by the polish of frequent feet and the broken bottles of thirsty souls, aspirants with the true faith at heart have been forced of late years to seek new sensations on the artificial erections of man.[5]

A few years later, Young expounded how different architectural styles and materials ought to be approached by aspirant climbers. His new tract, *Wall and Roof Climbing*, dispensed advice to the uninitiated while asserting that colleges and monasteries offered 'the best training academies for those who desire to become masters of the art'.[6] In the inter-war period, these precepts were followed by a group of Cambridge students whose exploits were documented by Noël H. Symington, their self-appointed chronicler writing under the pseudonym of Whipplesnaith. In *The Night Climbers of Cambridge*, Whipplesnaith praised a nocturnal activity that invigorated students with 'sheer ecstatic enjoyment'.[7] The town's historical architecture allowed them to exercise in the art of balance, a predominantly male practice that was shot through with moral overtones. The ability to overcome the dread of altitude was deemed to be essential in order to fortify a climber's character:

> The fear of heights is the easiest of all fears to cure, though one of the most troublesome while it exists. Giddiness, the mental paralysis which

> makes its victims unable to do simple things when there is a drop below them, blind fear of heights, all can be cured in two or three outings, starting with easy climbs and small heights.[8]

This account was based on the underlying assumption that everyone could easily develop a head for heights and relish the thrill of danger. With a romantic inflection, Whipplesnaith proclaimed that 'a climber is a man standing on the edge of an abyss'.[9] For the Cambridge students, however, treading on the edge did not evoke the horror of the precipice but a realm of adventure in which architecture was reconfigured as a field of gravity play.

A year after *The Night Climbers* was issued, Johan Huizinga published *Homo Ludens*, a seminal essay on the social function of play. All manifestations of the play instinct, he argued, occur in a particular sphere akin to a sacred place in which the norms and customs of everyday life are suspended. Crucially, every playground is governed by a set of rules: 'All are temporary worlds within the ordinary world, dedicated to the performance of an act apart.'[10] Accordingly, play ought to be considered not only as a ludic activity but as a veritable state of mind: 'It proceeds within its own proper boundaries of time and space according to fixed rules and in an orderly manner. It promotes the formation of social groupings which tend to surround themselves with secrecy and to stress their difference from the common world by disguise or other means.'[11] This definition applies well to the pursuits of climbers who turned the built environment into a gravity playground. Their nocturnal ascents reveal another way in which social norms have historically been transgressed through acts of balance. While the pursuits of a group of students in the 1930s might be dismissed as an eccentric and rather elitist fancy, they show another facet of a wider cultural phenomenon by which architecture became a stage for games of vertigo – one which would prove influential in the long term.

STUNTS ON CAMERA

The practice of urban climbing emerged at a time in which the American metropolis was redefining the experience of verticality. In the inter-war years, vertigo became an inherent aspect of city life and was absorbed into a modern culture of spectacle that sought to neutralise its sense of instability – and fear of falling. Cinema became a popular medium to represent the thrills and anxieties associated with metropolitan life, and architecture was the stage on which those conflicting emotions were played out. At that juncture, gravity performers came to represent the quest for balance in the vertical city.

The construction of skyscrapers fuelled a modern imaginary populated by bridge jumpers, 'human flies' and sundry entertainers who braved tall structures in sensational fashion. A key role was played by stunt performers, many of whom were trained in construction. As cultural historian Jacob Smith points out, they often plied their trades in the shadow of film celebrities, as the spectacle of gravity plays was incorporated in Hollywood's repertoire: 'the amusement parks, circuses, fairgrounds, and cinema screens of this era were also the sites of embodied performances that were part of rich historical traditions of popular entertainment'.[12] The heroics performed by those 'thrill makers' reflected the dominant values of masculinity but also the vitality of working-class subcultures that were overshadowed by the Hollywood star system. Moreover, they contributed to exorcise the anxiety of the metropolis as a vertiginous place that was growing at breathtaking pace.

The conception of manhood underlying this particular film culture was intertwined with the heroic image of construction labourers (see Chapter 2). In the 1920s, the fear of falling associated with high-rise buildings became a trope of silent comedies featuring the likes of Laurel and Hardy, Buster Keaton and Harold Lloyd.[13] The latter's thrill comedies constitute a prime example of this genre. Most memorable among Lloyd's acrobatics is the scene in *Safety Last!* (1923) in which the actor hangs precariously on the hand of a big clock as he climbs a building facade, grappling over the urban abyss in slapstick fashion. With his popular screen performances, Lloyd embodied the possibility of survival in the urban jungle.[14] Although his stunts were not simulated by photographic tricks, those scenes were often realised through miniature sets built on rooftops in order to enhance the perspectives from above. His body, permanently scarred by accidents which had occurred on set, bore witness to the hazards involved in a business that thrived on urban heights.

A remarkable balancing act features in *Feet First* (1930), one of Lloyd's early sound films. Here the actor plays a shoe salesman who somehow ends up on a window cleaner's cradle hoisted up by workers on a building roof. This rough-and-ready device, made only of wooden planks and ropes, provides the protagonist with a precarious refuge as he crawls along the facade. In an exhilarating sequence, he tries, in vain, to break in through various windows (fig.15). As soon as he reaches the rooftop, he accidentally inhales ether and begins to wobble dangerously on the edge, then falls down to the street hanging on a rope. The salesman's mishaps are an allegory of social climbing, a tortuous path that happily ends with his promotion. Shot in a tall building overlooking a busy Los Angeles street, the climactic scene brings out the perception of vertical urban space in all its vertiginous aspects as Lloyd skilfully treads on architectural edges, cornices and mouldings.

Apropos of the thrill comedy genre, art historian Steven Jacobs has remarked that 'the skyscraper can be seen as a slapstick crazy machine'.[15] In addition, *Feet First* reinforces an interpretation of Hollywood's thrill makers as anti-heroes who embodied with their antics and acrobatics the quest for balance in the metropolis. By taming vertigo, screen performers fuelled new forms of mediatised entertainment, while city dwellers could enjoy the thrills of engineered falls in bespoke amusement parks (see Chapter 5). Taking a thrill ride or watching a movie were complementary experiences that simulated the conditions of urban modernity and thereby exorcised its inherent dangers: by purchasing a ticket and taking a seat, it was possible to be transported into another sensory dimension that validated the relative safety of one's place in the world.

In parallel, the 1930s crystallised the perception of skyscrapers as urban mountains, a trope of narrative cinema epitomised by a classic Hollywood film like *King Kong* (1933).[16] After breaking free from the shackles that enslaved him to a freak spectacle, the giant ape climbs an apartment block as though it were a tree, then moves on to scale the Empire State Building. The tallest architecture in town, and in the world, was the location chosen for the dramatic ending: the Empire's pinnacle becomes the place of Kong's demise as a squadron of military planes encircle him in a lethal vortex of gunfire. His downfall restores the primacy of Western civilisation over the wild beast, its symbolic 'other' loaded with meanings.[17] The final scene lays bare the psychology of gravity associated with the skyscraper, its verticality being entangled with the double movement of rising and falling that pulls the viewer's imagination in opposite directions.

It is significant that in the 1976 remake of *King Kong,* directed by John Guillermin, the topical scene was situated at the World Trade Center. If compared with the original version, the film marks a distinct shift towards the postmodern zeitgeist. The plot, in which the ape is poached from an

Indian Ocean island by explorers in search of black gold, was scripted in the aftermath of the 1973 oil crisis. While the storyline informs a colonial narrative of subjugation, the special effects, designed by Carlo Rambaldi, yield a series of giddy-making scenes. When Kong grabs the captive woman (Dwan) who has been offered up in sacrifice, and lifts her into the air, she pleads to be released: 'I can't stand heights! Honest, I can't!' – she screams – 'When I was ten years old, they took me up in the Empire State Building and I got sick in the elevator.' In the lead-up to the film's dénouement, a view of the Twin Towers dissolves into a flashback of two boulders, as the vertical architecture reminds the primate of his natural habitat. Shortly afterwards, Kong summits the South Tower by climbing along one of its corners.

The architectural complex allows for a final plot development, as Kong jumps to the opposite building, crossing the gaping void as he would have done in the jungle. Here the rooftop of the North Tower stands in lieu of the Empire's pinnacle for the summit of modern civilisation. While the ape on the loose is attacked from the air in a high-tech version of the original showdown, the final blow comes from a commando who has been hoisted to the roof via a window-cleaning scaffold, the same apparatus which Harold Lloyd had harnessed to comic effect. The untameable creature is killed and order is eventually restored. This time, however, the sacrifice exposes the cracks of the Western subject, whose Faustian hubris is symbolised by the imposing towers: a low-angle shot depicts Kong's downfall through the space between them. The sombre ending shows his dying body surrounded by crowds on the plaza, a portent of the collapse that would take place a quarter of a century later.

CLIMBING TOWERS

The real-life practice of buildering reached new levels in the 1970s, when skyscrapers became the targets of urban ascents.[18] In 1977 the World Trade Center was the theatre of another stunt that revealed the modern abyss in all its magnitude. Less than three years after Philippe Petit had walked on a wire between the Twin Towers, an amateur rock climber called George Willig gained a moment of fame by scaling the 110 floors of the South Tower, aided by rope and clamps, using the window-cleaning channel that ran along a corner of the facade. As with Petit's coup, his climb took advantage of the surprise effect as well as the prominent location.

From its inception, the World Trade Center had been described with analogies to natural landscapes. In May 1968, before construction began, *The New York Times* carried a full-page advertisement, headed 'The Mountain Comes to Manhattan', illustrated by a picture of the Twin Towers with a plane flying by. It was sponsored by a group of real estate developers led by Lawrence Wien (the Committee for a Reasonable World Trade Center) who warned of the dangers that such a gargantuan complex might pose to air traffic. While the ad came to public attention post-9/11 due to its uncanny presage, its title is interesting for another reason as well: it aligns the perception of the skyscrapers with that of urban cliffs which had permeated the vertical growth of Manhattan, reaching new peaks in the 1970s.

Against this background, Willig's ascent added a further element to the conquest of urban heights by engaging with the tower's material surface. He climbed his way up in front of incredulous crowds and camera crews that rushed to the scene. News reports at the time revived the trope of the human fly while hailing the first man ever to have scaled a skyscraper. Whilst the event was linked with new ways of conducting rescue operations, its imaginative power transcended practical matters. It was a distinctly architectural experience insofar as it entailed the close encounter of the climber's body with the surface of the building, whose materiality and texture allowed him room to manoeuvre. Hijacking the tracks installed for window washing, he reproduced the vertical motion of a cleaning scaffold along the curtain wall. This oft-neglected device was employed on that occasion by the police in a vain attempt to halt the climber. Television channels reported that Willig had joked with security officers that he would rather complete his ascent than take the risk of stepping onto the cradle, while a policeman on the rescue mission avowed his fear of heights: two antithetical stances that represent in clear-cut terms the perception of the abyss.

Willig was inspired by Petit's 1974 coup and, in retrospect, their stunts might be seen in conjunction. If the latter had walked on a wire between the skyscrapers much in the same way as his forerunners used to cross natural gorges, the former scaled a tower as though it were a mountain face. In some respects, these dangerous games with vertigo were complementary: the funambulist treaded a thin horizontal line that formed an ephemeral bridge, whereas the climber moved along the vertical axis to reach the summit. While confronting the abyss of Lower Manhattan in different ways, they both transgressed the boundaries of corporate urban space.

Moreover, Willig's stunt drew comparisons with another, lesser-known event. In July 1975, a construction worker had jumped off the roof of the North Tower with a parachute, landing less than two minutes later on the adjacent plaza. Owen Quinn, a trained skydiver who had worked on the World Trade Center site, calculated that he had to drop in freefall for a height of 60 floors before opening the chute. Pictures of the dive show the bright cloth canopy against the vertical towers. An arresting shot immortalised the moment at which Quinn was about to jump from the rooftop, his body bent forward against New York's skyline. The picture, titled 'Point of No Return', captures the instant of highest tension in which the diver leaves the zone of safety enclosed by the skyscraper's edge and steps forward, looking down into space. The tension between anguish of falling and desire to jump embodied by the cliff edge here was firmly resolved in favour of the latter.

Willig's later climb was not an isolated episode: the practice of scaling towers was taken forward by climbers motivated by different purposes. In the 1980s, Dan Goodwin took on some of the tallest skyscrapers in the world, including the Sears Tower and the John Hancock Center in Chicago, using suction cups and sky hooks. While the parachute jump had given Quinn a stage for calling attention to world hunger, Goodwin used his visibility to raise awareness of other issues such as the vulnerability of skyscrapers to terrorist attacks. His 1983 ascent of the World Trade Center's North Tower, for instance, exposed the inadequate measures for firefighting.

A decade before, this theme had furnished the plot of a popular disaster movie, *The Towering Inferno*. Directed in 1974 by John Guillermin, who two years later would remake *King Kong*, the film centres on the operation mounted by firefighters to rescue the people trapped within a glass tower in San Francisco, gone ablaze during its inauguration. The suspense is conveyed by multiple states of suspension, notably in the scenes where the rescuers climb up a shaft, a scenic elevator hangs precariously on a cable, and people are eventually saved by rolling on a wire held in mid-air by a helicopter. Echoes of Hitchcock's *Vertigo* can be detected from the opening sequence, an aerial shot that frames the Golden Gate Bridge from the sky. In the closing scene, the Fire Department's chief (Steve McQueen) passes by the project architect (Paul Newman) and wonders in front of the smouldering edifice when building designers will ever consult the fire brigades. His final words compound the message: 'You know where to reach me. So long, architect.'

Centrepoint climb

SYDNEY'S HUMAN FLY

300m straight UP!

SCALED: Tower

A DAREDEVIL human fly dangles 300m above certain death — clinging from Sydney's Centrepoint Tower by a single rope.

Below him is a dizzying plunge to the streets of the city . . . above a head-spinning climb to the top of the structure.

This dramatic picture was snapped by a stunned onlooker who spotted the madcap stunt from the roof of another building.

The fly, clad in a flame-red climbing suit, inched his way up

Continued page 6

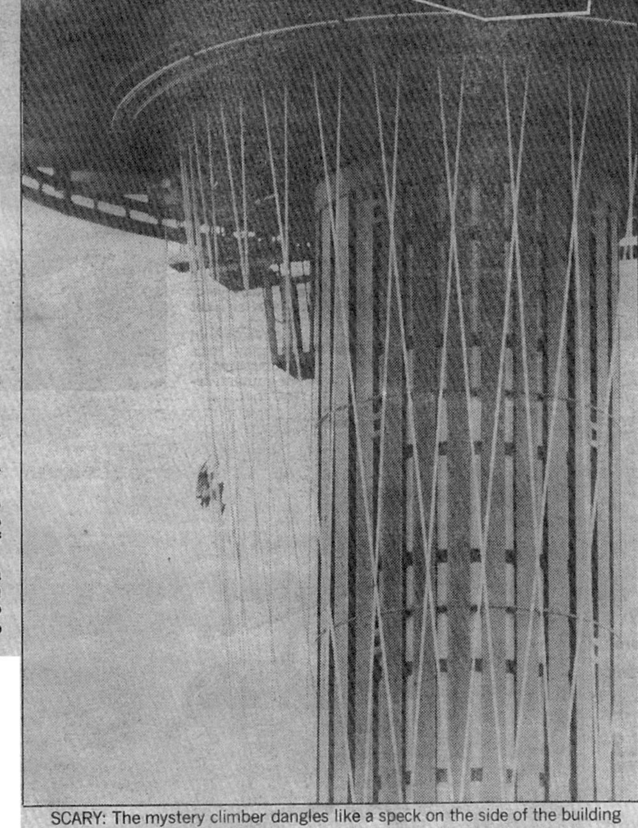

SCARY: The mystery climber dangles like a speck on the side of the building

16 'Human fly' Chris Hilton climbs the Centrepoint Tower in Sydney. Front page of *The Daily Mirror*, Sydney, 2 February 1987.

This cinematic tour de force became part of the vertical urban imaginary as much as Petit's coup of the same year. Subsequently, over the 1980s high-rise towers were targeted by climbers spurred on by Willig's and Goodwin's feats. In 1987, traffic engineer and mountaineer Chris Hilton climbed the Centrepoint Tower in Sydney (known today as Sydney Tower), the tallest structure in the southern hemisphere at the time. After meticulous preparation, Hilton achieved his goal by scaling overnight the steel cables that surround the central column with the aid of ropes and climbing gear; he completed the ascent by sliding his rig around the glass-cladded turret (fig.16).

This carefully planned act, which was filmed from three different cameras, became the subject of a documentary directed by Hilton himself with Glenn Singleman, which was televised by Australia's national broadcaster the following year – *A Spire: The Story of the First Climb of Sydney Tower*. Hilton's intent was to make a statement about the rapid vertical growth of the urban environment: by taking on the tallest structure in town, he wanted people to see 'just one individual under their own power bringing down a massive building which sets itself up as being huge and impenetrable and intimidating'.[19] Cultural theorist Meaghan Morris interpreted his climb, and the televised performance based on it, as 'an act of social criticism' which manifested 'a refusal of entrepreneurial aspirations to dominate and divide up city space'.[20] Alert to the subject positions involved in this all-male adventure, Morris nonetheless recognised its capacity to enact a symbolic response to the process of neoliberal urban development.

By shifting the scene of climbing from natural rocks to high-rise architecture, the documentary based on Hilton's climb raised questions about power and ownership at the peak of the property boom that transformed Sydney in the 1980s. This transient occupation of the city's tallest landmark was in stark contrast with the subsequent refurbishment of its observation deck, whose new set of features included an open-air, glass-bottomed platform jutting over the edge where thrill seekers could enjoy a state of suspension at 260 metres above ground. Claiming to offer 'the ultimate outdoor view of Sydney', the skywalk exemplifies a wider trend for vertiginous spaces that emerged in the noughties (see Chapter 7). Here the privileged position on top of the tower is no longer the reward for a perilous ascent but a themed experience that is staged in a safely controlled environment.

The practice of buildering has retained its critical agency well into the 21st century. A notable example is the protest staged in London by a group of Greenpeace activists in 2013, when six women climbed The Shard aided by ropes and, upon reaching the 310-metre-high top, unfurled a banner with the message: 'Save the Arctic' (plate 10). The glass skyscraper, which was opened to the public earlier that year, was reportedly chosen not only for its landmark value but also because of its resemblance to a shard of ice – the tip of an urban iceberg that was symbolically occupied in protest against oil drilling. Its exterior, realised with an innovative 'building envelope technology', provided an unwitting guide to the activists, who exploited the architectural elements to execute their plan. Walking along the bars that protrude from its corners to support the open-edge facades, they turned the building into a gigantic ladder.

The 16-hour ascent was widely reported in the media and broadcast on live streaming through cameras placed on the climbers' helmets, attracting the attention of global news channels as well as, inevitably, the local police. As in other unannounced climbs and high-altitude urban performances discussed above, the commotion caused by the scene led a multitude of passers-by to stare up at the skyscraper: the collective act of beholding the tower from street level was itself a vertigo-inducing challenge, one that conjured up the magnitude of the ongoing climate emergency.

In the urban ascents discussed above, displays of utmost equilibrium allowed the climbers to neutralise the dangerous effects of vertigo and accomplish their feats. The ability of these practitioners to keep a steady balance signals the resolution of the conflict between life and death drives which Freud identified as the elemental forces of psychic activity. A dissociation between these drives is common among amateurs – also described as 'vertigo junkies' – who perform extreme anti-gravity stunts. Conversely, gravity masters do not toy with death but seek a vital affirmation by mediating between their impulses. As Quinodoz suggests, their actions are wrongly dismissed as merely reckless feats, while in fact they are often animated by life-affirming dispositions.[21]

Accordingly, balancing at heights requires an ability to reconcile the inner voices that speak in conflicting registers of 'omnipotence' and 'realistic power'.[22] While the former is the legacy of an infantile drive, the latter countervails it with the rationality of the evolved self. Therefore, the equipoise attained by gravity-defying practitioners who tame vertigo derives from a consonance between their perception of external and internal spaces, a vital balance that is all the more admired by the public as it vanishes from everyday life. As high-rise construction expresses the relentless drive to conquer the sky, bodily practices that engage with urban heights give new expression to the challenge of gravity.

FREE REIN IN THE CITY

Climbing has prompted philosophical musings on the perception of balance. In *Variations on the Body*, Michel Serres argues that our longing for movement is expressed through corporeal activities, from dancing to cycling, that manifest a 'chaotic heart'.[23] With reference to Caillois's notion of *ilinx*, Serres claims that vertigo relates to the vitalism of human life. An upward élan makes us yearn for elevation and suspension, since losing contact with the ground can conduce to states of 'mystical elation' and self-discovery. Writing at the cusp of the digital revolution, the French philosopher rued how sensory experience had become increasingly disembodied within consumer societies: 'Transformed into obese pigs by the drug – soft in a hard way – consumption, we have been forgetting [. . .] the extent to which our body knows how to escape gravity by obeying it.'[24] These reflections were sparked off by Serres's own experience in the mountains. In order to rediscover an intimate relation with the environment, he maintained, it is necessary to embrace the animal gestures of the body-in-motion, starting from the primordial act of climbing on all fours that led to the evolution of *homo erectus*.

If 'climbing reveals space', as Serres put it, buildering sheds light on its social production. This is particularly evident in the practice of free solo, which is conducted without ropes or other safety equipment. This extreme sport was adapted to the urban environment by Alain Robert, a professional rock climber whose ascents earned him the sobriquets of 'human spider' and the 'French Spider-Man'. Robert began to scale tall buildings unroped in 1994, when he summited the Citicorp Citibank Center (now Citigroup Center) in downtown Chicago for a documentary titled *No Limits*, which contrasted the illicit urban escalation with a more conventional rock climb in Utah. Extending a popular 20th-century trope, Robert's double act marked the shift from natural to manmade environments as the terrain of gravity challenges.

In his autobiography, Robert describes the physical training, preparation and execution of a number of stunts.[25] Trained in the mountains of southern France, he began to see architecture in a different way when he undertook to scale buildings. The curtain-wall facades of office towers are designed to protect the interiors from the elements while allowing maximum natural lighting, and their glass-and-metal surfaces can easily become slippery for a climber: far taller and often harder to negotiate than walls of brick and stone such as those described by Geoffrey W. Young in his early guides to buildering. Surface details such as window frames and mullions provide anchor points, along with other elements on the facade. Finding stability in gaps, grooves, joints or ledges requires a fine-grained knowledge based on technical research as well as site visits. In preparation for the ascent of what he calls 'urban rocks' and 'urban mountains', Robert studies the texture of materials and develops an ad hoc approach to each building (plate 11).

Urban free solo is under constant threat by external circumstances that lie beyond the climber's control. Besides many incidents that undermined Robert's efforts, his stunts have often been affected by rain and winds that have made him lose his grip, but also by the startling reflections of light on surface panels. These performances foreground aspects of skyscraper facades that are seldom noticed by anyone but cleaners and maintenance workers. Among the structures more amenable to be scaled is the Eiffel Tower, a climber's favourite that Robert likens to 'an immense ladder'; but also the New York Times Building, designed by Renzo Piano's office (completed in 2007), where the protruding ceramic rods on the facades are analogous to ladder rungs.[26] Conversely, the Sears Tower in Chicago proved forbidding when moisture gathered on its surfaces during an ascent, as did the cables of the Golden Gate Bridge, San Francisco, which Robert took on amid major difficulties.

Robert's ability to scale buildings as well as rock faces did not make him immune to falls. He resumed climbing after a debilitating accident left him partly disabled, showing a determination that his surgeon described as 'a medical enigma'.[27] This case is all the more remarkable since Robert suffers from attacks of height vertigo as well as spells of dizziness caused by the injuries. The risks of perceptual instability manifested dramatically at the Elf Tower (now Tour Total) in the business district of La Défense, the first step of a 'Tour of Paris by Façades' that he undertook in collaboration with *Paris Match* magazine which included the Montparnasse Tower and the National

Library of France: 'Soon I start losing my bearings. The multitude of mirrors all around makes me dizzy and disorientates me. My vertigo kicks in and I fight to regain my wits. I feel lost in a vertical labyrinth. The escalation is certainly challenging and it is more physical than I expected.'[28] Through overcoming the dangerous effects of *ilinx*, Robert has taken on glass-cladded skyscrapers in precarious conditions amid slips, losses of balance and near falls.

Similarly to the funambulist, the climber humanises buildings that are typically perceived to be hostile and often inviolable. Echoing Petit's reflections on wire walking, Robert's account of free soloing acknowledges that vertigo is a human sensation that ought to be confronted rather than denied. Gliding across the surfaces of high-rise towers with carefully poised manoeuvres, urban climbers reassert a visceral engagement with the material world. Their ascents may therefore be considered a riposte to the perceived loss of bodily engagement in a society that is saturated with a culture of spectacle and simulation: in a vicarious way, these extreme performances may affect their spectators too.

Often documented by press photographers and television crews, Robert's stunts gained the 'French Spider-Man' global fame. He scaled some of the tallest buildings in the world including Shanghai's JinMao Tower – where he defied strict police surveillance after being denied permission – and Dubai's Burj Khalifa, which he climbed with rope and harness as required by security. The latter stunt, realised in 2011, shortly preceded the release of the action film, *Mission: Impossible – Ghost Protocol*, whose climax is announced by a vertiginous drone shot that pans across the 830-metre-high tower and ends with an overhead view. In the following scene, agent Ethan Hunt (Tom Cruise) jumps off a window and runs down the curtain wall tethered to a cable until he is finally rescued in dramatic fashion. Whether or not Robert's stunt was an inspiration for this film, the coincidence exposes the tenuous boundary between his dangerous games with vertigo and a burgeoning thrill culture fuelled by action movies, animation and video games which have reconfigured the image of the human fly in the computer age.

Nor are these heroics without contradictions, entangled as they are in a realm of visual representation that contributes to fetishise the sleek surfaces of skyscrapers. While Robert's escalations transgress the boundaries of corporate architecture, they rely on media exposure in order to be sustained. His popularity has grown in parallel with the revival of the Marvel Comics superhero designed by Stan Lee in the 1960s, whose adventures have reached new audiences since the noughties through a popular film franchise. Whereas Spider-Man's character is inseparable from the cityscape of New York, however, Robert has performed his art of balance in skyscrapers all over the world, sometimes dressed up as the web-shooting character.[29]

Climbers who scale buildings in the guise of urban mountains invite us to re-imagine those symbols of global power and the spaces they produce. Laying bare the abyss of vertical cities, free soloists demonstrate that even the tallest constructions can be trumped by human skills. Robert, in particular, has cast in a different light not only the exteriors of corporate skyscrapers but also the institutions they house. While acts of trespass led to his arrest on numerous occasions, one of them had an unexpected twist. After the lawsuit filed by Elf Aquitaine against Robert for scaling the company's Parisian headquarters ended in his acquittal, the trial turned against the accusers as the prosecutor put the spotlight on a business that was embroiled in a major corruption scandal: the 'affaire Elf' led to the downfall of its top executives, in a reversal of fortune that lent an added symbolism to the climber's ascent. Laying claim to places that are supposed to be unassailable, Robert deliberately seeks to shake from its doldrums a society addicted to passive consumption. Implicitly, his stunts draw attention to the privatisation of public space that has been affecting cities around the world.

Although the art of balancing on the facades of tall buildings requires the conquest of vertigo as well as physical impairments, for Robert, climbing is never a mere demonstration of skills: he focuses instead on the dynamic beauty inherent in every corporeal gesture. This aesthetic dimension is bound up with the challenge to gravity that climbers share, to varying degrees, with practitioners of other extreme sports. As the philosopher Bernard Andrieu suggests, these practices affirm the agency of an 'immersive body' that plunges into the depths of lived experience and re-emerges with the awareness of sensations and emotions that were previously unknown.[30] For Andrieu, vertigo is central to a 'corporeal ecology' that transcends the conscious pursuit of balance in order to explore the pleasures derived from gravity plays. When we are invaded by such feelings, our consciousness loses control and lets us precipitate in a fluid state that plunges deep into our body.[31] In this respect, climbing is aligned with the thrills of circus acrobatics but also with urban practices such as skateboarding, *parkour* and freerunning that reclaim a space of transgression to the body as agent of ecstatic experiences.

UP ON THE ROOFS

Urban scholars have been appraising the potential that various embodied practices have to unsettle the instrumental logic of cities. Shifting the focus of architectural research from the study of buildings to the social production of space, Iain Borden has developed a critique of the capitalist city that foregrounds the agency of lived experience. His seminal work on skateboarding highlights a way of performing space that subverts the coordinates of everyday life: for Borden, the marginal role of this practice with regard to mainstream design culture allows it 'to function historically as a critical exterior to architecture'.[32] This work has informed subsequent research into the role of public space in enabling playful behaviours and activities that can invigorate social interactions.

While the sensory stimulation that characterises urban life can lead to withdrawal and alienation, Quentin Stevens points out the function of play 'as a form of risky bodily engagement with physical edges'.[33] Citing Caillois, he evokes a range of experiences that derive pleasure from a challenge to gravity (*ilinx*): 'In vertigo, people "lose themselves" and are transported to new forms of experience. Some experiences of vertigo come through bodily actions which generate intoxicating physical sensations of instability and distorted perception: "mad, tremendous and convulsive movements" such as falling, sliding, jumping, climbing, dancing, spinning and moving quickly.'[34] These perspectives open up a critical space in which the rise of vertical cities might productively be re-imagined.

While the feats of renowned climbers uncover the scale of the urban abyss, there are myriads of explorers whose fleeting activities fly under the radar. During the noughties, a diverse and global community set about hacking out-of-bounds spaces ranging from underground tunnels to skyscraper rooftops. While this phenomenon grew out of youth sub-cultures in 1970s Europe and North America, the umbrella term Urban Exploration (abbreviated as Urb-Ex or simply UE) only surfaced in the mid-noughties to denote a networked community. Its members are animated by different motives but their intent is often the same: to infiltrate urban spaces that are forbidden to ordinary people. Buildings under construction, abandoned or awaiting transformation are among their favourite targets (plate 12).

Urban explorers seek to reclaim the right to the city by asserting the values of free play that are denied by the spatial logic of capitalism. In *Explore Everything: Place-Hacking the City*, the geographer-cum-explorer Bradley Garrett claims that this transient reappropriation of urban space amounts to a 'cultural renaissance'.[35] Garrett's unique position as 'the scribe for the tribe' offers at once an insider's perspective on the movement and a critical reflection on its methods and practices. His ethnographic study reveals a diversity of approaches: while some explorers are primarily moved by the sheer pursuit of thrills, others are driven by social and political ideas. In all cases, the play element is key to understanding what brings expedition crews to discover tall structures or abandoned tunnels.[36] Situationist tactics allow them to infiltrate off-limits sites and thereby to reterritorialise the vertical city through collective actions that push the boundaries of what is perceived to be accessible. Trespassing thus becomes a form of symbolic reappropriation: not only of urban spaces but, at a more fundamental level, of the conditions of freedom and curiosity that fuel the play instinct.

Within this broad movement, the specific practice known as 'rooftopping', or 'roofing', is fuelled by a desire to enjoy the view from above. Reclaiming a liminal space on the edge of buildings, rooftoppers use their bodies to assert a fleeting mastery over the city: climbing cranes, towers and sundry vertical structures yields vantage points that would otherwise be unattainable. The writer Katherine Rundell, for instance, was inspired by the trailblazers of Cambridge to climb urban architecture, relying on the ever-present scaffoldings to contemplate London's cityscape from aloft. She considers the lack of premeditation to be an integral aspect of this practice: 'Night climbing, when it goes well, works on the joy of quick and necessary decisions, on improvising in the two seconds in which your stomach and brain are in conflict. It is unmooring your sense of fear and self-preservation from your sense of hope and danger and adventure.'[37]

The means of documenting urban explorations vary as much as their motivating forces. Since the early 2010s, image-sharing platforms based on user-generated content (such as Flickr and Instagram) have provided a popular means of communicating place-hacking campaigns via photographs and videos. This trend was boosted by the advent of online social media and the widespread diffusion of action cameras. In the meantime, the boom of vertical construction around the world multiplied the range of opportunities for urban explorers. The circulation of so-called 'vertigo-inducing images' taken from high points heralded an image culture in which the transgression of boundaries is intertwined with the modes of performance and presentation of self that are fostered by social media.[38] This image culture emerged soon after photographers such as Gabriele Basilico and André Lichtenberg revived the plunging shot in their engagements with architectural vertigo (see Chapter 2). While these artists sought out a visual language that would capture the dizzy spaces of cities, rooftoppers embraced the camera in order to disseminate, and implicitly validate, their spatial practices.

Today, the web is awash with images taken from vantage points that bear witness to the hazardous feats of their makers. At the core of this trend lies an inextricable link between the act of representation and the embodied practices that make it possible. This convergence endows rooftoppers' photographs with a distinct architectural content: not so much in the canonical sense of detached views of buildings, but rather as subjective views that capture the embodied experience of space. The usual intimation that precedes these pictures in the media, 'Don't look down!', should in fact be reversed: these pictures invite us to stare into the urban abyss and, by inducing a vicarious vertigo, rejoice in the thrill of high-rise urban environments.[39]

The dangerous nature of rooftopping is part and parcel of its controversial appeal. With the invariable warnings that alert viewers not to emulate those stunts, the online media routinely reproduce these spectacular images. Such moral undertones echo the reactions of the Victorian press to the craze for gravity plays which purportedly elicited a morbid fascination in their spectators. While 19th-century acrobatics were typically conducted in front of crowds assembled for the events, the unannounced acts performed by the likes of Petit and Robert have drawn incredulous spectators to the scene. The spirit of those illicit endeavours is carried forward by urban explorers who act away from the public gaze, mostly at night, and share their 'trophy shots' with online viewers. By conveying the visceral experience of climbing and treading on the edge, this imagery gives credence to their ability to neutralise the dangerous effects of *ilinx*.

At a time when new narratives are required to make sense of vertical urbanism, this practice has exerted a powerful hold on the imagination. Rooftoppers have been hailed as 'humanizing vectors' that expand the representation of tall buildings beyond the hyper-realistic renderings made by architects.[40] Evoking the photographs of 1930s' ironworkers balancing on beams, they embody a shift from the sphere of labour to that of play. Urban explorers often depict themselves as solitary figures beholding the cityscape. A night shot of Toronto taken by Tom Ryaboi in 2014, titled 'Highlife', is emblematic of this panoramic self-portraiture (plate 13). Shot from a low angle, the picture alludes to the Romantic genre of landscape painting epitomised by Caspar David Friedrich's *Wanderer above the Sea of Fog* (plate 14). Lacking reference points in the landscape, the figure standing on the edge of a precipice embodies a sense of bewilderment in front of the might of nature. Conversely, today's urban wanderer is intent on contemplating the city from a tower crane, couched in the atmospheric effects of lights and haze. Once again, the cityscape is re-enchanted as an expression of the technological sublime.

The popularity of rooftopping has led to multiple variations on the theme of the selfie at height. A series of self-portraits taken by the photographer Lucinda Grange atop a gargoyle of the Chrysler Building in New York references the well-known pictures of Margaret Bourke-White taken in the same spot by her assistant in 1934. Grange, for whom climbing is a cathartic experience driven by a desire to interact with places, has asserted her place in a predominantly male field. The Chrysler series challenges gender stereotypes about rooftopping while at the same time evoking a symbolic continuity with the history of urban photography from above that emerged in the early 20th century. The contrast between the subject and the scenery gives them a surplus of meaning that transcends the common regularities of an increasingly codified genre.

Over the 2010s, rooftopping images spread from online platforms into the realm of exhibitions and publications. A case in point is *London Rising: Illicit Photos from the City's Heights*, a photo-book in which Bradley Garrett and two fellow explorers document a decade of expeditions in a city that has embraced the model of corporate verticality. This volume is at once an homage to the ever-changing metropolis and a critique of the ideology underpinning its rampant growth.[41] While showing views from elevated vantage points that are off-limits to most of us, the book sanctions the popularity of a class of images that, in Garrett's words, 'contain a kernel of power inversion'.[42] This appropriation of urban heights draws its visual power from the acts of trespassing which make such images possible in the first place. The very fact that the photographer is there implies a subversive act, and the images that result from it 'have the effect of dissipating privileged scopic power'.[43] The body is at once an agent of resistance and an index of the missions accomplished.

As the practice of hacking places became gradually normalised, and its imagery co-opted for commercial purposes, its spirit of adventure began to wane. By the time *London Rising* was published, the Urban Exploration movement was showings signs of fatigue; indeed, the authors themselves felt that 'a particular era of rooftopping may be coming to a close'.[44] Meanwhile, the image culture fuelled by it posed a dilemma to explorers driven by a deeper impulse to reclaim the spaces of vertical cities as well as the views they afford. If their overt aim is to sabotage consumer culture through the active occupation of space, this purpose has become entangled with the allure of self-representation.

In parallel, urban theorists began to consider climbers as the agents of new subjectivities. Andrea Mubi Brighenti and Andrea Pavoni point out that the practice of scaling cities entails a bodily engagement with the environment that is inherently political, insofar as it rejects the passive forms of consumption associated with commodity capitalism: 'By pushing control to its limits, urban climbing questions the false security of comfort and the false freedom of the consumer.'[45] Through the specific relations between body and environment that emerge in the vertical city, we can re-imagine the power structures that are involved in the production of space and probe the forces that underlie regimes of property and use. Unlike wire walkers who momentarily inhabit the space between buildings, climbers engage with their surfaces in ways that reveal the materiality of vertical cities. Both practices have the potential to affect, and in some cases subvert, the perception of architecture.

The critical agency of urban explorations depends not only on their intrinsic nature, but on how their actions can empower viewers to comprehend and confront those spaces. In other words, embodied spatial practices can help us to reconfigure the relationship between architecture and vertigo. The sense of perceptual disorientation induced by the encounter with the abyss cannot be reduced to the intoxicating pleasure of heights, nor to the potential anxiety provoked by them. Beyond fear and elation lies the possibility of discovering a new consciousness of verticality; a cognitive awareness of our place in the environment that can be triggered, vicariously, by a moment of bewilderment. Thus, by countering the effects of *ilinx*, climbers and aerialists inhabit urban space in ways that bring forth alternate forms of resistance.

Plate 15 ArcelorMittal Orbit tower with tunnel slide and abseilers.

LEFT

Plate 16 Interior view of the Hyatt Regency Hotel, San Francisco.

ABOVE

Plate 17 View from observation elevator, Hopewell Centre, Hong Kong.

Plate 18 Interior view of the Reichstag Building dome, New German Parliament, Berlin.

ABOVE

Plate 19 Frame from *Gehry's Vertigo* (dir. Ila Bêka and Louise Lemoine, Spain, 2013).

RIGHT

Plate 20 Observation deck with security fence, 2 World Trade Center (South Tower), 1984.

Plate 21 Floating garden observatory atop the Umeda Sky Building, Osaka.

LEFT, TOP

Plate 22 Infinity pool, SkyPark at Marina Bay Sands, Singapore.

LEFT, BOTTOM

Plate 23 'Skywalk 100' observatory, World Financial Centre, Shanghai.

ABOVE

Plate 24 Treetop Walkway, Kew Gardens, London.

Plate 25 'The Ledge' at Willis Tower, Chicago.

Plate 26 'Tilt', 360 Chicago, John Hancock Center.

ABOVE

Plate 27 'Vessel', Hudson Yards, New York.

LEFT

Plate 28 'Sky Portal', One World Observatory, One World Trade Center, New York.

PART III

STAGING VERTIGO

5

THRILLS OF GRAVITY

Every form of vertigo goes with a particular form of pleasure.[1]

17 Ferris Wheel at the World's Columbian Exposition, Chicago, c.1893.

MECHANISED FUN

Vertigo names a sensation that is often associated with discomfort, yet may also relate to a frisson of excitement. As far as our perception of balance is concerned, anxiety and pleasure are opposite sides of the same emotional coin. We only need to walk by a recreation ground to be reminded that playing with gravity is a favourite children's activity: climbing, jumping, sliding and swaying are some of the bodily pursuits that engender feelings of contentment and even elation. Amusement parks are further reminders that such dynamic plays retain an allure for adults, too, as they challenge our bodily equilibrium within controlled environments. As a species that evolutionally acquired the upright posture, we tend to relish those motions that rouse kinaesthetic awareness by stimulating the vertebral column. Indeed, the word vertebra shares the same etymology as vertigo and vertical (from the Latin *vertere*, 'to turn').[2] Postural movements of the spine affect the coordination of physical stability, as our central nervous system processes information from peripheral nerves that are distributed across the entire body in order to maintain an overall equilibrium.

Neuroscience research has shed light on how sensations of vertigo are caused not only by pathological dysfunctions but also, more commonly, by simple physiological stimulation. The latter involves a wide spectrum of feelings that range from disorientation to euphoria, as is particularly evident in the experience of heights: from the variety of individual reactions to high places can be inferred the sheer complexity of our balance system. As we have seen in previous chapters, spatial practices in which equilibrium plays a vital role, such as climbing and rope walking, epitomise the human drive to challenge the constraints of gravity. All activities that push the boundaries of physical stability trigger psycho-physiological responses that may induce excitement or fear – or, indeed, the excitement *of* fear. While the child's impulse to play with gravity responds to an evolutionary process, adults channel a residue of that impulse towards ludic activities that make one's head spin. Not surprisingly, then, the leisure industry has harnessed technology to rouse the balance system through ever more intense stimuli.

In the 19th century, the fascination with gravity manifested itself not only through the spectacular feats of daredevil performers but also through a wealth of contraptions that fuelled a growing demand for thrilling experiences. In the wake of the Industrial Revolution, a plethora of machines were invented to defy gravity on the ground and in the air. While vertigo-inducing devices had already been popular since the 18th century, the mechanisation of thrills picked up momentum when urban industrial modernity came into full swing.[3] Alongside the advent of mechanised transport, a host of gravity plays were introduced in pleasure gardens, parks and exhibitions, notably at the world's fairs that punctuated the second half of the century. By eliciting heady sensations of rising and falling, these modern thrill rides invited people to abandon themselves to momentary states of rapture.

Chief amongst them, the roller coaster played on the effects of gravity by subjecting the riders' bodies to the shocks of abrupt jolts, twists and turns. This popular attraction applied railway technology to the practice of sledge riding on artificial hills of ice, the so-called 'flying mountains' which had delighted St Petersburg's citizens since the 18th century.[4] The use of wheels on tracks led to the development of switchbacks that could be used all year around, sparking off the French vogue for 'Russian mountains'. From the *promenades aériennes* built in Paris in the 1810s to the scenic railways that spread across American cities in the 1880s, the 19th century was awash with amusement rides that channelled the pleasure of falling.

The first successful coaster – the Switchback Gravity Pleasure Railway launched at Coney Island in 1884 – was promptly emulated in Britain where a similar contraption was built at the seaside resort of Skegness the following year. According to Garrett Soden, these inventions exemplified the new age of mechanised thrills: 'The roller coaster was more than the first machine to deliver the sensation of falling to the masses; it was a machine that *amplified* the sensation of falling. [...] By stripping away control, increasing the magnitude of the falls, and distilling it all into a few minutes, the roller coaster isolated, packaged, and fetishized the sensation.'[5] In some way, those fairground attractions reproduced the thrills and dangers of the modern industrial world in the comfort of safe environments. The mechanisation of fun was part of a wider social phenomenon which saw the emergence of a new 'leisure class'.[6] As Josephine Kane points out, mechanised thrills became part of 'a world of commercially produced leisure' that provided sources of entertainment for ever larger sections of society.[7]

Towards the end of the 19th century, the popularity of giddy-making machines fuelled the design of modern amusement parks. This shift brought about a new 'architecture of pleasure' that thrived on the enjoyment of gravity.[8] Its prime locations were resorts such as Blackpool, on the northwest coast of

England, where the imposing cast-iron tower erected in 1894 symbolised the rise of mass tourism in the late Victorian period. Amid the piers and promenades of Blackpool Pleasure Beach, the 'flying machine' inaugurated in 1904 catered for the growing market of thrill seekers while profiting from the novelty of powered flight.[9]

The variety of pleasures dispensed by modern contraptions often combined visual and kinaesthetic stimuli. A turning point, in every sense, was the panoramic wheel designed by George W.G. Ferris Jr. for the Chicago Columbian Exposition of 1893, which set a model for mobile viewing platforms soon to be replicated around the world. Having won the competition to realise a landmark that would rival the Eiffel Tower, Ferris engineered a steel structure with a diameter of *c.*76 metres (250 feet) capable of carrying over 2,000 passengers in 36 cars. The giant tension-spoke wheel encapsulated Daniel Burnham's ambitious plans for the Columbian Exposition: against the scepticism of its detractors, it was hailed at the time as 'one of the wonders of the age' and 'the biggest piece of revolving machinery in the world' (fig.17).[10]

Around the turn of the 20th century, with the spread of amusement parks, came along new types of playground in which mechanised thrill rides reproduced the dizzying pace and space of metropolitan life. By the onset of the First World War, every major Western city had its own entertainment district in which a heightened version of the modern urban spectacle could be experienced for a fee.[11] In parallel, a number of variations on the roller coaster were patented, as Luna Parks were animated by ever new inventions with evocative names such as 'giant aerial drop', 'spiral wheel', 'cyclone bowl', 'gyroplane', as well as sundry 'looping machines' (fig.18).

The Ferris Wheel spawned a number of European imitations that surpassed one another in height, from the Great Wheel unveiled in London in 1895 to the *Grande Roue* that was built in Paris for the Exposition Universelle of 1900. The original structure erected in Chicago was dismantled and rebuilt in St. Louis for the World's Fair of 1904. Two days after the opening, newspapers reported that a worker had fallen to his death while oiling the 45-ton axle – a stark reminder of the hazards involved in assembling and maintaining those attractions.

The variety of entertainments designed to thrill modern city dwellers reproduced the heightened sensory stimuli that Georg Simmel identified in the early 1900s as integral to metropolitan life. For Simmel, whose observations were primarily based on his experience of turn-of-the-century Berlin, life in the *Großstadt* was characterised by impersonal and indifferent behaviours that

18 'Loop the loop', Atlantic City, *c.*1901. Detroit Publishing Company photograph collection.

reflected the values of the money economy. Social relations were manifested by the *blasé* attitude (*Blasiertheit*), an adaptive response to the pressure of external stimuli on people's mental life. According to Simmel, this defence barrier explained the intensification of consciousness that was typical of the big city, where 'metropolitan types' resorted to shield their inner selves from external impulses.[12]

At the same time, modern cities offered a plethora of amusements that allowed their inhabitants to discharge their pent-up reserves of nervous energy. The sphere of mental life, which was desensitised for the sake of individual self-preservation, was thereby reawakened in purpose-designed spaces for the consumption of leisure. Amusement parks operated as social safety valves for urban populations loaded with increasing levels of stress and anxiety: their intense sensory stimuli reactivated, if only for brief moments, the play instincts that were largely repressed by the metropolis. To borrow Marshall Berman's words, the enjoyment of mechanised thrills embodied 'the maelstrom of modern life'.[13]

The experience of urban modernity laid bare the conundrum of vertigo as an ambivalent psycho-social phenomenon. If, on the one hand, the intensification of sensory experience induced a bundle of anxieties, fears and phobias, on the other, it triggered a set of practices and representations that playfully defied gravity. For thrill seekers, those sensory solicitations were challenges to be relished, as evidenced by the emergence of new forms of spectatorship as well as extreme sports, leisure activities and amusements that challenged the sense of balance. Although the built environment became increasingly fraught with vertigo, this ambivalent phenomenon was largely expunged from the heroic narrative of modernity predicated on the tropes of crowds, speed and skyscrapers. In the early 20th century, the perceptual world brought along by the metropolis was embraced as a source of visceral thrills.

THE MAELSTROM OF MODERN LIFE

The geography of the metropolis expanded in the early 20th century beyond Europe's imperial capitals to encompass fast-growing cities such as New York, São Paulo and Tokyo.[14] As modern culture was revolutionised by mass media, the dizzy conditions of urban life became the subject of representations that circulated widely through exhibitions, cinema and the illustrated press. Amid the visual experiments that came out of the avant-garde movements, film established itself as the medium that captured most vividly the maelstrom of modern life.

An exemplar of the 'city symphonies' that burgeoned in the late 1920s,[15] Walter Ruttmann's *Berlin: Die Sinfonie der Großstadt* (1927) depicts the capital of the German Reich from dawn to dusk. While the city's hustle and bustle signified its relentless industrialisation, it also signalled a deep-seated malaise, providing a counterpoint to Simmel's critique of the money economy. Motor traffic dictated the tempo of urban life: steamboats, trains, trams and aeroplanes were not only vectors of transport but also viewing platforms that reconfigured the buzzing city as a field of vision in motion. This is compounded by the film's rapid editing, which conjures up the intensification of stimuli in the *Großstadt*. Mechanised thrills were integral to this sensory landscape. By the 1920s the roller coaster had become the premier type of amusement ride in Western cities, and Ruttmann illustrated the attractions of Berlin's Lunapark through queasy point-of-view shots taken from its coaster and merry-go-round. While these pictures celebrated the dynamism of modern life, they also introduced a more sinister reading of the metropolis.

The tension between the fear and desire of falling reaches a climax in a bumpy sequence from the roller coaster, intercut with the shot of a woman who jumps off a bridge. Her horrified expression, looking down at the river into which she is about to disappear, reveals the Janus-faced paradox of the metropolis. The sudden swing reproduces the oscillation between pleasure and anxiety that is constitutive of vertigo, and which is echoed by spiral movements throughout the film. Cultural historian Sabine Hake points out that this staged scene 'briefly abandons the celebration of rhythm and tempo and allows for a rare acknowledgment of the shock of modernity and the violence of modernization'.[16] The exhilaration of metropolitan life and the sense of dizziness descending into despair are powerfully juxtaposed in a quick-cut montage. Subsequently, the confluence of opposite drives is depicted by a sequence in which the surface of water eddies into a whirlpool, forming the abstract pattern of a receding spiral.

Similar motifs pervade *São Paulo: A Symphonia da Metrópole* (1929), directed two years later by Adalberto Kemeny and Rudolpho Rex Lustig, which depicts the modernisation of the Brazilian city in a cinematic style inspired by *Berlin*. By merging various aspects of industry, commerce, construction, education and sport taking place amidst a restless traffic, the film conveys the spirit of a major South American city that could hardly be distinguished from its European counterparts. As announced in the opening titles, the film 'reveals to the people of São Paulo the grandeur of this superb metropolis, which was made vertiginously, thanks to the constructive energy of its people'. The tempo of urban life is emphasised by images of ticking metronomes and people looking at their watches intercut with the unabating movement of machines. But the film equally depicts the vertical rise of architecture in a city whose population had already exceeded one million. Using kaleidoscopic montage and superimposition techniques that recall Vertov's as well as Ruttmann's films, Kemeny and Lustig evoked the heady atmosphere that pervaded the Brazilian metropolis on the eve of political revolution.

The influence of *Berlin* reached beyond the city symphonies of the 1920s. Ruttmann's now-classic film anticipated a series of visual themes that would resurface in *Vertigo* three decades later, from the frequent spiralling patterns to the frightened gaze staring into the abyss. A closer parallel can be found in Hitchcock's lesser-known film, *Champagne* (1928), a silent comedy released one year after *Berlin* and one year before the Wall Street Crash, which somehow, it presaged. Here a champagne businessman (Gordon Harker) feigns to have lost his fortune on the stock market in order to impart a lesson to his daughter (Betty Balfour). The plot is punctuated by heady tropes of speed and flight. An impending loss of balance, evoked throughout the film by twirling spirals as well as nauseous camera movements, culminates in the restaurant scene in which a performer jumps off a balcony into her partner's arms and the two pirouette into a whirling dance. Moments of inebriation alternate with instants of bewilderment to evoke the maelstrom of modern life – the capitalist city being its bustling theatre.

Tensions between the thrill of the metropolis and its social malaise exploded after the 1929 crash, when New York's cityscape became the backdrop to several narratives depicting the highs and lows of urban modernity. Amidst the visual and literary works of the 1930s, an illustrated book encapsulates the mood of the Great Depression in eloquent fashion. First published in 1937, Lynd Ward's *Vertigo: A Novel in Woodcuts* is a paragon of the wordless novel, a neglected genre sitting between literature and fine art that paved the way for the graphic novel. Tracing the story of a young couple separated by dire economic conditions, *Vertigo* narrates their parallel vicissitudes along with those of an aged businessman who embodies the greedy face of capitalism. New York's architecture pervades the engravings with high contrasts, as the doom and gloom of the story unfolds in the ominous shadow of skyscrapers.

In Ward's intentions, the book title '"was meant to suggest that the illogic of what we saw happening all around us in the thirties was enough to set the mind spinning through space and the emotions hurtling from great hope to the depths of despair"'.[17] This emotional whirlwind builds up to the final scene, where the boy and the girl are reunited after he, unable to find a job, sells his blood to the 'elderly gentleman' (fig.19). The ending is intimate yet not quite happy: on a Sunday pleasure trip, the lovers embrace in the seat of a roller coaster that is tumbling at full speed, as though united against a frightening menace. The boy's wide-open eyes, staring into the void, express the sense of dejection with which Ward depicted the bustling American metropolis.

Amid the well-documented race to the sky, with ever-taller skyscrapers embodying the power of industrial capitalism, in the inter-war years New York saw a culture of verticality spring up through an amalgam of technological advances. According to Adnan Morshed, the combined advent of high-rise architecture and powered flight fuelled a new 'aesthetic of ascension' in American culture.[18] The experience of altitude was imbued with spiritual, and

19 Illustration from Lynd Ward, *Vertigo: A Novel in Woodcuts* (1937).

invariably gendered, overtones: 'The aesthetics of ascension implied a peculiar blend of godlike spectatorship, technological utopianism, and evolutionary idealism – all converging to create the subversive myth of a master builder, able to redeem a chaotic world from his high perch of authority (this was a masculinist discourse).'[19]

This phenomenon took a spectacular form in the New York World's Fair of 1939, a display of technical progress designed to celebrate the 'World of

Jack NORWORTH

20 Parachute tower, Coney Island, New York, *c.*1941.

Tomorrow'. Its best-known highlight was the Futurama designed by Norman Bel Geddes and sponsored by General Motors: a giant animated model of an urban agglomeration that visitors could admire from above, perched on a conveyor belt that simulated the view from a moving aircraft.[20] This exhibit marked a contrast with the gloomy picture that was painted in *The City*, a documentary by the American Institute of City Planners which advocated centralised measures to address the plight of urban poverty. Meanwhile, on the exhibition grounds of Flushing Meadows, the geometric structures of the Trylon and the Perisphere were bright landmarks that symbolised a forward-looking spirit. Amidst thousands of exhibits, the sky-bound structures expressed the mood of a country that sought to shake off the gravitas of the Great Depression. This sense of lightness was emphasised by spectacles of acrobatics and free diving that were performed atop giant ladders held by metal wires in the amusement zone.

Above all other structures stood the Parachute Jump, a 76-metre steel tower sponsored by the Life Savers candy company in which riders were hoisted up on cables then dropped into a freefall until the chutes were released. A similar attraction had graced the International Exposition held in Paris two years prior, yet it was the New York tower that gained widespread acclaim. Its inventor, James H. Strong, was a retired US Navy commander who had initially devised the structure for training purposes before he realised its potential as a source of amusement. The prototype, which had electric engines and shock-absorbers preventing the impact of landing, was expanded from six to 12 chutes for the World's Fair, where it offered fleeting yet unrivalled views of the fairgrounds.[21] The Parachute Jump was so popular that, shortly after the fair, it was moved to Steeplechase Park in Coney Island and eventually listed as a historical landmark after its activity was terminated in 1968 (fig.20). Its first iteration, however, is historically significant since it adapted one of the foremost inventions of the gravity century to a vertiginous thrill. While the 1939 World's Fair was designed to project the United States towards a bright technological future, a new war loomed in which airpower would play a decisive role.

A VOLUPTUOUS PANIC

Tropes of vertigo became rife in Western art and literature after the Second World War, reaching a peak in the late 1950s (see Chapter 1). Along with

Hitchcock's *Vertigo*, those years saw a flurry of cultural production around issues of gravity and stability emerge against the background of an economic recession that hampered the efforts of post-war recovery across the industrialised world. While the precariousness of balance prompted reflections and representations, at the same time there arose a new interest in gravity-related thrills. In his study of games and play, Caillois referred to a variety of rituals – from the Mexican *voladores* to the whirling dervishes of Turkey – that embody the challenges posed by the force of gravity. The simple observation that children take delight in spinning around themselves until they fall testifies to our innate attitude towards *ilinx*. In the incipit of *Homo Ludens*, Huizinga had already noted that 'Play is older than culture', as its primary impulse could be observed in other animals as well.[22] But what interested Caillois were the social and cultural practices whereby humans seek to voluntarily alter their physical stability.

The term *ilinx* refers to those games 'which consist of an attempt to momentarily destroy the stability of perception and inflict a kind of voluptuous panic upon an otherwise lucid mind'.[23] With this category, Caillois identified the realm of play that more than any other corresponds to the machine age, for it was only after the Industrial Revolution that 'vertigo could really become a kind of game'.[24] Among its modern forms were the contraptions installed at fairs and amusement parks, which were designed to induce a 'pleasurable torture'. With the acceleration of speed in the first half of the 20th century, the mass production of cars, airliners and other means of powered transport brought about a revolution of mobility that had profound consequences on the perception of space. Furthermore, the intoxicating effects of modern technologies were set side by side with the alterations of consciousness caused by alcohol, smoking and recreational drugs.

Caillois regarded the pursuit of *ilinx* not only as a form of play but, importantly, as a strike on the normative structures of the social world. In parallel to the physical sensation of losing one's bearings, he wrote, 'there is a vertigo of the moral order, a transport that suddenly seizes the individual. This vertigo is readily linked to the desire for disorder and destruction, a drive which is normally repressed.'[25] These words make plain why the author aligned *ilinx* with a play instinct that is fundamentally undisciplined. Such an unruly tendency resonates with the concept of *jouissance* developed by Jacques Lacan between the late 1950s and the early 1960s. The French psychoanalyst, who was influenced by Caillois's study of animal camouflage, discussed at length the quest after pleasure that leads individuals to live out their drives in disregard of their potential consequences.[26] In Lacanian terms, this form of 'deadly enjoyment' would transcend the balancing function of the pleasure principle while pulling the subject towards chaos and destruction. The linkage between the concept of *jouissance* and that of *ilinx* sheds further light on a realm of human play that rests on a deliberate loss of balance.

Concurrently, the excitement derived from vertigo-inducing practices was investigated by Michael Balint, who put forward a psychology of thrills based on object relations theory. His 1959 book, *Thrills and Regressions*, refers to popular amusements that are typical of funfairs, namely 'pleasures connected with dizziness, vertigo, impairment or loss of stability, such as swings, roundabouts, switchbacks'.[27] Balint related the feelings of rapture aroused by thrill rides to the longing for visceral experiences in which the sense of balance is momentarily destabilised. In a compelling passage, he remarked on the different psychological responses elicited by funfair thrills:

> All the amusements in this group are connected with giddiness and vertigo; that is to say, with a situation in which a particular form of anxiety is aroused and borne. The form of this anxiety can be described as loss of balance, of stability, of the firm contact with the safe earth, and so on. Some people react instinctively, almost reflex-like, to this kind of anxiety by clutching at something firm, or, in still greater anxiety, by pressing their whole body against a firm and safe object. While normally the planting of the feet firmly on the ground gives them enough security, in 'giddy' situations this does not seem to be sufficient.[28]

For Balint this state of perceptual instability stemmed from the exposure to an external source of dread that was at once intentional and controlled. Key to mastering the ensuing anxiety was the consciousness that any perceived risk would remain within tolerable margins: 'This mixture of fear, pleasure, and confident hope in face of an external danger is what constitutes the fundamental elements of all *thrills*.'[29] Accordingly, emotions of fear and pleasure are mediated by an inner safety mechanism that presides over the perception of danger.

Our responses to hazardous situations, however, vary widely on the basis of different personality types and Balint distinguished between subjects who enjoy the thrills of gravity ('philobats') and those who shy away from them ('ocnophils'). Taking a historical outlook, he classified as philobatic the gravity plays performed by acrobats since ancient times in front of audiences who would rejoice in vicarious pleasures. In the course of the 19th century, growing numbers of people longed to challenge gravity themselves rather than acting as mere spectators, a development which Balint ascribed to the modern tendency 'to live dangerously'.[30]

A sustained interest in this psychological impulse had emerged after the Second World War within the British Psychoanalytical Society, of which Balint was a member. Another of its exponents, Donald Winnicott, investigated in parallel the 'counterphobic character', an attitude that draws the subject towards the source of fear or anxiety, rather than shunning it as happens in phobic behaviours. This personality trait leads to the pursuit of activities that are considered to be dangerous, such as those involving the risks of falling from height. Winnicott associated it with the formation of an idealised self which stands as a defence mechanism in the way of the true or original self.[31]

Within this context, Caillois's anthropology of play and Balint's psychology of thrills evince a new awareness of the subjective as well as socio-cultural aspects of vertigo that crystallised in the late 1950s. Moreover, the terminology they put forward attests to the search for a vocabulary that would describe the playful dimension of this phenomenon. While Balint focused on the mechanised attractions that populated modern amusement parks, he also remarked on the ability of performers such as acrobats and rope walkers to convey the synthesis of fear, pleasure and confidence that lay at the core of his psychology: vicariously, their acts arouse in spectators the thrills of defying gravity at dangerous heights.

These theories informed subsequent studies of vertigo and, by the end of the 20th century, it was widely acknowledged that this category encompassed a broad emotional spectrum. Building on Balint's psychology of thrills, Danielle Quinodoz went on to regard anxiety and pleasure to be opposite poles of an emotional pendulum.[32] Her insights into psychic vertigo open up new ways of understanding extreme games of vertigo that are performed by scores of thrill seekers as well as by trained practitioners.

More recently, psychology researchers have considered a wide scope of responses to high places that are not limited to vertigo-related pathologies but extend to the emotional realms of thrill and pleasure.[33] It has been established that the perception of danger varies greatly between subjects who avert heights and those who actively pursue them: 'Height-tolerant individuals perceive the physical danger of heights but compensate either by habituation or a comfort level with their sense of physical danger. Height-seeking individuals actually enjoy the sense of physical danger when exposed to heights.'[34] Therefore, the full spectrum of height (in)tolerance should include subjects who cope well with altitude and encompass those who keenly embrace its risks. This prompts us to consider the role of contemporary architecture in fostering gravity plays, as buildings themselves are turned into thrill machines.

MEMORABLE EXPERIENCES

The rise of adventure tourism, a sector which has grown significantly since the last quarter of the 20th century, shows an increasing tendency to cast high-rise architecture as a playground. While mechanised thrills have moved to specialised themed parks that are often located outside towns, various amusements that engage with the experience of the abyss – such as bungee jumping, tunnel slides and 'edgewalks' – have been incorporated in urban environments. Rather than thriving on the power of machines, these attractions foster the play of *ilinx* by stimulating an active bodily engagement with space. Such kinaesthetic experiences cater for, and in turn reproduce, a desire to defy gravity through variations of children's games or simulations of professional acrobatics. The rise to popularity of these games of vertigo has coincided with a wider socio-cultural shift in the latter part of the 20th century. In the words of sociologist Zygmunt Bauman: 'The mark of postmodern adulthood is the willingness to embrace the game wholeheartedly, as children do.'[35]

The exhilarating thrill of falling through space, in particular, has driven a whole industry of visceral plays epitomised by the craze for bungee jumping. This practice originated in the Dangerous Sports Club at Oxford University, where in the late 1970s a group of students revelled in extreme stunts such as leaping off bridges with the aid of parachutes, thus paving the way for the development of BASE (Buildings, Antenna, Spans and Earth) jumping over the following decade. In parallel, bungee gained momentum in New Zealand from A.J. Hackett, who caused a sensation by throwing himself off Auckland Harbour Bridge with a rubber cord harnessed to his ankles. An illicit stunt performed at the Eiffel Tower in 1987 (fig.21) helped Hackett to popularise this practice, and his commercial venture was propelled by a jump off Auckland's Stock Exchange Tower the following year. While typical bungee locations were initially bridges over gorges and valleys, urban structures were later

21 A.J. Hackett's bungee jump from the Eiffel Tower, Paris, 26 June 1987.

retrofitted with facilities for adventure tourists: before the end of the century, it became possible for thrill seekers to jump off from a height of 190 metres at Auckland's Sky Tower.

Since its early days, bungee jumping was inspired by ancient rituals associated with male identity formation, such as the land-diving ceremony performed on Pentecost Island in the archipelago of Vanuatu (formerly known as New Hebrides). This ceremony caught the attention of Western travellers

22 Illustration from David Frederick Attenborough, 'The Land-diving Ceremony in Pentecost, New Hebrides', *Philosophical Transactions of the Royal Society* (1966).

in the early 1950s, hence the first reports on the gravity stunts performed in the South Pacific began to appear.[36] In 1960, David Attenborough published an ethnographic study of the ritual, traditionally staged in the harvest season, whereby men dived off a wooden tower with vines harnessed to their ankles as safety ropes (fig.22).[37] Their bodies are subject to one of the highest levels of g-force experienced by humans in the absence of machines, making the challenge of dropping without touching the ground notoriously dangerous.

A similar ceremony involving music and dance has taken place for centuries in Mexico, where men let themselves fall from a wooden pole to which they are attached through ropes. This ancient rite, known as *danza de los voladores* ('flyers' dance'), was cited by Caillois as a historical example of *ilinx*. Soon after these traditions caught the attention of Western researchers, in the second half of the 20th century, they became tourist attractions; and it was only a short step before they were adapted to the pursuits of modern thrill seekers.

The AJ Hackett group has operated bungee sites and various other gravity-defying activities around the world since the late 1980s, contributing to refashioning urban observation towers into playgrounds for games of vertigo. This trend is typified by Macau Tower, a high-rise concrete structure modelled after Auckland's Sky Tower and designed by the same architects (Craig Craig Moller) which embodied the boom of extreme sports around the turn of the millennium. A record-breaking jump by Hackett himself, in 2006, was followed by the launch of a new attraction branded 'The World's Highest Bungee Jump Facility'. This 'skyjump' was joined by other gravity plays including a 'skywalk' around the outer edge of the observation deck. Macau Tower signals how, turning some of the tallest urban structures into sites of visceral thrills, the tourist industry redefined the experience of vertical space as an extreme form of entertainment. The success of this practice signals that the act of falling, which for the greatest part of history had retained negative connotations of danger and death, became associated with a modern pleasure.[38] Once the impulse to master gravity shed off its hubris, it fuelled a growing market for visceral experiences that gained traction in the last quarter of the 20th century.

The gravity plays that can be found atop amusement towers today embody the myths and rites of contemporary culture. Namely, the rise of adventure tourism is an expression of the wider phenomenon that is known as the 'experience economy'. This term was coined in the late 1990s by the American economists Joseph Pine and James Gilmore to describe the latest step in the progression of values that marked the evolution of capitalism. After the modern economy shifted from extracting commodities to manufacturing goods, then on to delivering services, a new phase emerged in the late 20th century based on a distinct function: staging experiences.

Pine and Gilmore recognised that the main factor in the creation of economic value was no longer defined by characteristics, features and benefits, as in previous eras, but rather by *sensations*. Hence, they recommended that businesses seek a competitive edge by staging 'memorable experiences'.

Architecture played a key role in the rise of this new economy owing to its capacity to stimulate experiences with a strong aesthetic component: 'In such experiences, individuals immerse themselves in an event or environment but themselves have little or no effect on it, leaving the environment (but not themselves) essentially untouched.'[39]

One of the main functions of this economy, *immersion* was defined by Pine and Gilmore as the act of 'becoming physically (or virtually) a part of the experience itself'.[40] Accordingly, it is essential to stimulate strong sensory responses in order to attract visitors to immersive environments: 'The more effectively an experience engages the senses, the more memorable it will be.'[41] A notable precedent can be found in the theme parks that were built after the Disneyland model in post-war America. Indeed, the tourist industry was ahead of its time and blazed the trail for the experience economy. In the 1970s, the sociologist Dean MacCannell had already noted in his semiotic analysis of tourist attractions: 'Increasingly, pure experience, which leaves no material trace, is manufactured and sold like a commodity.'[42] Later, Bauman remarked that tourists, unlike other social types of travellers, are often moved by the pursuit of goals that are at once transient and controlled:

> the tourist is a conscious and systematic seeker of experience, of a new and different experience, of the experience of difference and novelty – as the joys of the familiar wear off and cease to allure. The tourists want to immerse themselves in a strange and bizarre element [...] – on condition, though, that it will not stick to the skin and this can be shaken off whenever they wish.[43]

In the latter part of the 20th century, memorable experiences became the main commodity of one of the fastest-growing industries in the world. They fostered the cycle of desire that Bauman identified as a key feature of liquid modernity. Accordingly, in consumer societies the body is reconfigured from a means to an end (the instrumental logic of industrial capitalism) to an end in itself: that is, an 'autotelic' body that is constantly bent in the pursuit of pleasure and wellness. Far from expressing a care of the self, leisure activities are often spawned by an advanced form of capitalism that sees the body as an endlessly profitable source, fuelling what has been called the 'happiness industry'.[44] Thus, the goal of marketing language is not the satisfaction of desires but, in Bauman's terms, '*arousing* desire for ever more desire'.[45] As this perverse cycle spins ever faster on the free market's wheels, the quest for commodified pleasure is bound to generate stress and, as a consequence, to cause frustration: 'The consumer's body [. . .] tends to be a particularly prolific source of perpetual anxiety, exacerbated by the absence of established and reliable outlets to relieve it, let alone to defuse or disperse it.'[46]

This state of anxiety is inextricably bound up with the imperatives of an ideology that promotes solitary forms of enjoyment for subjects-consumers. Such a hedonistic and self-centred subject, which Bauman called *homo consumens*, is predicated upon the search for immediate gratification. Its conundrum is that it must never be truly satisfied in order to continue its course. As illusions of omnipotence nourish the will to conquer time and space for the self's own satisfaction, the value of the 'other' is progressively eroded in the process.[47] Those very pleasures that are marketed as collective often mask a deeper individualistic nature: 'Consumption is a supremely solitary activity (perhaps even the archetype of solitude), even when it happens to be conducted in company.'[48] With its promise of memorable experiences, adventure tourism is deeply implicated in a cycle of desire that caters for an incessant pursuit of novelty. As part of this process, amusement towers stage the abyss as a site of immersive thrills.

SLIDING AWAY

The trend for staging immersive experiences has had ripple effects across the art world as well. In 2006, Carsten Höller realised an installation at London's Tate Modern that played on the thrill of falling through space. Located within the vast Turbine Hall, *Test Site* consisted of five semi-transparent coiling tubes in which visitors could slide down from different heights. Often cited as an example of relational art, the work was meant to foster public interaction in antithesis to the passivity of consumer culture. By throwing bodies off balance, Höller sought to challenge the normative order of society: the dizzying experience elicited by the slides was deemed to provide 'a model or prototype for change in our urban environment'.[49] In the exhibition catalogue, art historian and curator Dorothea von Hantelmann wrote:

> The somatic phenomenon of vertigo signals the failure of a coherent coordination of self and world perception. As an aesthetic and cultural

concept, however, it comprises a narration that goes from the fragility of the self to the evanescence of the senses and a sense of dizziness, to finally reach the joyful experience of vertigo, an attraction that confronts us with the limits of our sensual disorientation.[50]

Test Site was endowed by critics with political agency since it acted as a catalyst for doubt. In conjunction with this project, a regeneration consultancy carried out a feasibility study in East London and concluded that tunnel slides could provide a means of public transportation while creating opportunities for communal enjoyment. Their case study of Stratford Town Centre (an area that was later redeveloped for the 2012 Summer Olympics) suggested that slides could be used to integrate existing transport links, animate underused spaces, connect buildings and enhance circulation systems through new forms of 'collective descent'.[51] Adapting the spirit of the original artwork to the public realm, this research advocated new forms of play and spontaneity that could enhance the experience of buildings such as stations, office blocks and shopping centres. A parallel application was explored by Foreign Office Architects, who designed a visionary tower in which users would ascend by elevators and descend through a web of tunnel slides criss-crossing its outer perimeter. The Hypothetical Slide House project anticipated an outcome that would materialise a decade later.

Among the slides that were installed by Höller at international galleries and various other sites, most prominent is the giant version realised at London's ArcelorMittal Orbit, the observation tower at Queen Elizabeth Olympic Park designed by the artist Anish Kapoor with the engineer Cecil Balmond (plate 15). Unveiled for the 2012 Olympics, this topsy-turvy structure was intended to convey a sensation of instability, so much so that Kapoor himself likened it to the Tower of Babel. In a bid to revamp East London's new landmark after the Games, in 2016 the longest tunnel slide in the world began to channel visitors down 178 metres of twists and turns over a 40-second descent.

Höller's intent was to induce a mix of fear and fun that, in a way wholly different from roller coasters, would enable adults to enjoy the subversive power of gravity plays that are usually confined to childhood: 'It proposes the idea not only of the slide as a means of transportation, but also as a tool for introducing a moment of real madness into daily life. If slides were everywhere – if architects would listen to me and stop building only stairs, escalators, and elevators – it would be a different world.'[52] The utopian thrust of this statement is at odds with an installation that is seemingly aimed at an enterprising *homo consumens* rather than an idealised *homo ludens*. Arguably, The Slide indicates that Höller's artistic concept, which originally engaged with the social as well as experiential aspects of falling, has been turned into a source of entertainment aligned with the imperatives of the experience economy: its aesthetic value commodified into a kinaesthetic experience for thrill seekers.

Another gravity attraction, a roped descent from the topmost viewing gallery (80 metres above the ground), had been installed in the same tower the year before the giant slide. Guided by trained instructors, adventure tourists could experience the highest freefall abseil in Britain, as a typical mountaineering practice was revamped into an urban thrill. Höller's subsequent intervention sealed the new function of the ArcelorMittal Orbit as an amusement tower specialising in gravity plays.

Trained as a biologist, the German artist had been concerned with issues of gravity well before *Test Site* and cited the notion of *ilinx* as inspiration for his first slides. Upon closer scrutiny, however, this category reveals a deeper insight into the pursuit of vertigo. For Caillois, this class of games belongs to a domain in which the player 'gratifies the desire to temporarily destroy his bodily equilibrium, escape the tyranny of his ordinary perception, and provoke the abdication of conscience'.[53] This critical undertone seems to have been lost on artists and writers who overlook the ambivalent nature of *ilinx*, reducing it, somewhat nostalgically, to a primordial instinct to be reawakened by artificial means.

By claiming to channel a ludic impulse through a purportedly spontaneous and liberatory experience, Höller's installations are caught up in a leisure industry that reproduces the imperatives of neoliberal subjectivity rather than questioning it. While the design of tunnel slides relates to a history of gravity plays which elicit the voluptuous panic of *ilinx*, it also signals a more recent tendency to convert urban structures into sites of vertiginous thrills, as the providers of immersive experiences vie for shares of a lucrative tourist market.

UP TO GIDDY HEIGHTS

Since the turn of the 21st century, the experience economy has played an increasing role in the production of urban space. An instance of this process is the makeover of existing buildings into gravity playgrounds that are embedded in the economy of vertigo. The Millennium Dome in southeast London is a notable case in point. Located in the Greenwich Peninsula, on a symbolic place traversed by the prime meridian, it was designed by Richard Rogers Partnership with Buro Happold engineers to house the Millennium Experience in 2000. Its cable-net structure, forming the largest tensile structure of its kind in the world, added a new landmark to London's skyline. Besides referencing the Dome of Discovery erected upstream for the 1951 Festival of Britain, the design harked back to a longer history of circular buildings that catered for the demand for urban entertainment over the 19th century: it echoed historical precedents, from circuses to panoramas, designed to enhance the public's sensorial engagement with spectacles.[54]

The original exhibition revolved around a 'body zone' designed by Nigel Coates in which visitors traversed the giant model of a human organism via walkways and escalators. Prior to the 2000 events, the construction of the Dome had already involved a distinct type of balance-testing experience. The roof was installed by a team of professional climbers who had to assemble 144 fabric panels weighing more than one tonne each and secure them to the cables. The acrobatic feats of those workers became integral to its architectural imagery.[55] Failure to convert the Dome after the millennial celebrations led it to become a white elephant, a fate it shared with a spate of buildings designed for urban entertainment which arose to public interest and declined just as swiftly.

Eventually, in 2007 the site was regenerated into an entertainment district with shops, restaurants, cinemas and an arena under its new sponsor's name: 'The O2'. Despite its modest height (52 metres symbolising the weeks of a year), the canopy covering the roof lent itself to an original gravity play. A themed attraction called 'Up at The O2' was launched before the 2012 Olympics, allowing tourists to climb the tent-like surface in a roped party for an urban mountaineering experience (fig.23). After a safety demonstration at the base camp, participants are shepherded on a bouncy mat suspended two metres above the roof and walk up to the summit where expansive views open up all around the observation platform; they then descend the walkway on the river side down another steep incline that reaches 30 degrees.

At a time of major vertical growth, with panoramic terraces and sky gardens springing up around London, 'Up at The O2' offered an alternative way of experiencing the cityscape in a simulated group expedition. Visitors who are afraid of heights are welcomed on the official website with a warning:

23 Up at The O2, North Greenwich, London.

'remember, what goes up, must come down. [. . .] Once you've started the climb, you have to complete it.' Such a disclaimer acknowledges that, while promising the thrill of *ilinx*, this attraction relies on the uncertainty of our response to spatial depth. The routine unfolds as a scripted performance taking place in public view, as the building's exterior is turned into an unlikely walkway. Its marketing slogan, 'Climb an Icon', lays emphasis on the landmark value of the location in order to enhance its tourist appeal. More broadly, though, it illustrates how a strand of contemporary architecture has become an instrument of the experience economy.

In staging architecture as a field of outdoor experience, 'Up at The O2' draws its venturous proposition from the analogy with mountaineering, yet also prompts comparisons with the feats of urban climbers. In actual fact, the organised activity of walking on the Dome is the polar opposite of those illicit practices in which climbers risk life and limb to transgress the spatial order of the city. In its ersatz version, the narrative of conquest is staged within a highly controlled environment. The roped expeditions embody the logic of the experience economy in a patent way by offering a kinaesthetic way of knowing and appreciating architecture. This staged experience is premised on the idea that *everything is possible*: enacting the supposed liberation of the individual within safe and secure boundaries, it promotes a form of consumerism in which, to cite the psychoanalyst Paul Verhaege, 'we all cherish the illusion that we are unique'.[56]

A notable precedent is 'BridgeClimb Sydney', an attraction opened in 1998 when the theory of the experience economy was inchoate. The roped ascent of Sydney's Harbour Bridge along a walkway heralded a unique way of enjoying the city views while ascending a major landmark. An even closer parallel, in architectural terms, might be drawn with the roof climb at Munich's Olympiapark, the site of an innovative system of tensile structures designed by Frei Otto for the 1972 Olympic Games. Here visitors can trek on platforms suspended along the curved structure and contemplate the expansive vistas: not only the architecture itself but a sweeping landscape in which the peaks of the Bavarian Alps blend with the city's skyline. The adventure is described on the official website with all the trappings of the experience economy: 'You climb with a small group up to giddy heights. You'll be gone for 120 exciting minutes and we promise you that every minute will be unforgettable.'

Once again, the ascent is key to an aesthetic experience that relies on the allurement of *ilinx*, bringing visitors into contact with the surfaces and details of an extraordinary structure that would otherwise be inaccessible. These guided expeditions belong to a set of activities that reconfigured the Olympic Stadium and adjacent park into a field of gravity plays as well as a venue for sports and cultural events. Securely strapped to a harness, you can also abseil down a pylon to the stadium lawn and even glide across it suspended on a zip wire.

Themed experiences of this kind tend to blur the historical divide between work and leisure. Indeed, contemporary forms of adventure tourism adapt to the urban environment techniques and practices that were developed in mountain sports, but also in the field of building construction. The impulse to re-enact the gestures of workers who climb tall structures is the result of deeper changes in the leisure industry. As Brian Lonsway points out, traditional boundaries have become increasingly tenuous and hybrid forms of 'leisure-work experience' have emerged in the early 21st century.[57]

Similarly, the tourist practice of climbing architecture simulates those activities on ropes conducted by construction, maintenance and cleaning workers which are coterminous with mountain sports. Urban mountaineering draws its inspiration from a repertoire that encompasses extreme sports as well as labour activities, extending to the realms of action films, comics and video games. In the domain of thrill tourism, however, the act of climbing is stripped of any instrumental reason and reduced to a form of spatial play: a scripted adventure that leaves little room for individual agency or improvisation.

In London this phenomenon has been spreading since the noughties, when a new impetus to high-rise construction reshaped the city's skyline.[58] The new millennium was heralded by another landmark erected on the South Bank, the London Eye, which sparked off a race for the construction of ever bigger panoramic wheels around the world. Later on, amid the tall-building boom that reshaped the capital, the Olympics provided a further catalyst for gravity plays. In June 2012, the Emirates Air Line cable car was opened in Greenwich, carrying passengers over the Thames to the Royal Victoria Docks on the northern bank. Designed by Wilkinson Eyre Architects with the same engineers of the Millennium Dome, the gondola line enables sweeping vistas from a height of up to 90 metres. Although the cable car link is integrated into the public transport network, its main purpose is arguably to create a mobile viewing platform as much as an aerial bridge across the river, as pledged by the slogan: 'discover a unique view of London'.

In line with the sponsor's interests, the marketing narrative evokes images of flight that recall the campaign with which the London Eye was launched by its original patron – British Airways. If, in its capsules, the views from above come at the risk of height dizziness, that possibility is accentuated in the Air Line gondolas due to the sway caused by winds, which can quickly turn the thrill of altitude into an awkward sensation of imbalance. Designed by exponents of British high-tech architecture, both these structures are expressions of a market that promotes immersive experiences of urban space. They manifest a hyper-hedonistic desire to enjoy the cityscape not only through its aesthetic contemplation but through a kinaesthetic act.

While the cases mentioned above relate to forms of passive transport, there are also instances of static aerial experiences. This phenomenon takes multiple forms in which the user's body is carried into the air and, unlike in urban mountaineering, is not required to perform any physical effort. In summer 2014, the 'London in the Sky' attraction was brought to the northern side of the Greenwich Peninsula by the Dinner in the Sky group. For a hefty price, it became possible to have a dinner party set up around a table, suspended on a crane, right next to the Dome. London's cityscape provided the scenery for an exclusive social activity performed in a state of suspension ('the most high-end experience in the world'). This seasonal attraction, which had been staged in various locations since 2006, attests to a wider shift in the branding of vertical cities whereby urban heights are no longer conceived as platforms for panoramic views but, increasingly, as sites of immersive gravity-defying experiences. Through stimulations of the balance system, these variations on the theme of *ilinx* are designed to challenge the user's equilibrium in ever more intense ways.

The regeneration of North Greenwich endowed the former Millennium Dome with a new set of symbolic as well as economic values. Ironically perhaps, the structure designed to celebrate the human body as an agent of creativity and innovation has become the stage for gravity plays that reinforce, in Bauman's words, the autotelic character of a 'consumer's/consuming body'.[59] By emboldening a dynamic and enterprising subject to enjoy a seemingly boundless degree of freedom, these new games of vertigo embody the dominant values of neoliberalism. As architecture becomes the site of activities that turn the experience of the abyss into a packaged thrill, it is implicated in a cycle of desire that capitalises on the body as a virtually unlimited source of profits.

If play is an inherent aspect of human life, the social values attached to it are subject to continuous evolution. Even before the publication of *Homo Ludens*, Huizinga had noted that the boundaries of this sphere were already being eroded: 'nowadays play in many cases never ends and hence is not true play'.[60] These words resonate deeply today, as the pursuit of *ilinx* fuels a growing economy of vertigo. While the new brand of attractions is linked with the thrills and amusements that emerged in the 19th and 20th centuries, their latter-day versions are no longer confined to funfairs and parks but have become pervasive features of the urban environment; they thrive on the visceral experience of cityscapes in which the subject-consumer is immersed.

6

LOSING THE GROUND

'Vertigo' could be said to express an inescapable ambivalence and indeterminacy.[1]

24 Suspended walkway providing visitors with bird's-eye views of a relief map of Belgium, Expo 1958, Brussels.

URBANISME
STEDEBOUW
URBANISME

MODERNISM IN THE AIR

Our built environment is fraught with places that elicit sensations of dizziness. The impact of architecture on the sense of balance is often underestimated, though, and its capacity to trigger perceptual instability has long been neglected. Historically, this mismatch was widened by the advent of modernism, which brought about a whole range of design concepts as well as built spaces with significant implications of vertigo. The user's sense of balance was deeply affected by spatial devices enabled by modern technologies and building materials: along with their functionality came a new realm of sensory experiences imbued with thrill and anxiety. Revisiting some key moments in the canon of architectural modernism and the subsequent postmodern shift will allow us to reappraise the significance of these issues.

Although it remained largely unspoken, vertigo pervaded the modernist design culture. The concept of *ilinx* – which names the impulse to elicit a state of perceptual disorientation akin to vertigo – allows us to unpick a thread that runs through the history of 20th-century architecture. The Modern Movement was animated by an impetus to overcome the gravitas of the past through ideals of social progress coupled with an almost inexhaustible faith in technology. The upward élan of the 'new architecture' (*nouvelle architecture* or *Neues Bauen*) was integral to the aerial aesthetic that emerged in the 1920s, when modern architects and planners called into question the earth-bound conventions of building. Leaving the ground was a symbolic as well as material way of overcoming gravity; the sky was the frontier of the brave new world.

As powered flight opened up a new field of vision, an air-minded ethos permeated avant-garde movements, ranging from Italian Futurism to Russian Constructivism, while the artists' fascination with aeroplanes and aerial views was shared by a generation of architects intent on liberating the art of building from the burden of the long 19th century. This longing for weightlessness is epitomised by the Bauhaus Building, designed by Walter Gropius in Dessau and inaugurated in 1926. It is particularly evident in the two-storey bridge structure where the architect himself had his office; in the adjacent student workshop, Gropius deployed the industrial aesthetic of the glass box to flood the interior with light, typifying the functionalists' use of glass as a transparent membrane.[2]

As Adrian Forty remarks, transparency is 'a wholly modernist term, unknown in architecture before the twentieth century'.[3] This notion became popular in the 1910s and 1920s when advances in manufacturing and frame construction made it possible to build self-standing glass enclosures.[4] Modern glass technology enabled architects to dematerialise the building mass and achieve new levels of lightness, structurally allowing greater spans to be achieved while also allowing interiors to be flooded in daylight. If buildings could not quite fly, their relationship with gravity was nonetheless radically transformed.

The coupling of structural frames with large glass panes – whose ancestors were the windows of Gothic cathedrals – had such an impact on the construction industry that it has been described as nothing less than 'the most significant development in architecture in the last millennium'.[5] In addition to brighter interiors, this advancement enabled a range of textural effects that contributed to the emancipation of architecture from gravity, an ideal encapsulated by Ludwig Mies van der Rohe's 1922 unbuilt project for a glass skyscraper. Light and lightness were intertwined aspects of an aesthetic that privileged the airy element over the earthly one. In breaking off with tectonic traditions, modern buildings were often designed to stimulate new sensory engagements with space, thereby challenging the user's perceptual stability.

The new aerial aesthetic crystallised in 1928 through a series of paradigmatic projects such as the Villa Savoye in Poissy, the concrete house in which Le Corbusier gave plastic form to the *esprit nouveau*: pilotis, ribbon windows and the ramp leading to the roof terrace accentuated its sense of lightness. Concurrently, the first European skyscraper complex (the House of State Industry, also known as Gosprom Palace) was erected in the Ukrainian city of Kharkiv. This cluster of office blocks linked by skybridges asserted the structural ambitions of Soviet architecture and paved the way for the megastructures of the post-war period.[6]

While elevated walkways had featured in European architecture since the Middle Ages, they took on new significance as part of the modernist quest for weightlessness. This ethos was given radical expression by Georgii Krutikov in the diploma project presented the same year at Moscow's Vkhutemas, the leading art and technical school of the Soviet Union. Krutikov's project for the 'City of the Future', an airborne structure suspended in the air, was praised by Le Corbusier during his visit to Moscow.[7] As avant-garde architects embraced the design of gravity-defying structures, flying machines became integral to the modern urban imagination, along with suspended bridges and skyscrapers.[8]

In parallel, the spirit of modern construction came to the fore of architectural criticism. A milestone was Sigfried Giedion's *Building in France, Building in Iron, Building in Ferroconcrete* (1928), which was published in the same year as the International Congress of Modern Architecture (CIAM) was inaugurated, with Giedion in charge as secretary-general. This book presented the main achievements of the new architecture against the background of engineering structures of the 19th and early 20th centuries. Giedion hailed an art of building based on weightless volumes, as traditional architecture couched in historicist styles gave way to 'a new oscillating harmony'.[9] Countering the gravitas of the past with a sense of airiness, this modern development laid emphasis on the thrill of perceptual experience.

An exemplar was the experimental housing project designed by Le Corbusier at Pessac, near Bordeaux (1926), which created a fluid transition between interior and exterior. Despite their modest heights, the residential units attained a level of spatial interpenetration that Giedion described in giddy terms: 'There arises – as with certain lighting conditions in snowy landscapes – that dematerialization of solid demarcation that distinguishes neither rise nor fall and that gradually produces the feeling of walking in clouds.'[10] This somewhat esoteric passage evokes the emergence of a modern aerial aesthetic that stood against the gravity of the 19th century.

Echoing Le Corbusier's influential manifesto, *Vers une architecture* (1923), Giedion compared the task of the modern architect with that of the engineers who had brought industrial techniques and materials to fruition. Iron constructions such as the Eiffel Tower and the Transporter Bridge in Marseille – a cable-stayed bridge that straddled the Old Harbour – expressed the dynamic properties of *fluctuation*, *connection*, and *interpenetration* that constituted a new architectural experience.[11] Giedion's own photographs strived to capture these spatial qualities through views up, down and through the iron works in a visual language that echoed the experiments in 'new vision' conducted by Moholy-Nagy, who curated the layout of *Building in France*. The permeability of iron lattice structures allowed for the 'fluid transition of things' that made them look almost weightless.[12] Indeed, Giedion went so far as to consider the state of suspension created by iron construction as a precursor of the experience of flight:

> Through the condensation of the material to a few points, there appears an unknown transparency, a suspended relation to other objects, a creation of the airspace. [...] This sensation of being enveloped by a floating airspace while walking through tall structures (Eiffel Tower) advanced the concept of flight before it had been realized and stimulated the formation of the new architecture.[13]

25 Double spread from Herbert Bayer, Walter Gropius and Ise Gropius (eds), *Bauhaus, 1919–1928* (1938).

The Eiffel Tower opened up new expansive vistas while, at the same time, eliciting the impression of floating in the air. Le Corbusier himself had previously described his ascent of that structure with elation:

> If I climb up to the platforms of the Eiffel Tower, the very act of mounting gives me a feeling of gladness; the moment is a joyful one, and also a solemn one. And in proportion as the horizon widens more and more, one's thought seems to take on a larger and more comprehensive cast: similarly, if everything in the physical sphere widens out, if the lungs expand more fully and the eye takes in vast distances, so too the spirit is roused to a vital activity.[14]

The analogy between broadening outlooks and spiritual uplifting was imbued with metaphors of elevation, as the Tower constituted – for Le Corbusier – the summit of human civilisation. In Giedion's view, a similar sense of liberation was conveyed by the platforms that cantilevered out of the pylons of Marseille's ferry bridge: an 'unconscious' precedent of the balconies that would later become a key feature of *Neues Bauen*, as exemplified by the Bauhaus Building in Dessau. The projecting balconies of the five-storey studio wing (*Prellerhaus*) played a central part in the Bauhaus iconography, providing the stage on which students and masters alike were pictured in playful and sometimes acrobatic poses that conveyed an impetus of creative freedom (fig.25).[15] These concrete platforms manifested the thrust of the new architecture, which Giedion considered an ethical as well as aesthetic pursuit: 'there exists the need to live in buildings that strive to overcome the old sense of equilibrium that was based only on fortress-like incarceration'.[16]

As established by the canon of 20th-century historiography, the machine aesthetic infused modern design culture with a dynamic spirit. While concrete and iron structures allowed architects to explore spatial, visual and sensory environments with unprecedented freedom, however, their endeavours were largely unconcerned by the implications in terms of perceptual stability. If the new architecture challenged the human sense of balance, that was a measure of its ability to reconfigure the built environment in radical ways.

STRUCTURAL ACROBATICS

The longing for weightlessness was integral to the critique of monumentality that surfaced within architectural discourse in the 1940s, when Giedion drew on theories of perception, and in particular on Gestalt psychology, to codify 'the growth of a new tradition'.[17] Following a series of trips to America, he championed the role of modern materials and techniques in giving expression to shared cultural symbols. For Giedion, the function of monuments had declined in the 19th century, leading to a 'pseudo-monumentality' that was ill-suited to express the modern spirit.[18] In order to foster a sense of civic identity, future monuments would have to integrate art and architecture in public places. The emphasis on community life reflected a shift of focus in the agenda of the Modern Movement from building design towards the more inclusive endeavours of city planning.

Giedion's call for a new monumentality went hand in hand with his quest for a new equilibrium. His praise for a skyscraper complex such as the Rockefeller Center in New York, for instance, highlighted its civic spaces and landscaped areas in antithesis to 'the tyranny of the tower'.[19] But the modern age did not need grandiose buildings to express its spirit. The 'Nine Points on Monumentality', jointly written by Giedion with Fernand Léger and Josep Lluís Sert, referred to 'light elements like ceilings which can be suspended from big trusses covering practically unlimited spans'.[20] Light-and-sound displays, fireworks and other examples of ephemeral architecture symbolised the zeitgeist in forms that were quite apart from traditional monuments. By carrying forward the avant-garde aerial aesthetic, this manifesto signalled a yearning for multisensory experiences that challenged the stability of perception. After the war, Giedion drew an analogy with funambulism in order to expound the necessity of a new balance:

> Our period demands a type of man who can restore the lost equilibrium between inner and outer reality. This equilibrium, never static but, like reality itself, involved in continuous change, is like that of a tightrope dancer who, by small adjustments, keeps a continuous balance between his being and empty space. We need a type of man who can control his own existence by the process of balancing forces often regarded as irreconcilable: man in equipoise.[21]

This longing reverberated through the 1950s, when the technical and functional properties of modernism became increasingly popular. The concept of new monumentality found an original expression in the Festival of Britain, which was staged in London in the summer of 1951 amidst the shortages of post-war reconstruction. Under the direction of Hugh Casson, modern art and design set the scene for a festive exposition that provided 'a tonic to the nation', as the South Bank offered exhibits, fairground rides and sundry spectacles culminating in firework displays.[22] Its main attractions – the Skylon, the Dome of Discovery and the Royal Festival Hall – displayed an aesthetic of lightness that sought to overcome the weight of two world wars while reviving the glories of the Great Exhibition staged in Hyde Park a century prior. Daring feats of engineering were meant to herald a new era of peace and prosperity.

The spirit of progress was symbolised by the Skylon, a 90-metre-high sculpture suspended on wires that appeared to float in the air (fig.26). Made of steel and aluminium, and tapered at both ends, its streamlined shape invited playful responses: a group of students climbed the structure before the festival opening, leaving a flag on the top after the prank. Later on, the Skylon was the background for a wire-walking performance in which the funambulist Charles Elleano walked across the Thames on a steel cable. These gravity plays evoked a desire to take off from the ground that was given built form by the festival's architects.

Elevated platforms and open stairways created new vistas across the South Bank, while at Battersea Park, a 'tree-walk' made of wooden gangways allowed visitors to float over the Pleasure Gardens. Meanwhile the Festival Hall, with its glazed walls on all sides, free-flowing spaces and an auditorium floating inside the structure like an 'egg in a box', epitomised the application of modern principles and materials to the design of public architecture. The only remnant of the 1951 event, the building (designed by a team of London County Council

26 The Skylon at the Festival of Britain, 1951.

architects led by Leslie Martin) stands as a monument to the democratic ideals of post-war Britain, but also as a startling example of how they were embodied by airy and transparent structures.

The quest for weightless architecture reached its peak in 1958, when the first World's Fair since the war was staged at the Heysel Plateau in Brussels. Dedicated to 'A New Humanism', the Brussels Universal and International Exposition (Expo 58) was animated by a constructive outlook that beckoned a new age of progress (fig.27).[23] Echoing the 'Festival style' of London, the 'Style Expo' of Brussels was defined by bold structural achievements. Several pavilions were built with lightweight construction systems that included an

bruxelles 58

1 | 2
3 | 4

1. Détail de la couverture du pavillon de France, à la fin des travaux (photo J.P. Lenoir). 2. Flèche du pavillon Eternit (photo J.P. Leloir). 3. Porte des Nations. 4. Atomium (photo J.P. Leloir).

27 Structures exhibited at the Brussels World's Fair (Expo 58), from *L'Architecture d'aujourd'hui* (1958).

assortment of hanging roofs and other eye-catching structures. With its technical prowess, Expo 58 resumed a time-honoured tradition interrupted by the war. While at the New York fair of 1939 the aesthetic of ascension was confined to particular exhibits, in Brussels, however, it permeated the entire event.

Highlights included the suspended roofs of the French Pavilion and the glass boxes of the German one, along with several variations on the hyperbolic paraboloid which came to epitomise the 'Style Expo'. This geometric form was given a striking interpretation in the Philips Pavilion, designed by Le Corbusier's office with Yannis Xenakis in charge of the project. Similar in appearance to a giant tent, the pavilion was in fact made of precast concrete panels hung in tension by steel cables. Multiple effects of disorientation were achieved by its structure and contents alike. A multi-media spectacle awaited the public inside the cavernous space, where the *poème électronique* composed by Edgard Varèse was played out while pictures were projected on screens in rapid sequence.

This experimental design reflected the barrage of sensory stimuli which immersed visitors to the Expo. The patterns of mobility contributed to arouse their kinaesthetic experience through cantilevered stairs and suspended walkways – most notably the 58-metre-long walkway, suspended from a cantilevered 'arrow' made of reinforced concrete, that allowed bird's-eye views of a relief map of Belgium spreading underneath (see fig.24). Further, it was possible to glide over the Heysel in the open cabins of the Telelift, a tub-like variation of the cable car system built a year before at the Interbau Exhibition in Berlin. The pavilions shared the ground with a multitude of leisure attractions under the giant model of the Atomium, the extant landmark made of nine spheres connected by tubes traversed by stairs and escalators. An amusement park including a roller coaster and other gravity plays complemented the exhibition.

The engineering tour de force of Expo 58 was described at the time as a challenge to gravity, yet the architectural press was divided over its merits. The *Architectural Forum* hailed the 'acrobatic exhibitionism' on display in Brussels as a celebration of the freedom enabled by steel and concrete, the modern materials that were used in tension to achieve new spatial forms. At the same time, *The Architectural Review* regarded the features of Expo 58 as a repertoire of 'structural acrobatics': focusing on the formal variations on the theme of the hanging roof, its reviewer observed how the experiments with new structures revealed a desire to be exciting at any cost. Several observers, including Bruno Zevi, André Bloc and Frei Otto, variously criticised how the prowess of modern engineering had turned the art of building into a mass spectacle. While the playful atmosphere was intended to lift the world's mood, those structural acrobatics were seen by critics as a pointless extravaganza that failed to tackle the pressing socio-economic issues of the time; so much so that Expo 58 came to embody the experimental play of construction for its own sake. Taking a broader historical outlook, the event might be placed in relation to the search for a new equilibrium in the post-war period, as structural innovations contributed to shape a modern perception of balance – and a novel monumentality.

STATES OF SUSPENSION

The design of living spaces suspended above the ground took manifold shapes and forms after the Second World War. New ground was broken by the *Unité d'habitation* designed by Le Corbusier in Marseille (1952), the 12-storey housing block raised on massive concrete pilotis that included two elevated shopping streets as well as a rooftop terrace encircled by a running track. After Le Corbusier demonstrated that the sky was a place for modern living, this idea became a feature of Brutalist architecture. Inspired by the outdoor walkways of inter-war social housing, the 'streets in the sky' concept was given impetus in Britain by Alison and Peter Smithson, who applied it to their 1952 unbuilt scheme for the Golden Lane Estate in London. They eventually realised it two decades later at Robin Hood Gardens, after Jack Lynn and Ivor Smith had given it built form at Sheffield's Park Hill Estate. While the influence of the *Unité* on these projects has been debated, they clearly illustrate a new conception of ground that gained currency in the post-war period.[24]

These architectural experiments were concomitant with the research on vertigo that was conducted independently by Michael Balint and Roger Caillois (see Chapter 5). Free-span constructions, streets in the sky and bridge-like buildings that appeared to float in the air might be regarded as analogues of the wire walkers' ephemeral bridges. While aerialists tamed the dangerous effects of *ilinx* through their embodied acts, architects put forward a challenge to gravity through spatial concepts that aspired to new forms of balance. If structural stability could be achieved by technical means, however, their implications in terms of sensory perception were far more elusive. Vertigo was embraced as a heady sense of liberation, but its distressing aspects were largely ignored or denied.

An area in which the dizziness of modern construction could not be eluded is that of high-rise architecture, which attained new levels of transparency in the post-war period thanks to developments in curtain wall design. The separation of glass facades from load-bearing structures was accomplished by two skyscrapers that were built around the same time in New York, where a number of institutional and corporate headquarters were built. The United Nations Secretariat Building, designed by Le Corbusier and Oscar Niemeyer (1953), was the first to feature a fully glazed curtain wall, whereas Lever House, by SOM's Gordon Bunshaft and Natalie de Blois (1952), was sealed in such a comprehensive way that even the spandrel panels were clad with wired glass.

28 Ezra Stoller, view from the top floor of the Seagram Building, New York, 1958.

The latter's frame of stainless-steel mullions was indebted to the sleek high-rise aesthetic that Mies had brought to America.

In 1957, *The Architectural Review* hailed 'a new vernacular' brought about by the spread of glass-clad skyscrapers.[25] The following year this trend reached a new high at the Seagram Building, designed by Mies with Philip Johnson, on the East Side of Park Avenue, across the street from Lever House. Whereas both the latter and UN Secretariat had masonry spandrels on their facades – in compliance with the city's building code in force at the time – Seagram was the first office tower in New York to have a floor-to-ceiling glass curtain wall.[26] The brown-gold glass plates endowed the building's exterior with a sculptural value that contrasted with the brightness of its neighbour's blue-green hue. Although the tinted plates, produced by the Franklin Glass Company, were made using a traditional 'batch casting' technique, the Seagram's interiors were characterised by remarkable levels of transparency which were enhanced by the lack of horizontal glazing bars.[27] These effects were vividly captured by the photographer Ezra Stoller, whose documentation of the newly completed building included giddy-making views from the top floor (fig.28). At the time of construction, the absence of visual barriers raised issues of perceptual stability.

The combination of transparency and height (157 metres to the roof) brought up legitimate concerns about sensations of dizziness that the building might cause for its tenants. Phyllis Lambert, the client's daughter and consultant on the project, recalls that the real estate agency in charge of renting the office spaces had doubts: 'They worried that potential occupants would balk at being able to stand close to the window and be terrified or suffer vertigo in looking out and especially down without any element to retain them, and therefore would not rent space in the building.'[28] Mies devised an ingenious solution to allay those concerns: he placed the air distribution system all along the window walls, running at floor level with louvres at the horizontal plane. The diffuser was encased within a bronze unit in order to minimise its visual impact on the facade. By keeping users at a distance from the glass panes, the architect believed this 'would be sufficient to obviate the fear of falling or jumping or any other feelings associated with vertigo'.[29] The effects of transparency achieved through the full-height curtain wall transcended the functional and aesthetic aspects of design, revealing an underlying issue of height perception that remained suppressed for a long time.

By the end of the 1950s, the Modern Movement was on the wane and new tendencies that challenged the orthodoxy of functionalism led to the dissolution of CIAM. The radical thrust of the early 20th-century avant-garde, which found an expression in the pursuit of lightness and transparency, had given way to the ubiquitous glass boxes that became symbols of corporate capitalism. While the International Style went mainstream, the neo-avant-garde movements of the 1960s sought to revive the spirit of modern construction in dynamic ways. The play element was central to the work of architects such as Yona Friedman and Cedric Price, as well as groups such as Archigram and Superstudio. With varying levels of social commitment, they all reclaimed the spontaneous and often transgressive spirit of play from an urbanised world that was increasingly caught up in the logics of capitalist production and consumption.

Technology was a close ally in their quest for emancipation. A creative use of high-tech devices and lightweight materials enabled Price's design of the Fun Palace, while Kenzo Tange and fellow Metabolists envisaged new urban megastructures, and Friedman imagined 'a new world created in the sky, purified of the *membra disjecta* of past and exhausted civilizations on the ground below'.[30] Visionary projects such as Archigram's Instant City, Friedman's *Ville Spatiale* and Constant Nieuwenhuys's New Babylon situated play at the centre of an alternative urbanism that promised to liberate humankind from its utilitarian mindset. Inspired by Huizinga's writings, several architects brought the concept of *homo ludens* to bear on their design work. However diverse in conceptual terms, their projects shared an impulse to lift up the space of everyday life in order to instigate play and creativity. This tendency is aptly summarised by Rodrigo Pérez de Arce: 'A progressive disengagement from site led their schemes to rise free from the ground, sometimes drift or move impelled by mechanical contrivances, rendering futile any concerns about locality. A renovated nomadic experience now fostered by technology became a common ground.'[31]

New Babylon exerted a profound influence on the architectural imaginary. Over its long period of development, Constant envisaged a habitat based on 'units of ambiance' that invited chance and interaction, an idea that fellow situationists practised through the tactics of *dérive* and *détournement*.[32] Inspired by the circus environment and nomadic lifestyles, New Babylon consisted of a series of interconnected platforms without a prescribed function: these were raised from the ground so as to deny the stability of rational cities, but also the doctrinaire character of modernist planning (namely the separation of functions sanctioned by the Athens Charter of 1933). Open stairs and ladders populate Constant's drawings, evoking the act of displacement: 'The relentless derive from one unit of ambience to another, the fluid and ungraspable nature of the urban labyrinth, the absence of landmarks nurtured those feelings that Caillois had classed as *ilinx*, claiming the value of subjectivity against rationalist expectations.'[33]

Constant was adamant that, once liberated from the physical constraints of ground and barriers, life would begin to shape the human environment, rather than being shaped by it. The embodied experience of space, however, would have demanded of New Babylonians not only a great deal of physical effort but also the ability to negotiate vertiginous environments. While the architect was opposed to the orthodoxy of the Modern Movement, his vision recuperated the radical values of weightlessness that marked its heyday. Indeed, situationist life was conceived as a perpetual state of suspension: plays of gravity were inherent to this and other radical visions for a modern *homo ludens*.

NEW INCLINATIONS

A notable exception is the work of Claude Parent, who approached the relationship between body and ground in a wholly different way. Working in collaboration with Paul Virilio – with whom he founded the *Architecture Principe* group in 1963 – Parent articulated a critique of modern urbanism centred on the 'oblique function'.[34] Their premise was that, by designing around the Cartesian axes, functionalist planners had brought about a two-dimensional city in which dwelling had become dissociated from circulation and hindered the flow of human activities. A 'peaceful urban revolution' was therefore invoked to rescue cities from an inexorable decline.

Parent's 1970 manifesto, *Vivre à l'oblique*, sketched out the lineaments of a new spatial order based on inclined planes. Its core concept was the *inclisite*, an oblique structure unfolding along a continuous path on which circulation and living spaces would blend seamlessly. This multi-purpose infrastructure offered a 'new way of taking possession of space' whose possibilities were seemingly unlimited.[35] In lieu of stairs and elevators, a system of ramps was devised to activate the body's motor function and restore freedom of movement. Extending the topography of natural reliefs through artificial hills and cliffs, this new 'ground for living' (*le sol à vivre*) would have reshaped the human habitat at all scales, from the public realm to interior furniture. Once again, consumer capitalism was the target. The 'dynamic instability' provoked by oblique infrastructures was supposed to spur people into action, providing an antidote to the regime of passive consumption that was held responsible for numbing citizens into apathy.

Although Parent was conscious that the *inclisite* would have caused 'psychological discomfort' in users, he believed that a level of distress was necessary to foster interaction. The architect expressed his concern with issues of stability, since an environment made exclusively of inclined planes had inevitable implications for the body's motor function. The movement of ascent required an effort to counter the force of gravity, whereas the descent was meant to engender a euphoric acceleration that was akin to *ilinx*. In his commentary on the *inclisite*, Parent referred to vertigo as 'the fact of diving into a space while discovering it during the descent', a definition that hinted at a cognitive experience of space. Conscious of its complexity, he called for neuroscientists to shed light on this phenomenon.[36]

Parent's vision shared with Constant's the desire to stimulate pedestrian mobility and a more active engagement with urban space. Unlike the floating structures of New Babylon, however, the *inclisite* was firmly grounded. Indeed, Parent proclaimed that the oblique function had the capacity to stabilise architectural form and to engender a new type of monumentality. A far cry from the lightweight structures envisaged by Giedion, this was instead an attempt to reinstate the ground as the medium of human life. By professing

29 Interior view of the French Pavilion at the Venice Biennale, 1970.

the agency of gravity, Parent marked a departure from the modernist search for weightlessness that culminated in the structural acrobatics of the post-war period. Ironically, this appreciation of vertigo came from an architect intent on re-grounding the experience of space.

Although the oblique function led to few built projects – notably the Brutalist Church of Sainte Bernadette of Banlay in Nevers – it went on to influence leading architects ranging from Jean Nouvel (who cut his professional teeth in Parent's office) to Rem Koolhaas and Zaha Hadid. Above all, this concept brought forward an alternative way of imagining the human habitat around the body's sensorimotor functions. A public demonstration was the French Pavilion designed by Parent for the 1970 Venice Biennale, where visitors were invited to walk and sit on a series of sloping surfaces (fig.29). Gravity was no longer the enemy to be defeated but an integral component of life that architects should design around, rather than against. While this idea remained central to a strand of architectural culture that absorbed the principles of phenomenology, it was soon overshadowed by a new spatial paradigm that took the dynamic effects of gravity into a wholly new direction.

LOST IN HYPERSPACE

Issues of perceptual stability were central to the emergence of postmodern 'hyperspace', a concept theorised by cultural critic Fredric Jameson in the mid-1980s. In the realm of architecture Jameson found the most eloquent signs of how commodity production was taking over Western culture. Accordingly, the advent of postmodernism was marked by 'a new kind of superficiality in the most literal sense', a suppression of depth that could be detected across a range of arts and cultural forms.[37] The emotions and affects underlying modernist art had been replaced by the surface values of consumer capitalism, as a culture of simulacra manifested the logic of the spectacle in all its force. Concurrently, Jameson detected a veritable 'mutation in built space itself'.[38]

The reduction of cultural practices to the surface value of the commodity was apparent in the reflective glass facades of high-rise buildings that had begun to crop up since the 1970s. A startling example was the Crocker Bank Center, a cluster of prismatic towers designed by SOM on Bunker Hill, Los Angeles. Seen from the nearby hill, their sharp-angled volumes stood like alien objects in the landscape: 'This great sheet of windows, with its gravity-defying two-dimensionality, momentarily transforms the solid ground on which we climb into the contents of a stereopticon, pasteboard shapes profiling themselves here and there around us.'[39] Behind their facades Jameson detected a deeper ideological shift, whose clearest expression was the emergence of large urban complexes designed as a self-enclosed world.

In order to illustrate this tendency, Jameson singled out another building in downtown Los Angeles, the Westin Bonaventure Hotel designed by John Portman (1977). Its labyrinthine atrium made it difficult for visitors to apprehend the intricate patterns of circulation that unfolded on multiple levels, leading to 'bewilderment and loss of spatial orientation'.[40] A web of escalators and elevators was designed to draw the visitor into an immersive environment which Jameson dubbed *hyperspace*. Static and mobile elements traverse the atrium and connect it with the viewing gallery on top of the building, where a rotating restaurant frames the cityscape:

> the glorious movement of the elevator gondola is [. . .] a dialectical compensation for this filled space of the atrium – it gives us the chance at a radically different, but complementary, spatial experience: that of rapidly shooting up through the ceiling and outside, along one of the four symmetrical towers, with the referent, Los Angeles itself, spread out breathtakingly and even alarmingly before us.[41]

While the reflective glass panels on the hotel's exterior suppressed the sense of depth, its interior activated an intense sensory stimulation that could be overwhelming. For Jameson, that spatial arrangement was not intended to affect its users in any meaningful way but rather to draw attention to itself: in other words, it was an architecture that asserted its own superficiality. His account of traversing the Bonaventure at different levels evokes dizzy sensations. In particular, his feeling of disorientation was accentuated by the experience of riding in a glass elevator up and down the atrium: 'The descent is dramatic enough, plummeting back down through the roof to splash down in the lake. What happens when you get there is something else, which can only be characterized as milling confusion, something like the vengeance this space takes on those who still seek to walk through it.'[42]

At the Bonaventure, the glass elevators augmented the visual experience of the atrium with a kinaesthetic one, heightening the sense of an imaginary fall. Hyperspace was overpowering not only in sensory terms but also from a cognitive standpoint: indeed, Jameson's architectural analysis underpinned his critique of a socio-spatial condition whose subjects become unable to map their position in the world. Such a bewildering experience signalled the 'alarming disjunction point between the body and its built environment' that, in turn, reflected the cultural logic of the post-industrial age.[43] The Bonaventure was symptomatic of a wider state of disorientation: 'the incapacity of our minds, at least at present, to map the great global multinational and decentred communicational network in which we find ourselves caught as individual subjects'.[44] In response to this, the critic called for a new aesthetic of 'cognitive mapping' that would enable a reorientation of the subject's position, not only in their immediate environment, but within a wider social world.

In actual fact, the postmodern atrium made its appearance well before it was held as a distinct architectural space. Portman's majestic entrance halls had become the signature of American high-end hotels since the mid-1960s, heralding what Charles Rice has called 'the atrium effect'. In his study of interior urbanism, Rice argues that 'the atrium became the characteristic architectural space of this period'.[45] This concept was introduced in 1967 at the Hyatt Regency in Atlanta, where five high-speed elevators were inserted in the 22-storey glass-roofed atrium. Enclosed by glass panels allowing a full view of the interior, the lifts were designed to perform a dual function by creating mobile viewing platforms while also freeing up service space through the elimination of shafts. Although the scenic elevator dated back to the early 1900s, in the hotels designed by Portman it became 'an integral visual element of the building [...] like a giant, sculptural mobile', allowing visitors to enjoy ever-changing views of the interior.[46] Those features transformed a means of vertical transportation that was commonly associated with dark interiors into streamlined capsules befitting of the space age.

Portman's idea was widely adopted in the design of office towers as well as hotel buildings, so much so that it was hailed as '[t]he elevator's architectural salvation'.[47] After the success of the Hyatt in Atlanta, riding on glass elevators became an attraction in its own right. Typical destinations were the panoramic bars and restaurants that crowned urban observation towers, a trend popularised by the Space Needle built in Seattle for the 1962 World's Fair. A few years later, in Atlanta, the elevators became part of a composite spatial arrangement in which they traversed the atrium and reached the hovering disc on top, where the scenic experience shifted from the interior to the urban panorama. From the beginning, they were considered to 'make the scenic vertical ride part of a uniquely memorable experience', thus anticipating an economic principle that would establish itself over subsequent decades.[48]

The postmodern atrium – with its dizzying gamut of suspended walkways, cantilevered bays and glass elevators – features in Mel Brooks's parody of Hitchcock's suspense films, *High Anxiety* (1977), which dates to the same period as the Bonaventure. Brooks himself plays the leading character, Dr Thorndyke, a psychiatrist who suffers from a severe form of acrophobia and is called to direct 'The Psycho-Neurotic Institute for the Very, Very Nervous' (*sic*). A topical scene is shot at the Hyatt Regency Hotel in San Francisco, designed by Portman and Associates and completed four years earlier (plate 16). As Thorndyke arrives for a psychiatric convention, the glass elevators running through the lobby deliver a comic take on the Hollywood murder mystery plot. Upon reaching the hotel's 17th floor through a dizzy-making elevator, he crawls along the inner wall of the walkway in the grip of an acrophobic episode; meanwhile, his chauffeur looks into the atrium and exclaims with excitement: 'Hey Doctor! Look at this . . . what a view . . . this is spectacular!' In a slapstick scene, the protagonist is accidentally pushed over the parapet and, horrified, stares down into the void.

Beyond the film's humour, the atrium is cast as an ambivalent place which draws out the dual nature of vertigo. Thorndyke is an overt parody of Scottie's character in *Vertigo*, who was paralysed by acrophobia when he climbed the bell tower (a scene that is mimicked at the end of *High Anxiety*). Two decades later, Brooks reiterated the stigma of a spatial phobia that was exacerbated by the rise of postmodern space. The location of the hotel scene reasserts the perception of Portman's interiors as vertiginous spaces, which was corroborated by other dystopian films that found ideal sets in his large, other-worldly buildings.

The risks of vertigo and motion sickness did not deter designers nor developers from embracing the disorientating effects of hyperspace. In fact, spatial devices that challenged the sense of balance became increasingly common at a time, between the 1970s and the 1980s, when the physiology of height vertigo was investigated by neuroscientists. Glass elevators were built into high-rises around the world and began to feature on their exteriors as well. At the Hopewell Centre in Hong Kong (1980), two panoramic lifts connect the 17th floor lobby with the restaurant lounge 40 storeys up (plate 17). The semi-cylindrical capsules are enclosed by full-height curved glass panels with a single handrail to hold onto. During the ride, the lack of fixed visual objects in one's field of view, which would normally help to provide an input to the balance system, can make it difficult to maintain equilibrium. Here vertigo is triggered not only by the rapid vertical movement, but also by the close proximity of neighbouring buildings of varying heights that appear to stretch out abruptly during the ascent. Conversely, on the way down one may experience the visceral feeling of plunging into a yawning abyss.

A more renowned case is perhaps the Lloyd's Building in the City of London (1986), where Richard Rogers and Partners installed 12 lifts enclosed by glass panels on the outside, next to the spiral staircases that shape the tower's corners. The dynamism elicited by the lifts is known to affect onlookers at street level as well as workers inside the block. Architectural critic Tom Dyckhoff recalled his first encounter with it in ecstatic terms: 'I couldn't get enough of the place. It was brash, it was sleek, it was romantic. [...] Just the sight of the outside was thrilling enough, the dizzying spirals of its staircase towers delivering a rush to the head.'[49] The aesthetic appeal of the Lloyd's Building is tempered by the awareness that passive transport can provoke motion sickness or imbalance due to the simultaneous overload of all three perceptual systems that regulate our balance; moreover, the elevators' transparency is liable to induce visual vertigo in users who are susceptible to it.

The design of scenic elevators and escalators contributed to shape built environments that make ever greater demands on the user's perceptual stability. In Paris, a century after the Eiffel Tower was erected, the theme of vertical mobility returned with prominence at the Grande Arche de la Défense, designed by Johan-Otto von Spreckelsen (1989), where glass elevators lift visitors to the panoramic rooftop terrace atop the building. Renowned for its dizzying effects, the 100-metre ride on the free-standing lifts is announced to prospective ticket buyers with a disclaimer: 'As visitors who access the Grande Arche roof via the panoramic elevators and the promenade in outdoor areas may experience feelings of vertigo and perception issues, people sensitive to these issues are advised not to access the roof.'

A marker of the growing consideration for health and safety that has emerged in recent decades, this warning is also an implicit acknowledgement of the complexities involved in the experience of heights. However, 'feelings of vertigo and perception issues' are ostensibly attributed to the susceptibility of subjects rather than to the instinctive and often unforeseen responses that may be triggered by the combined experience of elevation, speed and transparency. Hence, the architectural monument designed to celebrate the bicentenary of the French Revolution (initially named *La Grande Arche de la Fraternité*) has come to encapsulate the ambivalence of vertigo, as the pleasure of its roof terrace remains precluded to many.

A STRANGE NEW WORLD

On the eve of the new millennium, architectural practice was so diversified as to render any attempt to subsume it under a single category all but pointless. The tendency to build large-scale and self-reliant complexes, which had prompted Jameson to detect the signs of a spatial mutation, was by then widespread. This global trend was represented in the 1999 exhibition, *Vertigo: The Strange New World of the Contemporary City*, which brought together in Glasgow an assortment of projects ranging widely in function and scale, from Tate Modern in London to the Ontario Mills shopping mall in California. Although none of these buildings constituted a new typology per se, they eclipsed traditional notions of hierarchy and scale. According to the curator, Rowan Moore, they were inspired not so much by feats of engineering as by an 'imagineering' process.[50] The new architectural landscape showed a tendency to adopt common design solutions with scant reference to local contexts: 'This landscape is manifest in shopping malls, theme parks, airports, new residential enclaves and in hybrids like the themed shopping mall or the airport retail area. Each element creates a self-sufficient, artificial, all-embracing experience that is both controlled and controlling.'[51]

Moore applied the notion of spectacle to a pervasive tendency that was driving late-20th-century design. In the 1960s, Guy Debord had observed that architecture embodied the contradiction between the material progress of Western society and a diminishing ability to control or even comprehend its powers. Insofar as architects and planners perpetuated the identification of social life with a realm of appearances, they were integral to the society of the spectacle: that is, in Debord's words, complicit in 'the empire of modern passivity'.[52] The Glasgow exhibition showed how that logic had been forging the built environment ever more deeply. Drawing from the repertoire of fairgrounds and amusement parks, architects were intent on designing buildings that harnessed the user's sensorium towards specific types of experience. This strategy led to a widespread sense of disorientation – hence the exhibition title was meant to capture the ambivalent feelings elicited by the new architectural landscape:

> There is also a dizziness, sometimes exhilarating, sometimes frightening, that comes when the certainties on which we stand are blown away. Such dizziness is intensified by the speed, scale and sometimes height of new development. It is also created, in a more literal sense, by the devices used by shopping malls and theme parks to disorient their visitors, of which the rollercoaster is only the most extreme example. This dizziness is, by another name, vertigo.[53]

The Glasgow exhibition did not identify a consistent design approach but rather an unsettled condition in which architecture faced up to the new millennium. Its provocative and somewhat prophetic title was a nod to Hitchcock's masterpiece and the spiralling tension that runs through it. Having lurked under the surface of architectural discourse throughout the 20th century, with only sporadic utterances, the concept of vertigo was enunciated to define how built environments had become all the more disorientating. Tate Modern architect Jacques Herzog remarked apropos of this:

> The word 'vertigo' does not have auspicious connotations. In fact, it would seem to address the sinister and even dangerous side of things: fear of heights and the attendant dizziness. Or even a double anxiety: the fear of falling passively through no fault of one's own, and the fear of responding quasi-actively to the magical attraction of the abyss and thereby succumbing to its vertiginous appeal.[54]

If one building showcased in Glasgow is singled out to illustrate the multiple layers of this phenomenon, it would be the New German Parliament in Berlin by Foster + Partners, which opened the same year as the exhibition. The renovation of the former Reichstag included the controversial glass dome (a radical departure from the canopy initially proposed by the architects in the winning competition design), through which the public can walk over the glazed roof of the debating chamber and reach an observation deck (plate 18). In order to celebrate the unification of Germany after the fall of the Berlin Wall, the chosen architectural form was that of a spiral walkway revolving around a cone of mirrors that multiplied the feelings of lightness and transparency. The ramp allowed citizens to occupy a symbolic position of sovereignty over their representatives, evoking a double movement in time as well as space. Indeed, the renovation of the Reichstag preserved the traces of its violent past but equally embodied the collective élan towards a brighter future. Its symbolic resonances ran deeper, though, as the spiral unfolding through the dome alluded to the ambivalent nature of vertigo.

This motif was reinterpreted by the same architects in the project for London's City Hall, completed in 2002. Although the building lacks the historical layers of the Reichstag, its interior has drawn explicit parallels with Hitchcock's *Vertigo*. Mark Dorrian, in particular, has compared its disorientating experience with the dissolution of ground represented in that film. The rounded shape of City Hall is defined by a helical ramp that spirals around the glass-walled assembly chamber situated in its midst. At the bottom level, visitors can stand on a large aerial photomap of London, taking symbolic possession of the city from a vantage point that signifies power and control. Here Dorrian sees 'an attempt to architecturally stage [...] democratic transparency' in a similar vein to the Reichstag's dome.[55]

At City Hall, the miniaturisation of London produced by the photomap is perceptually at odds with the act of walking on it while looking down in search of familiar clues. If, on the one hand, this bodily experience provides the visitor with an impression of physical grounding, on the other, the aerial view triggers an opposite effect: a vertiginous feeling amplified by the act of walking in circles along the ramp. Once again, we are reminded of the dialectical way in which Bachelard defined verticality, as a double movement of ascent and descent that is key to the psychology of gravity. A moment of perceptual imbalance caused by the tension between walking up and looking down triggered the acrophobic episode that traumatised the French philosopher, and a similar tension later infused the climactic scenes of Hitchcock's *Vertigo*. Dorrian, however, plays down the spatial discomfort felt by its protagonist: 'Scottie's dizziness in high places is really only a minor motif: the real vertigo felt by him in the film is that emanating from the erasure of death as the ultimate surety of existence.'[56]

The analogy between London's City Hall and *Vertigo* stems from the embodied experience of the photomap as a walking surface on which the lack of perceptual bearings can elicit impressions of falling. Spreading over the floor, the vertical view of the city impedes any visual hierarchy and draws the visitor into a field of 'vertiginous multiplicity'.[57] Although the spatial experience of heights is arguably of greater import to Hitchcock's *Vertigo* than Dorrian suggests, this analysis offers valuable insights into the loss of grounding that came to pervade Western architecture around the turn of the century.

If weightlessness was a central tenet of modernism, and depthlessness the main attribute of postmodern space, a condition of groundlessness appeared to define the edgy architectural landscape at the dawn of the new millennium. To some degree, this phenomenon may be related to the anti-gravitational impulse that animated a strand of 20th-century architecture, giving spatial form to the play of *ilinx*. However, the pursuit of groundlessness reflects a specific moment of social instability that has led several thinkers to define vertigo as the malaise of our age: in Bruno Latour's words, the widespread feeling 'that the ground is in the process of giving way beneath everyone's feet at once'.[58]

VERTIGO IN BILBAO

The perceived loss of grounding is bound up with a design strategy that stimulates immersive experiences to the detriment of cognitive and reflective ones. This slippage can be detected from a combination of factors – such as mobility, transparency and verticality – that define the architecture of the experience economy. The design of so-called 'brandscapes' has co-opted the repertoire of phenomenological and situationist principles in order to foster corporate identities that are increasingly globalised.[59] As Brian Lonsway notes, architecture plays a significant role in this process: 'It is literally an economy of branded emotion, where the spatio-temporal production of sites of experience correlates to brand affiliation and repeat consumerism.'[60] What Lonsway calls 'architecture of persuasion' developed over the second half of the 20th century –

30 Interior view of the Guggenheim Museum, Bilbao.

from the theme parks of the 1950s to the entertainment complexes of the 1990s – paving the way for the consumer chain stores that dot the high streets of contemporary cities. Under the rampant forces of neoliberalism, architecture has been reconfigured as brand, while the commodification of experience has spread far beyond the entertainment industry.[61]

A symptom of how deeply the experience economy has seeped into architectural culture is the so-called 'Bilbao effect', a phenomenon with a deep relevance to the perception of balance. The term has come to describe the ability that certain buildings have to attract symbolic as well as financial values capable of regenerating urban districts and, in some cases, entire regions. Frank Gehry's design for the Guggenheim Museum Bilbao (1997) greatly contributed to a rebranding of the forlorn industrial city as a tourist destination while pioneering a global commercial franchise with one of the foremost institutions in the culture industry.[62] The Guggenheim epitomises the 'architecture of spectacular circulation' that rose to prominence around the turn of the millennium (fig.30).[63]

By fetishising the culture of circulation, Gehry's architecture reproduces the logic of flows, networks and digital transactions that underlie financial capitalism. The buildings he designed for cultural institutions – from the Weisman Art Museum in Minneapolis to the Louis Vuitton Foundation in Paris – are based on a fluid circulation that elevates the concept of flow to an allegory of our times.[64] The integrated circulation systems that define these projects (stairs, ramps, walkways, escalators, elevators) embody a global imaginary based on the model of capital, in which everything must incessantly flow in order to ensure the reproduction of value. This 'space of flows', as Manuel Castells pointed out, is the dominant form of a society based on global information networks.[65] Within this context, Gehry's architecture reaffirms a socio-spatial condition of instability while loading the experience of gravity with new values.

This phenomenon is reflected in the essay film *Gehry's Vertigo*, by Ila Bêka and Louise Lemoine, which revisits the Guggenheim Museum Bilbao from the perspectives of three climbers charged with cleaning the building.[66] Having honed their skills in the Basque mountains, the young men perform their daily routines in front of the camera, ascending and abseiling on ropes through the building's hollow interior as well as its curved outer surfaces (plate 19). Their closely observed gestures highlight a neglected aspect of the museum, which requires acrobatic manoeuvres in order to reach every nook and cranny. As a result, materials and surfaces that are often fetishised in architectural magazines are re-imagined through the experience of workers who operate in close contact with them.

The states of suspension involved in this process are shown in a segment of the film, titled 'Vertigo', that was shot from a helmet-mounted camera while a climber-cum-cleaner performed his routine. If the museum's interior is known to elicit sensations of dizziness in visitors affected by visual height intolerance (in particular the suspended walkways and glass elevators traversing the atrium), the point-of-view sequence reproduces those feelings in a graphic manner. After carrying out a series of tasks that are precluded to mechanical equipment, the acrobatic cleaner proudly says on camera: 'where man reaches, the machine can't'.

Somewhat ironically, this is the consequence of an architecture whose complex geometry could only be generated with the aid of advanced computer software. Bêka and Lemoine comment in an interview: 'In front of a "special" building, as they like to call it, the game consists in finding straight away the best routes and techniques to reach the hardest locations to get to. Wouldn't it precisely be the existence of teams of the sort that gives architects such creative freedom?'[67] The intimation that acrobatic workers might liberate the architect's imagination is consistent with the ludic atmosphere that pervades the film. Even the most vertiginous scenes give the impression that the climbers are on top of their job. Their roped actions are ever-present in the life of the building and frequently catch the attention of curious visitors.

Moreover, the editing of *Gehry's Vertigo* echoes its subject in an interesting way. As Bêka explains, its fragmentary structure harks back to a visual space in which '[b]odies, buildings, everything used to float in the air', a space that was born in medieval painting and was reinstated, in different forms, by modern art. Then he adds: 'what I like is to reach a certain state of vertigo, of imbalance and disorientation. Instead of explaining, I prefer confusing, creating uncertainty, so that this floating could be felt.'[68] Throughout the film, this approach brings out the dizzying aspects of the Guggenheim Museum by dissipating the aura that enshrouds the building. Laying emphasis on the workers' bodily actions, the film manages to de-fetishise the architecture of spectacular circulation while showing how its fluid spaces and flowing surfaces are negotiated by those who know them most intimately.

However partial, the survey of architectural concepts presented in this chapter has shown how various attempts to leave the ground, and to regain it, have punctuated the trajectory of modernism and postmodernism since the early 20th century. While the modernists' yearning for weightlessness brought about 'streets in the sky' and sundry states of suspension, the postmodern turn heralded new types of immersive environment that made ever greater demands on the sense of balance, paving the way for contemporary designs that relinquish the ground in dizzying ways. The strange new world represented in the 1999 *Vertigo* exhibition has become increasingly familiar as the pursuit of visceral experiences takes centre stage. In keeping with the precepts of the experience economy, the built environment professions have embraced the design of spatial features that play with the sense of balance, contributing to the spread of a phenomenon that might be characterised as architectural *ilinx*.

7

ARCHITECTURES OF VERTIGO

It was all very beautiful, but when you are standing on a glass floor looking down, it gives you a nasty feeling.[1]

31 Covered walkway of the Eiffel Tower (first floor), Exposition Universelle, Paris, 1889.

CONQUERING THE URBAN SKY

The rise of vertical cities over recent decades has been accompanied by a proliferation of design features that play on the sense of balance. After the concept of vertigo was invoked to describe a generic condition of the architectural landscape, it went on to define a specific brand of spaces that push the boundaries of perceptual stability in ever more extreme ways. This phenomenon emerged amid a surge of spatial practices and representations that variously engage with verticality. While the tourist industry turned the impulse of living on the edge into thrill adventures, architecture became involved in the production of spaces that engender visceral experiences, bolstering the rise of a new economy of vertigo. A conspicuous aspect regards the design of tall buildings, through which the abyss has been commodified in order to create value. Domesticating a cultural trope that has long represented the anxiety of life on the edge (see Chapter 1), contemporary towers have increasingly become the sites of vertiginous thrills.

In order to appraise this development, it is useful to begin by tracing its historical genealogy. The ambivalent nature of height vertigo was precipitated by the rise of skyscrapers between the late 19th and the early 20th centuries, when the advent of the hydraulic elevator functioned as a catalyst for the construction of office blocks and observation towers. After the introduction of freight hoists in the 1850s, when Elisha Otis demonstrated the safety devices that prevented freefalls, it was only a matter of time before passenger elevators transformed the design of office buildings, in the 1870s, paving the way for the skyscraper age.[2] With the application of electricity, in the last decade of the century powered elevators brought this technology to full fruition. Its impact was later recognised by Le Corbusier when he asserted: 'The elevator is in fact the keystone of all modern urbanization.'[3]

The very idea of elevation was redefined by the wrought-iron lattice structure engineered by Gustave Eiffel for the 1889 World's Fair in Paris. The heated debate around its construction testifies to the controversy of a project that, in the eyes of its detractors, evoked the Tower of Babel. Although the 300-metre-high structure was a ground-breaking project in more ways than one, it had a notable precedent in the Latting Observatory built in New York for the 1853 Exhibition of the Industry of All Nations; moreover, it was inspired by the iron towers designed for the Centennial International Exhibition held in Philadelphia in 1876, one of which was later rebuilt at Coney Island.[4] But no construction rivalled the Eiffel Tower, which embodied the triumph of technology over nature by nearly doubling the tallest structure ever built until then. A historical index of its magnitude is that it took more than 40 years for an American skyscraper (the Chrysler Building) to surpass it in height.

The Tower par excellence, as Roland Barthes called it, set out a new model for urban observatories (fig.31). Its system of vertical mobility allowed visitors to reach the viewing platforms through hydraulic elevators as well as open stairs. Despite the wide range of responses elicited by that engineering marvel, the literature of the period understated its destabilising impact on the human sensorium. In order to reassure prospective visitors, a booklet on sale at the exhibition site advertised the novel experience while dispelling the common fears that altitude and sway would make people dizzy. The author played down the dangers involved in climbing the structure and waxed lyrical about views which had hitherto been reserved for aeronauts: 'It's a very pleasant feeling that of going up to a great height, without fatigue, without jerking, without vertigo and without any danger. It seems like everything sinks around you; you see the horizon slowly widen, you discover at each instant a greater expanse [...] Finally, you enjoy a quite extraordinary spectacle.'[5]

A more dispassionate argument was expressed by the polymath Eugène-Melchior de Vogüé, whose remarks on the Exposition Universelle included the first comprehensive review of the Tower at night (fig.32). The writer extolled the virtues of the new structure by narrating what he imagined to have heard from the Tower itself, a structure so eloquent in its modernity that it was personified. Reporting on the magnificent views from the top, de Vogüé admitted in passing to feelings of vertigo, yet ascribed them to a momentary state of hallucination rather than to the perceptual uncertainty caused by the experience.[6] The panoramic vistas were tied up with a new perception of vertical space: with its intricate system of stairs, elevators and open-air platforms, the 300-metre structure was the harbinger of the modern architectures of vision. However, anecdotal evidence suggests that climbing the Tower was not as pleasant for everyone. *Le Monde illustré* reported that a French MP did not want to miss the inauguration although he suffered from acrophobia; eventually, he was persuaded to join the first ascent, led by Eiffel himself, blindfolded and holding onto a fellow's arm.

Meanwhile, the parallel rise of skyscrapers in 1880s Chicago made the conquest of the urban sky a sustained and pervasive process with a lasting

32 The Eiffel Tower at night during the Exposition Universelle, Paris, 1889.

impact on the experience of space. This new building type provided not only a means to colonise the airspace and profit from its rentability, but also an unrivalled symbol of modernity. Skyscrapers went on to reconfigure the emotional as well as material landscapes of American cities, embodying the fears and desires elicited by the modern metropolis. Around the turn of the 20th century, it became fashionable in New York to enjoy the expansive vistas afforded by new vantage points, as roof gardens attracted a flurry of social activities. As pointed out by Meir Wigoder, those heterotopian places made it possible to contemplate the urban spectacle away from the hustle and bustle of the streets: 'they offered the possibility of standing at the edge of the roof and looking down at the city as if it were a sublime, romantic view enjoyed from a mountain crag'.[7] Transposing the experience of the abyss from nature to the city, the rise of the 'skyscraper-viewer' established a new mode of spectatorship attuned with the American technological sublime.

Tall buildings brought along a modern version of the abyss that replaced the dizzy ravines conjured up by the Romantics. Urban mountains, cliffs and canyons became the modern analogues of natural sceneries in the Western cultural imagination, spawning an appetite for ever more thrilling viewing platforms. In the first age of the skyscraper, architecture formed the scene of a new urban precipice which, in turn, became a site of vertiginous experience. Catherine James sums up the implications of this shift: 'One effect of the new skyscraper landscape was that falling became psycho-social reality, and vertigo, that dizzy preparation for the fall, was rehearsed in the wider cultural imagination, moving between potent metaphor and lived condition. [...] Vertigo, as condition, sign and image, was a valve through which to mediate a darker malaise at the heart of modernity.'[8] The production of vertical space brought about a new mode of perception that, coupled with the advent of mass tourism, went on to exalt New York's status over the 20th century.

ON TOP OF THE WORLD

As skyscraper architecture expanded the field of vision, urban observatories enabled new ways of contemplating cities from above. A race for the most spectacular vistas was tied into the construction of tall buildings throughout the 20th century. The skyward élan of the 1970s took the panoramic experience to new levels. An exemplar was the late World Trade Center (WTC) complex in Lower Manhattan, named after an exhibit of the 1939 World's Fair that championed international commerce as a means of achieving peace. When completed, in 1973, the South Tower (415 metres) nearly equalled the world record of height recently established by its northern twin. The multi-level observatory combined the outdoor panoramic deck typical of early-20th-century skyscrapers such as the Empire State Building with the indoor viewing galleries that became popular in the second half of the century, as epitomised by Chicago's John Hancock Center.

The observation deck atop the WTC South Tower, named 'Top of the World', significantly raised the bar. From the enclosure of the 107th floor, which afforded expansive views, an escalator led visitors to the rooftop three storeys up. Here, an elevated walkway was set back from the edge of the building, while a security fence at a lower level pre-empted the imagined agency of throwing oneself off. Built in response to the growing number of suicide attempts taking place from skyscraper rooftops, this device shifted the danger zone away from the public area, which was bordered with a simple metal railing.[9] The measures introduced on 'Top of the World' were designed to fend off the hazards of a potential fall from a site that thrived on the pleasure of sightseeing from above (plate 20).

At the time of its construction, the Twin Towers marked a departure from the predominant 'glass box' aesthetic of high-rise architecture. Given their unprecedented height, engineers had to find new ways of stabilising the structure. They devised a damping system similar to the shock-absorbers of automobiles in order to reduce the sway caused by winds on the metal frame, which was not as stable as the stone-cladded facades of earlier skyscrapers. But the most interesting aspect of the project, with respect to vertigo, is related to its architect. In 1962, the Port Authority of New York and New Jersey gave Minoru Yamasaki the commission to revitalise Lower Manhattan following his acclaimed design for the U.S. Science Pavilion at the Seattle World's Fair, where he had inserted Gothic arches and narrow vertical windows overlooking a plaza. An avowed humanist, Yamasaki drew upon diverse cultural references in search for architectural beauty, a quality that was seldom associated with the 'glass box' aesthetic of American skyscrapers (fig.33). For the curtain wall of the Twin Towers, the architect developed a module with narrow windows (56cm wide) to minimise the uncomfortable feelings that could be induced by full-height glazed panels. Yamasaki elucidated this choice in his autobiography:

> These windows are narrower than one's shoulders; I've often gone to a high floor and comfortably placed my nose against the glass to view the plaza below. I can't do this in a building with floor-to-ceiling glass and mullions say five feet apart because, as experienced as I am in high-rise buildings, I still have a strong feeling of acrophobia.[10]

Such a frank admission remains unusual for skyscraper designers, yet it displays a sensitivity to the perception of vertical space that concerns a number of

33 Architect Minoru Yamasaki with model of the World Trade Center, n.d.

architects as users of buildings. James Glanz and Eric Lipton observe: 'Oddly enough, for an architect who was designing the world's tallest buildings, he was afraid of heights. Narrow windows meant Yamasaki, and the office workers in the towers, could approach a window and have the security of being able to rest arms against two vertical barriers.'[11] Consistently, where wider windows were required the architect had waist-high bars installed in order 'to give a sense of security to those who work in the building'.[12] The heady mix of verticality and transparency brought about an intensification of sensory stimuli that engendered different responses.

The South Tower observatory was not built until 1975, a year after Philippe Petit had staged his high-wire walk from the same rooftop. It soon established itself as one of the most popular tourist destinations in New York, and the following year the 'Windows on the World' restaurant opened on the 106th floor of the North Tower. The impulse to cast a totalising gaze from above came to symbolise the scopic regimes of spectacle and surveillance. Questioning the 'erotics of knowledge' involved in the view from above, Michel de Certeau criticised the power structure embodied by the World Trade Center with an emphasis on the voyeurism induced by its public observation deck (see Chapter 1). While this author laid emphasis on the act of reading the city from such an elevated vantage point, an alternate source of representation drew out the ambivalence of that position in more visceral terms.

A lengthy scene in Jon Jost's film, *All the Vermeers in New York* (1990), takes place on the same observation deck, where the two protagonists go out on a date.[13] As an elated Anna (Emmanuelle Chaulet) contemplates the views while holding onto the protection fence, Mark (Stephen Lack) speaks out an altogether different emotion: 'I hate it up here. It's like being dead. [...] It's like being dropped off on your way to hell. [...] I don't know how people could come up here for a thrill, it's disgusting. It's just too much.' A Wall Street broker on the brink of existential downfall, Mark expresses the malaise of a life driven by money in which only art provides a temporary refuge. Panning across the rooftop alive with tourists, the camera conveys the tension of a place where the unbound vistas are indissolubly linked with the anxieties of lives on edge. The experience of the city's apex ultimately precipitates the protagonist's demise.

The feeling of disjunction conveyed by this film echoes a sense of subjective and social instability that was widely registered in the 1990s. During that decade, the so-called 'spatial turn' reoriented the focus of enquiry in the humanities, as space became a central concern within postmodernist thought. Western cities were perceived to be places of increasing fragmentation where the foundations of social life established in the post-war period were breaking down. Against this background, humanities scholar Kathleen Kirby mobilised the category of vertigo in an attempt to redefine how the experience of space is embedded in subject formation. In her 1996 book, *Indifferent Boundaries*, Kirby explored the connections between psychic and social experiences of space by reflecting on her own history of post-traumatic vertigo, which, following an accident, had caused an enduring rift between her subjective perception and the surrounding environment. This vestibular syndrome led her to rethink the phenomenon of perceptual dissonance as a crucial aspect of subjectivity: 'First there is a mismatch – perception out of true with perceived: the swimming head confronted with an inassimilable depth, a failure to place the limits or judge the dimensions of an enclosing space, a failure to situate a surface in relation to the body and its surface, or the consciousness, and its surface ...'[14]

With the emphasis on 'failure', this passage speaks of a subjective condition that is out of sync with the external world. Thereby, Kirby asserted a corporeal language that embraces the body's agency in philosophical thinking: a gendered body that does not hide its flaws but thinks through them instead. The incongruity at the basis of this experience resonates with scientific definitions of vertigo formulated in those years. Writing from the perspective of medical psychology, Lucy Yardley observed: 'when an apparent mismatch occurs between the different sensory inputs to the balance system, the perceptual uncertainty this creates is itself experienced as a sensation, which may be described as dizziness, disorientation, or vertigo'.[15] Concurrently, Kirby questioned the formation of subjectivity in relation to socio-spatial conditions that are inherently unstable:

> Couldn't we see in vertigo, as Freud saw in dreams, an attempt to resolve, in imagination, an uncooperative environment? See in vertigo a sign of an unmanageable occurrence in the dimensional realm of the social, and a compensating attempt to manage it psychically? [...] Could vertigo – even simple disorientation – be called the product of a certain antithesis between the subject, and her internal spaces, and the external, material and social, spaces she occupies?[16]

These questions transcend the specialist definitions of vertigo based on somatic and psychogenic disorders and challenge the philosophical conceptions of space that assume an un-differentiated subject position. They provoke reflections on the discrepancy that arises from the sense of being out of place in a hostile environment, which is felt in particular at the margins of societies. As Kirby sums up, '"Vertigo," then, represents the experience of subjects out of step with the social order and the reality it sets up.'[17]

Weaving together social and experiential aspects, this argument echoes those of 20th-century writers and philosophers who related vertigo to the perception of existential instability (see Chapter 1). Through her emphasis on the spatial production of subjectivity, however, Kirby offered a corrective to a Western discourse in which vertigo had long been aligned with anxiety disorders that were traditionally construed as being primarily feminine. Her call for a politics of the subject reacted against a dominant social order that was symbolised, in the last quarter of the 20th century, by the towering complex of the World Trade Center. As shown by various cultural representations, the 'Top of the World' observatory became the place in which the desire to embrace exhilarating views of the city from above collided with the sense of anxiety and alienation provoked by the experience of dizzy heights.

VANISHING EDGES

High-rise architecture sets the scene in which the experience of the cliff edge is staged within modern cities, where urban crags and canyons engender new encounters with the abyss. The materiality of the edge plays a crucial role in experiences of vertigo. Its impact on the psychology of gravity is typified by see-through parapets that blur the boundaries of architectural space. Far from being a mere detail, the design of these elements has a bearing on the perception of safety and, as a consequence, can deeply affect our sense of stability. Individuals on the spectrum of visual height intolerance instinctively tend to keep away from the outer edges of roofs and balconies, as well as from sheer drops such as open stairwells and atria. Yet, the situations that may affect our sense of balance are not always predictable, nor are our psycho-physiological responses to them.

Once again, Hitchcock's *Vertigo* provides a reference point. After the rooftop chase that opens the film, in the following scene Scottie visits his friend and ex-fiancée Midge (Barbara Bel Geddes), who is drawing a new type of brassiere modelled on the structure of a cantilever bridge. This detail adds an architectural layer to the plot, further emphasised by the fact that Hitchcock cast in Midge's role the daughter of Norman Bel Geddes, reportedly to pay homage to him (by an uncanny coincidence, the renowned designer passed away the day before the film was released).[18] In that scene, Scottie explains his trouble with heights: 'I have acrophobia, which gives me vertigo, and I get dizzy. Boy, what a moment to find out I had it!' Although this causal chain may seem oversimplified in light of contemporary medical research, it draws a link between perceptual imbalance and irrational fear of high place which has lost none of its relevance.

Scottie then shares with Midge his 'theory' that he could gradually become accustomed to heights, and, in order to demonstrate it, he slowly climbs a three-step stool placed by the large apartment window. He then talks through his routine: 'I look up, I look down. I look up, I look down. I'm going to go right out and buy me a nice, tall stepladder. Here we go.' However, he feels nauseous the moment he looks down through the window from the higher step, as he seems to relive the trauma of the opening scene. The location of this seizure, a medium-rise block in San Francisco, is symptomatic of a built environment that is fraught with dizzying spaces – an impression reinforced by the steep hills in the background. Throughout the film, the episodes that afflict the male protagonist are precipitated by the experience of places that are bound either by thin edges or by transparent surfaces.

Owing to their bearing on the sense of balance, architectural edges are integral to the 'encounter spaces' that trigger acrophobia.[19] However, this anxiety disorder is still surrounded by prejudices and false beliefs that have long obscured its impact on lived experience. In addition to the psychopathological fear of heights, which according to a German study affects circa 3–5 per cent of the population, neuroscientists have mapped a broad range of non-phobic reactions on the spectrum of visual height intolerance: 'The distressing phenomenon [...] occurs when a visual stimulus causes apprehension of losing control of balance and falling from some height.'[20] Besides towers, typical precipitating factors are climbing a ladder, walking over a bridge and looking out of a tall building, all of which are conditioned by physical edges – or lack thereof.[21] Not only do those spaces involve a sheer drop which would make a fall potentially hazardous, but also a level of see-throughness that arouses the visual apparatus and therefore affects our multisensory balance system. In light of this, a key condition related to the sensation of height vertigo is what might be called vertical transparency, a characteristic of viewing platforms and other spaces that stage the thrill of altitude by effacing the edge or reducing it to its minimum terms.

A shift occurred in the late 20th century when the experience of vertigo became integrated in architectural practice as a means of generating value. After the urban observatory was redefined by the World Trade Center, new spatial constructs came about as the geography of vertical cities shifted towards Asia. A postmodern exemplar is the Umeda Sky Building in Osaka, where a floating garden observatory connects the tops of two office blocks clad in reflective glass (plate 21). Open in 1993 to Hiroshi Hara's design, the complex is a scaled-down version of a grander scheme which originally comprised four towers. In the central void, a cluster of panoramic elevators and escalators allows visitors to take in the shifting views while ascending to the 170-metre-high summit, where a multi-level observatory unfolds around a vast round aperture.

The Sky Building references the Futurists' urban visions of the early 20th century as well as the machinic architecture advocated by the Metabolist Movement in the 1960s, namely Arata Isozaki's 'cities in the air' concept. It was at that time that Hara developed his *yukotai* theory: an assemblage of interconnected spatial units conceived as separate domains in contrast with the homogeneous space of modernism.[22] This approach found a mature expression in the new landmark he designed for Osaka, conceived as the prototype for a future 'mid-air city' in which high-rise buildings would be connected at different levels.[23] Inspired by the tradition of hanging gardens, the observatory itself consists of a circular outdoor terrace lined with glass parapets, situated above an enclosed gallery bound by transparent walls: the superimposed rings are inscribed in a square platform allowing for a safety zone along its perimeter. While the viewing platforms are organised over multiple levels on the model of the World Trade Center, their design was based on the concept of a panoramic garden floating in the sky.

This concept was given a new twist at Marina Bay Sands, Singapore. The integrated resort, built in 2010 by Safdie Architects for the entertainment giant Las Vegas Sands Corporation, was the fulcrum of a major regeneration that created a new gateway to the city. Its three 57-storey towers are joined by a cantilevered structure, the SkyPark, that links their summits. The curved platform is divided into different areas whose degrees of exclusivity are commensurate with their potential for *ilinx*. Bordered by a typical glass parapet, the public deck at the northern end hangs over the bay. Adjacent to it runs the 151-metre-long 'infinity pool', from which residents can enjoy uninterrupted views of downtown Singapore (plate 22). Divested of any visible border, the pool gives the impression that water flows straight over the building's edge, and that one might fall down with it. It thereby exemplifies a brand of spaces that harness the experience of heights to original thrills.

The vanishing edge revives an architectural feature that was glamorised by John Lautner between the late 1960s and the early 1970s. His designs for luxury villas such as the Elrod House in Palm Springs, California (1968), and the Arango Marbrisa House in Acapulco (1973), which appears to float over the adjacent bay, adapted the *ha-ha* principle of English landscape design to modern residential architecture. In the 1770s, Horace Walpole conceived that an invisible boundary could be realised through sunk fences in order to achieve visual continuity between a garden and the surrounding countryside.[24] Two centuries later, Lautner grafted this naturalistic illusion onto the pools of sun-soaked villas along the Pacific coast. Subsequently, Safdie Architects lifted it to the summit of the most expensive resort ever built.

At Marina Bay Sands, the feeling of loftiness elicited by the Singapore skyline is somehow analogous to the assertion of ownership in 18th-century garden design, the impression of nature replaced by an expansive urban landscape. The SkyPark embodies, quite literally, the principle of immersion that is central to the experience economy. Its spatial arrangement shows that vantage points alone, such as those afforded by the public observation deck, are no longer the marks of a privileged subject position; in the infinity pool, the urban spectacle is augmented through an exclusive multisensory experience. The success of this concept, which vividly encapsulates the notion of architectural *ilinx*, is demonstrated by similar features that were built in other Asian metropolises ranging from Hong Kong to Kuala Lumpur.

A decade after Marina Bay Sands, Safdie designed a 'horizontal skyscraper' in the Chinese city of Chongqing, where the four mixed-use towers of Raffles City are connected by a rooftop park suspended at 250 metres. Shaped as a curved cylinder, the structure terminates at both ends with open-air terraces paved with glass flooring. Named 'The Crystal', it exemplifies the design of panoramic terraces that incorporate gravity-defying attractions amid an assortment of bars, restaurants, pools and gardens. As verticality drives urban development, luxury is associated with the escape into an elevated leisure experience. This trend is summed up by the slogan of Palm Tower in Dubai, the residential project that includes an infinity pool overlooking the highest skyline on Earth: 'This is elevated living.'

While the infinity pool is a glaring signifier of luxury, the dematerialisation of the edge is a widespread phenomenon that permeates the design of a wider range of building types including social housing. This is evinced by the ubiquitous glass-sided balconies that line the facades of residential blocks as well as the parapets of roof terraces in many parts of the urbanised world. A remarkable case is the Mirador Building designed by MVRDV in the Sanchinarro district of Madrid (2005), a stacked housing block with a semi-public 'sky-plaza' situated in its midst at 40 metres above the ground. Besides creating a communal platform that transposes the 'streets in the sky' concept to an outdoor terrace, the Mirador allows its residents to enjoy views of the cityscape and the nearby mountains. The pursuit of *ilinx* is inescapable, as the lookout embeds the prospect of inducing a frisson of excitement through the fully glazed parapets on either side.

A different scenario can be found again in Singapore, where communal 'skybridges' and 'skygardens' feature in tower blocks erected by the Housing and Development Board (HDB) since the noughties.[25] Marking a departure from 20th-century roof gardens based on the *Unité d'habitation*, the HDB promotes a model of vertical living that aims to fuse comfort with sustainability. The Pinnacle@Duxton (2009) has two skygardens linking together a cluster of 50-storey towers at their middle and on top: these bridge structures cater

34 Skygarden (50th storey), Pinnacle@Duxton, Singapore.

for multiple social uses – from children's playgrounds to running tracks – that normally take place on the ground (fig.34). This high-rise complex became a landmark of 2000s Singapore at a time when the South Asian city-state established itself as a global travel destination. On the national tourist website, the project is described in high-sounding words: 'The sky's the limit. The soaring lines and stunning views of majestic residential estate Pinnacle@Duxton will make you forget your fear of heights.' Although the skygardens are bound by two rows of safety rails at diminishing levels, the open decks can be difficult to navigate for those on the spectrum of visual height intolerance. While vertigo is an issue that is rarely discussed, the social perception and use of these spaces have been subject of debate.[26]

A mix of elation and anxiety is also induced by another housing complex in Singapore, the SkyVille@Dawson designed by WOHA Architects (2015). This HDB project includes communal terraces suspended between blocks and is topped by a continuous roof garden on the 47th level, bound all along its perimeter by a metal railing with flower beds as visual barriers. While ensuring greater air flow, the minimalist edge invites an unabridged experience of heights that exalts the thrill of verticality, a buzz that is intensified by the dizzying drone's-eye views in the promotional video. Public housing projects show that this phenomenon is not restricted to elite tourist attractions but has become an increasingly general trend. In the realm of the experience economy, the architectural edge has been turned into a see-through screen: as material boundaries dissolve in favour of unimpeded views, the implications of vertigo become palpable.

THRILLS OF TRANSPARENCY

The quest for vertical transparency is best exemplified by the proliferation of see-through platforms designed to induce the feeling of walking on air. A prelude of things to come occurred in 1994 when the first high-rise glass floor was fitted in the observation deck of Toronto's CN Tower, the tallest free-standing structure in the world at the time. This tourist attraction, comprising a horizontal grid of tempered glass panes, was mounted on the viewing gallery at 342 metres above the ground. What appeared to be merely an eye-catching novelty turned out to be the harbinger of a new architectural experience that challenges the perception of spatial depth.[27]

In the same year, the Oriental Pearl Radio and Television Tower was unveiled as part of the major development of Pudong New Area in Shanghai, the 'dragon's head' of the special economic zones that opened the People's Republic of China to foreign trade.[28] Owing to its multiple viewing galleries culminating in the upper sphere which features a sightseeing corridor lined with a glass-bottomed floor along the edge, the tower became a landmark of the city's skyline and a popular tourist destination. Although it has since been overshadowed by nearby skyscrapers, its iconic forms and vertiginous attractions symbolise the ascent of China's economy on the global scene.

Amid the rise of vertical cities, the design of viewing platforms is geared towards spatial experiences that are not only aesthetic but increasingly kinaesthetic. By exposing the depth of space beneath one's feet, these features brought the literal transparency of glass to bear on the experience of high places. The perceptual quality of this material is intrinsically tied up with a potential threat to the body's perceptual stability. As Li Shiqiao provocatively asserted: 'The use of glass is the danger aesthetic of our time.'[29] While Western conceptions of prudence and peril have historically differed from those prevalent in Chinese culture, the spread of architectural features such as the ubiquitous curtain walls, glass elevators and sundry transparent devices signals a globalised trend in the production of urban space.

By the turn of the millennium, glass had become a popular means of arousing the thrill of altitude as effects of transparency spread to oblique and horizontal surfaces. With the epicentres of vertical urbanism now situated in Asia, skyscraper design became involved in a new symbolic economy in which the search for original forms goes hand in hand with the design of exclusive attractions. A striking example is the Kingdom Centre in Riyadh (Omrania and Associates, 2002), whose Sky Bridge framing the top of the building is lined with slanted glass panes that make it possible to sit on a low edge and lean over the abyss. It is in South-East Asia, however, that designers have exploited the thrill of transparency to most sensational effect. A milestone in the quest for architectural *ilinx* was marked by the Shanghai World Financial Centre (SWFC), designed by Kohn Pedersen Fox in the business district of Lujiazui, a short distance from the Oriental Pearl Tower. The skyscraper, which gave form to the rise of Chinese financial markets, was featured in the 1999 *Vertigo* exhibition when only the foundations had been laid. Following a hiatus caused by the economic downturn of the late 1990s, construction was eventually completed in 2008 after design alterations increased its height to nearly half a kilometre (492 metres).

The observation gallery on the 100th floor offers not only panoramic views of the cityscape – as do other observatories at lower levels – but also vertical views through a series of glass panes built into the floor (plate 23). 'Skywalk 100' consists of a 55-metre-long, free-standing bridge that envelops visitors within a glassy enclosure from which they can gaze below as well as around, even though the downward views through the transparent panels are somewhat obstructed by the bulk of the building beneath. Sensory stimulations are further heightened by the reflecting ceilings and by the outward inclination of the side walls. While the glass floor at the Oriental Pearl Tower enhanced the appeal of an urban observatory, 'Skywalk 100' embodies its evolution to a fully fledged spatial device. Implicitly, this and similar structures allude to the art of funambulism: by staging a 'walk-on-air' experience, they entice tourists to challenge their sense of balance within immersive environments.

This spatial concept has been applied to natural settings as well. The cantilevered skywalk unveiled at Grand Canyon West, Arizona, in 2007 paved the way for a plethora of glass-bottomed bridges and viewing platforms designed to heighten the scenic effects of cliffs, gorges and mountains. Vertiginous structures of this kind – most notably the Zhangjiajie glass skywalk in the Hunan province of China, which broke all records with its 430-metre footpath suspended at 300 metres over a canyon – have since been involved in the promotion of landscapes around the world. As Nicole Porter has pointed out, they signal 'a tourist development which, like the quest for the tallest building, is a never-ending exercise in one-upmanship, leading further and further into exaggeration'.[30] Concurrently, the glass floors that are fitted in urban observatories provide an analogue to the experience of natural landscapes: indeed, the fact that these platforms were first introduced in cities is symptomatic of how vertical urban environments have taken centre stage in the geography of thrill tourism.

Nor is glass the only material employed to achieve vertical transparency. In subtler ways, this effect has crept into the design of elevated structures that embrace full visibility as their constituent factor. A compelling project is the Treetop Walkway, designed by Marks Barfield Architects and unveiled at London's Kew Gardens in 2008, around the same time as the glass skywalks at SWFC and Grand Canyon West (plate 24). With a nod to the tree-walk installed at Battersea Park for the 1951 Festival of Britain, the structure allows people to appreciate the biodiversity of the arboretum from the level of a tree's canopy. Designed to blend in with the environment, the walkway is lifted on weathering steel columns that reach up to 18 metres above the ground, while open mesh flooring and metal grillage endow it with a semi-transparent quality.

The Treetop Walkway became an instant attraction and was described by critics as uplifting, similarly to other structures designed by the same architects such as the London Eye. Several of their projects, from Brighton's i360 viewing pod to the Skyline cable car for Chicago (unbuilt), are driven by a desire to upraise bodies from the ground as a means to elevate the human spirit. Although their design for Kew Gardens is not comparable with the Grand Canyon Skywalk in terms of height or transparency, it elicits dizzying responses that may be aggravated by its tendency to wobble under use. A comment posted online at the time of its opening illustrates this point:

> Beautiful idea; beautiful building; beautiful materials. I'm an architect too, but I have problems with vertigo. For me it would be better if the floor was not open. In this case I would try, with a little time for adaptation, to walk along this wonderful thing. But for now I think that I will stay with my feet on the earth, feeling a bit of an idiot for not being able to do it.[31]

This message reveals as eloquently as any theoretical conjecture the dilemma of height-induced vertigo in contemporary architecture: a repressed issue that is bound to surface, time and again, from the unconscious mind of the profession. Although the Treetop Walkway was not intended to defy the user's perceptual stability in an overt manner, as do other platforms designed for thrill seekers, its drive to elevate bodies and minds throws into relief the sheer spectrum of psycho-physiological reactions to being lifted from the ground while still retaining a visual contact with it. As the same commenter noted: 'This happens with many other monuments in the world. The architects should think about the people who have vertigo and make little modifications that don't change the meaning of the project. I know that with this floor the work is most beautiful, but we, poor things, exist too.'[32] There is an emperor's-new-clothes ring to these words, proffered during a boom of design interventions that combine the thrill of heights with effects of vertical transparency. While boosting up the game of *ilinx* to a design principle allows for enthralling spatial experiences, this process unwittingly discloses the plight of subjects affected by visual height intolerance.

TOURIST BUBBLES

The pursuit of architectural *ilinx* crystallised in the late noughties through countless design interventions attuned to the values of the experience economy. See-through elements designed to increase lighting and visibility became standard features of museum interiors, carrying a load of perceptual implications along with practical functions. The extension of the Ashmolean Museum of Art and Archaeology in Oxford (Rick Mather Architects, 2009), for instance, exploits the technical possibilities of glass in the parapets of corridors and mezzanines, as well as in the full-height panels that line the suspended walkways. The open staircase is protected by a glass partition of diminishing height that makes it all the more challenging to navigate the interior space for subjects predisposed to height vertigo. As neuroscientist Michael Gresty noted, this feature 'gives the impression that one is threatened with the possibility of falling over the side'.[33] Not only this element but the whole interior is designed to achieve a maximum of natural lighting through transparent surfaces which have the collateral effect of potentially destabilising the user's balance.

Meanwhile, glass floors have become de rigueur in exhibition spaces such as archaeological sites as well as museums where objects are displayed under walking surfaces. Although these features are usually placed over shallow spaces, in some cases they engage a bodily interaction with deeper voids. At the Acropolis Museum in Athens (2009), Bernard Tschumi Architects made extensive use of transparent surfaces not only to exhibit the outdoor excavations, but also to allow light to filter into the atrium from the top floor. Walking over glass panes, visitors are held in a state of perceptual suspension.

The museum's circulation system exalts the dynamic qualities that have long been central to Tschumi's work. His influential ideas on architecture and disjunction, formulated between the 1970s and the 1980s, foregrounded the agency of the body in the experience of space while laying emphasis on the subversive power of actions and events. To recognise the fundamental instability of architecture, the 'state of uncertainty' that underlies its condition, was regarded at the time as a means of exploring its potential for social change.[34] The Acropolis Museum retains only a distant echo of those radical ideas. If the sensory qualities of suspended glass floors and see-through parapets call to mind the 'spatial aggression' previously advocated by the Swiss-French architect, they do so in ways that ostensibly reflect the values of the experience economy. Those spatial devices elicit a mix of excitement and discomfort that captures the precarious balance of our age.

Transparent walking platforms have also been retrofitted in historical structures with a view to enhancing their tourist appeal. In Britain, they were applied to listed monuments from the late Victorian period such as Blackpool Tower, where the 'walk of faith' glass floor inserted in the late 1990s was expanded during the refurbishment unveiled in 2011 by the global leisure giant Merlin Entertainments. Two glass-bottomed walkways were later installed at London's Tower Bridge with the aim of attracting visitors and commercial activities such as corporate events, private parties and yoga classes. Their relatively limited height (42 metres above the road bridge) allows for a closer visual connection with passers-by and the traffic unfolding below. The incongruous effect of transparency triggers a voyeuristic curiosity in people either side of the glass panes, as well as awareness of the reciprocal distances and positions within the vertical field of vision.

The transformation of floors into transparent surfaces calls to mind the notion of fifth facade that was formulated by Le Corbusier in the late 1920s, when he listed the roof terrace among the key principles of modern architecture. It

35 Glass floor, Eiffel Tower, Paris.

might be argued that, by overturning the vertical window-wall onto a horizontal surface, the glass floor ushers in a sixth facade. This epithet befits the lower side of elevated buildings and overhanging elements, insofar as they fulfil the condition of externality that is implied by the etymology of the word (denoting the front of a building): that is, in the case of glass platforms, the possibility of looking from outside as well as from inside – albeit through a sealed glass. Suspended walkways such as those installed at London's Tower Bridge and Shanghai's World Financial Centre typify this architectural feature.

In parallel with the Tower Bridge retrofit, an analogous intervention took place in the modern architecture of vision par excellence – the Eiffel Tower. The restyling of the first floor by Moatti-Rivière, also unveiled in 2014, included a series of glass platforms aimed at producing an 'augmented architecture'.[35] Besides improving the existing public spaces, the architects introduced a series of open-air terraces overlooking the central void. Their intention was to valorise the empty core that historically defined the Tower: a monument which Alain Moatti, with reference to Barthes, credited with 'the invention of third dimension in the city'.[36] The impression of floating over the void, at 57 metres from the ground, is amplified by the contiguity between the horizontal platforms and the inclined parapets, also made of glass (fig.35).

The experience of walking on those surfaces has been likened to levitation, an ancient practice imbued with myths and magic that possesses an enduring imaginative power.[37] In Paul Auster's 1994 novel, *Mr Vertigo*, the young protagonist learns to levitate after long and hard training, echoing the author's fascination with Philippe Petit's high-wire walks.[38] On the glass platforms that have sprung up since the noughties, however, the longing to overcome gravity is no longer associated with the search for one's limits but is packaged as a themed experience. At the Eiffel Tower, the effect of mid-air suspension immerses the visitor in the central void, providing an enhanced appreciation of its space. As stated on the official website: 'The project offers an improved experience of the Tower and Paris, an entertaining sensory experience, a journey of the senses and knowledge.'

The impulse to challenge our sense of balance is a pre-rational form of play and there is something fascinating, as well as frightening, about the possibility of looking down through an elevated glass floor. This ambivalence had already been captured by Roald Dahl in his children's narratives of Charlie Bucket and Willy Wonka on a 'great glass elevator', as hinted at the outset of the present chapter. Transparent walking platforms hold the potential to arouse an embodied awareness of verticality and reflections on the growth of cities. However, their intended function is usually an altogether different one. Far from inviting a reflexive aesthetic experience, the glass surfaces that dare us to walk on air operate as 'tourist bubbles' in which the encounter with the abyss underneath one's feet is reduced to a commodified experience.[39] In these self-contained and highly regulated spaces, thrill seekers can perform gravity plays within safe environments. Indeed, the idea of vertigo as a sudden loss of balance, which has historically been associated with a state of confusion and a darkening of the mind, is sanitised through devices that aim at maximum transparency and visibility.

This burgeoning trend fuelled a race between rival observatories for the most thrilling attraction. In 2009, Chicago's Willis Tower had its 103rd-floor Skydeck retrofitted with four retractable balconies designed by SOM Architects, the same practice that in the 1970s had designed the skyscraper formerly known as Sears Tower (plate 25). 'The Ledge' broke new ground in the field of viewing platforms, with its all-glass boxes protruding over one metre from the building facade at 412 metres above ground. On the Skydeck website, customers are promised a lasting reward: 'With glass on the ceiling, floor, and all sides, it is truly, an unforgettable experience.' Behind this marketing pledge lies a deeper strategy that pits skyscrapers vying for tourists against each other – globally as well as locally.

In 2014, in overt competition with the Skydeck, a new attraction called 'Tilt' opened across town at 360 Chicago, formerly known as the John Hancock Center observatory (plate 26). Branded as 'Chicago's highest moving experience', it consists of a glass-and-steel platform that moves 30 degrees outwards, stimulating a dynamic perception of the abyss. As you face the full-height glass panels and hold on to the side bars, you are slowly tilted off your upright posture by a sliding device that makes you lean over a 300-metre-high chasm. This game of *ilinx* effects a disruption of sensory stability that is at variance with other high-altitude thrills, insofar as it transports the visitor's body over the void through a slow inclination.

Even cities where verticality is comparatively less pronounced have tapped into the economy of vertigo. Notably, a supercharged attraction playing on the thrill of transparency was built in downtown Los Angeles. If the tilting mechanism at 360 Chicago introduced a slow-moving element, the dynamics of architectural *ilinx* picked up speed at the U.S. Bank Tower, located one block away from the Westin Bonaventure Hotel. Whereas the latter's atrium was held up as the epitome of spatial depthlessness, this new design intervention encapsulates the pursuit of groundlessness. The U.S. Bank Tower was the tallest skyscraper in town when, in 2016, it was remodelled by Gensler Architects to make space for a series of new observation decks named OUE Skyspace Los Angeles.

The makeover included 'Skyslide', a glass-clad ramp hanging on a facade that purportedly offers 'unparalleled views in a whole new way'. Although it is hard to imagine anyone pausing to contemplate the panorama when sliding down a glass box suspended 300 metres above the ground, this attraction offers an exhilarating play of *ilinx* by enacting a real drop in space. Augmenting the visual experience of height with a visceral one, albeit brief and controlled, the Skyslide marks a further step in the economy of vertigo that emerged in the early 21st century. Its extreme challenge to gravity, introduced in the same year as the giant slide at London's ArcelorMittal Orbit tower, epitomises a design trend that found in the sky a lucrative field.

FLOATING IN THE SKY

The designs outlined above call to mind the early experiments on spatial depth conducted in the late 1950s, at a time when issues of balance and vertigo came to the fore of Western culture. Through her pioneering research into space perception, the psychologist Eleanor Gibson shed light on how humans and other animals react to the experience of heights. Gibson and colleague Richard Walk tested children between six and 14 months on an ingenious set-up called visual cliff: 'a board laid across a sheet of heavy glass, with a patterned material directly beneath the glass on one side and several feet below it on the other.'[40] Prompted to crawl across the glass surface and reach their mothers at the other end, most children were deterred by the apparent chasm and stayed away from it. The experiment revealed that human behaviours are highly dependent on visual clues, since our consciousness of space develops faster than our locomotor abilities. When approaching the edge, our balance system alerts us to the danger of falling and triggers 'depth avoidance' behaviours.

The same phenomenon occurs on high-level glass floors, where the opaque frame holding the panels gives an impression of safety. Many people initially skirt around the glass surface and approach it through small and tentative steps. Although the vogue for transparent floors has proved extremely popular, and perhaps because of it, these features have flown above the radar of architectural criticism. Their proliferation, however, indicates the signs of a deeper change that warrants critical attention. Indeed, the thrill of vertical transparency has become increasingly central to high-rise buildings, with the play of *ilinx* informing and being incorporated into their design.

This trend is epitomised by the angled sky deck protruding from the 100th floor of the North Tower at 30 Hudson Yards (Kohn Pedersen Fox, 2020). Extending 24 metres into the air at 344 metres in height, the 'Edge' is a highlight of the real estate development on Manhattan's West Side that broke all previous records of size and cost (fig.36). In this elaborate set-up, the gravity challenge posed by the cantilevered structure is augmented by an all-pervading effect of transparency. A multimedia display prepares the visitor for the dramatic exit onto the observation deck, which is bordered by frameless glass parapets with an outward slant. Here the key features of contemporary urban observatories are brought to bear on the Manhattan skyline, and a flight of steps provides vantage points to top the outdoor experience. The marketing rhetoric is one of leaving the ground and embarking upon a journey through the sky:

> Edge is the highest outdoor sky deck in the Western Hemisphere, with a one-of-a-kind design. It's suspended in mid-air, giving you the feeling of floating in the sky with 360-degree views you can't get anywhere else. Look 100 stories down from the thrilling glass floor, lean out over

36 'Edge', 30 Hudson Yards (North Tower), New York.

> the city on angled glass walls and sip champagne in the sky. You've never experienced New York like this before.[41]

These words sums up the immersive experience offered by the new attraction, while at the same time, emphasising its location as a unique selling point. 'Edge' embodies the key principle, formulated by Pine and Gilmore, whereby the capacity to produce a memorable experience depends on its effectiveness in engaging the senses (see Chapter 5).[42] And yet, it is not the most extreme experience on offer at Hudson Yards. The sloping roofline of the same tower has been repurposed into a new attraction, 'City Climb', which invites tourists to walk along the edge and lean suspended over the abyss. While different 'urban mountaineering' and 'edgewalk' experiences had previously been introduced in various cities such as Sydney, London and Shanghai, this one combines those thrills into a single package, updating the New York tradition of skyscraper viewing to the contemporary tourist market.

Meanwhile, down on the ground, a barrage of sensory stimuli awaits the visitor to the 'Vessel', the 45-metre-high climbable sculpture designed by Heatherwick Studio as part of the first phase of the Hudson Yards development and inaugurated in 2019 (plate 27). A critic noted that this Escher-esque structure, comprising 154 flights of stairs and 80 landings bound by continuous glass parapets, 'might induce the same sense of vertigo found on construction sites'.[43] While the designers emphasised the public nature of this installation, its fate was soon thwarted by a spate of suicides which raised concerns over the height of the protective barriers and led to the temporary closure of the attraction.

The high-rise boom of the 2010s has revived New York's primacy as vertical metropolis and signalled the city's economic resilience as the tenets of the experience economy were adapted to the spectacle of urban verticality. Its ever-changing skyline, punctuated by the supertall luxury towers overlooking Central Park (the so-called 'Billionaires' Row'), reflects the relentless production of vertical space while paving the way for new forms of architectural spectacle. At a time when the geography of vertical urbanism has shifted its focal point to Asia, Manhattan's new skyscraper boom revives its historical pre-eminence. The development of Hudson Yards is particularly interesting in terms of vertigo: if 'Vessel' elicits giddy sensations through the vistas it opens inwards as well as outwards, 'Edge' takes the challenge of gravity to a new stage. In promoting an immersive experience of heights that is visceral as well as visual, it brings to fruition the pursuit of architectural *ilinx* that has burgeoned since the turn of the millennium.

This pointed terrace appears to reclaim a centre of gravity – or rather of *anti*-gravity – that harks back to the turn of the previous century, when the new skyscraper rooftops played host to a range of social activities. Although the panoramic view remains the predominant function of urban observation decks, their design is increasingly geared towards the production of multisensory experiences that find a parallel in the surge of technologies such as virtual reality and 4D cinema. This correlation is validated by the spectacles offered on top of several skyscrapers around the world. At Istanbul's Sapphire Tower, for instance, besides the views from the open-air observatory visitors can enjoy a 4D 'Sky Ride' which simulates a helicopter flight through the city in a multisensory movie experience.

A special place is held by New York's One World Trade Center (SOM, 2015), the landmark tower erected on the site of Ground Zero. According to Henriette Steiner and Kristin Veel, this skyscraper epitomises the syndrome of gigantism that continues to affect Western culture, albeit in new forms that merge high-rise construction with digital infrastructures: 'the building makes use of what we could call a trick of the contemporary urban experience economy: a tiny fraction of the building is open to the public (or that part of the public that is able to pay a significant entrance fee) and is heavily branded and swathed in mediatized experiences that attune the visitor to a particular set of narratives about the building.'[44] The observatory is reached via 'Sky Pod' elevators that climb more than two storeys per second, while an audio-visual display illustrates the city's historical development. Up above, the panoramic galleries are organised over three floors and reach up to 387 metres in height. An original feature is the 'Sky Portal', a walkable screen on which visitors can watch a real-time video image of the street from above (plate 28). Here the experience of vertical space is simulated through a high-definition live stream that invites you to confront the abyss in a state of vicarious suspension.

By replacing the walk-on-air experience with the ersatz version of a glass floor, the Sky Portal gives new meaning to the suspension of disbelief: it is the simulacrum of an embodied experience that is itself illusory. Its hyper-realism is implied in the marketing slogan: 'An experience above'. While the highlight of the former World Trade Center was the panoramic terrace that claimed 'top of the world' status, the new attraction is designed to draw tourists into an inward-looking realm of simulation. Extending the mediatised experience of the elevators, this high-tech simulacrum compounds the phenomenon of architectural *ilinx* that has burgeoned in the early part of this century. Immersive experiences that challenge the multisensory balance system have become integral to the design of urban observatories, complementing and in some cases superseding the panoramic views. Moreover, the Sky Portal bears an indirect allusion to the all-too-physical downfall that beset the late Twin Towers, suggesting a possible reason why the state of suspension was not directly induced but rather simulated at the site of such a traumatic event.

The range of spatial devices examined above indicate a shift from the modern architecture of vision towards a new architecture of vertigo. Although it remains, as Barthes noted, that while on high 'one can feel oneself cut off from the world and yet the owner of a world', the panorama alone appears to be no longer adequate to meet the demand for immersive experiences.[45] Initially conceived as a machine for seeing, the urban observatory has been reconfigured as a machine for thrilling: it combines the visual spectacle of the city with new effects of transparency that challenge the visitor's perceptual stability. The desire to experience the unknown is a powerful drive for the design of ever more extreme spaces that bring people in contact with the abyss, reflecting and actively producing a demand for visceral sensations.

The race for global primacy is evidence of how deeply architectures of vertigo are embedded in the structures of a buoyant experience economy. While the modernist 'streets in the sky' were aimed at fostering social interaction and new patterns of circulation, the vogue for glass-bottomed platforms is driven by the pursuit of intense individual experiences. Symptomatically, these devices have emerged along with a profusion of design features such as slides, swings, tilts and ledges that are increasingly turning cities into gravity playgrounds: promoting the heady excitement of heights, they embrace the glamorous image of living on the edge.

These immersive environments, whose names almost invariably start with a 'sky-' prefix, simulate the balancing acts performed by aerialists within hyper-secure bubbles. By summoning the user's perceptual stability, they embolden dynamic and enterprising subjects to enjoy a seemingly boundless degree of freedom, in reality an artificially staged one. Effectively, they are a notable instance of how architecture operates, to quote Douglas Spencer, as a 'spatial complement of contemporary processes of neoliberalization'.[46] Through its deceptive liberation from gravity, the architecture of vertigo seeks to exorcise the fear of falling that characterises our age of instability and insecurity. Reducing the abyss to a themed experience, it seeks to normalise an urban condition that, in reality, is increasingly unbalanced.

EPILOGUE

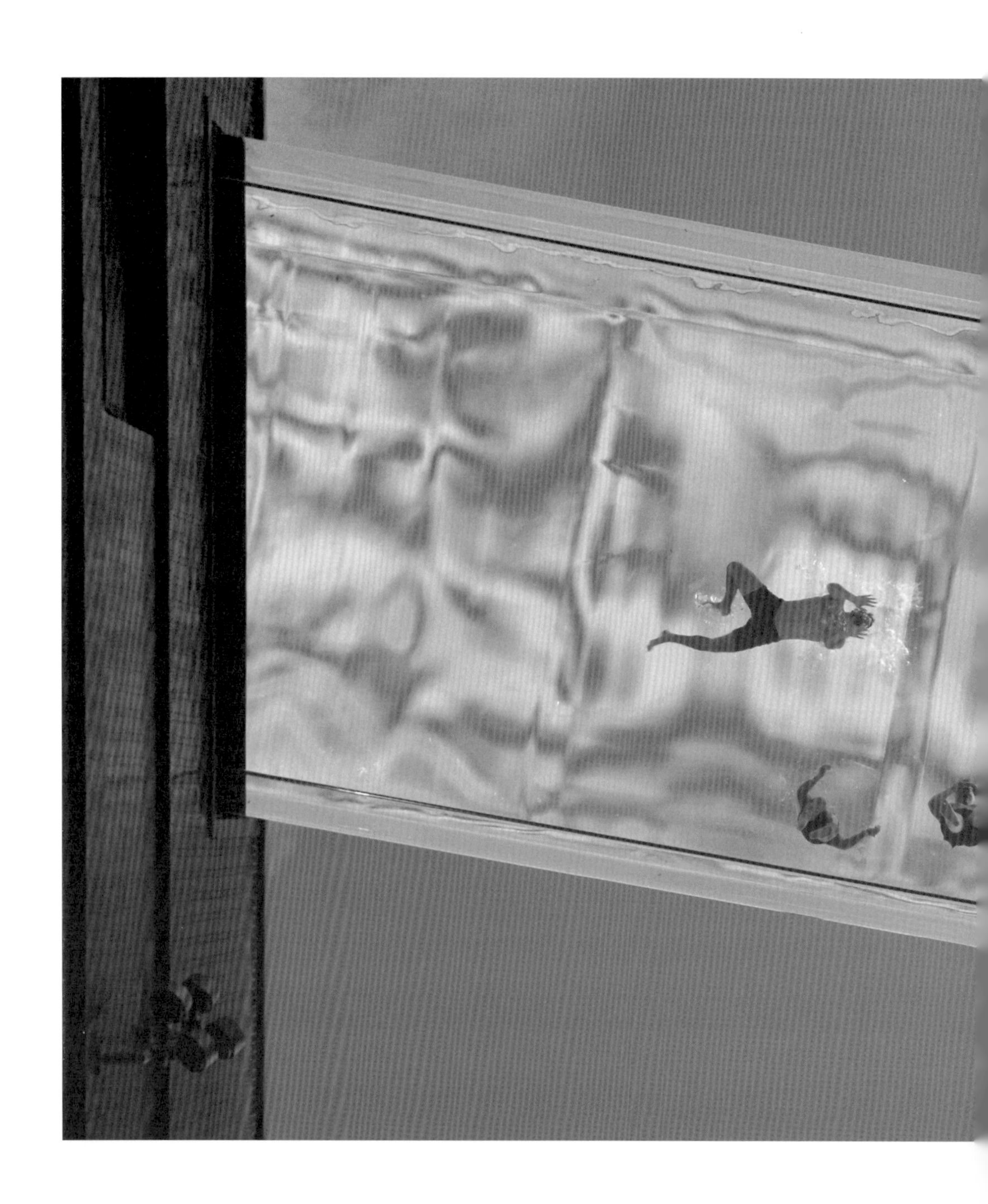

37 'Sky Pool',
Embassy Gardens,
London.

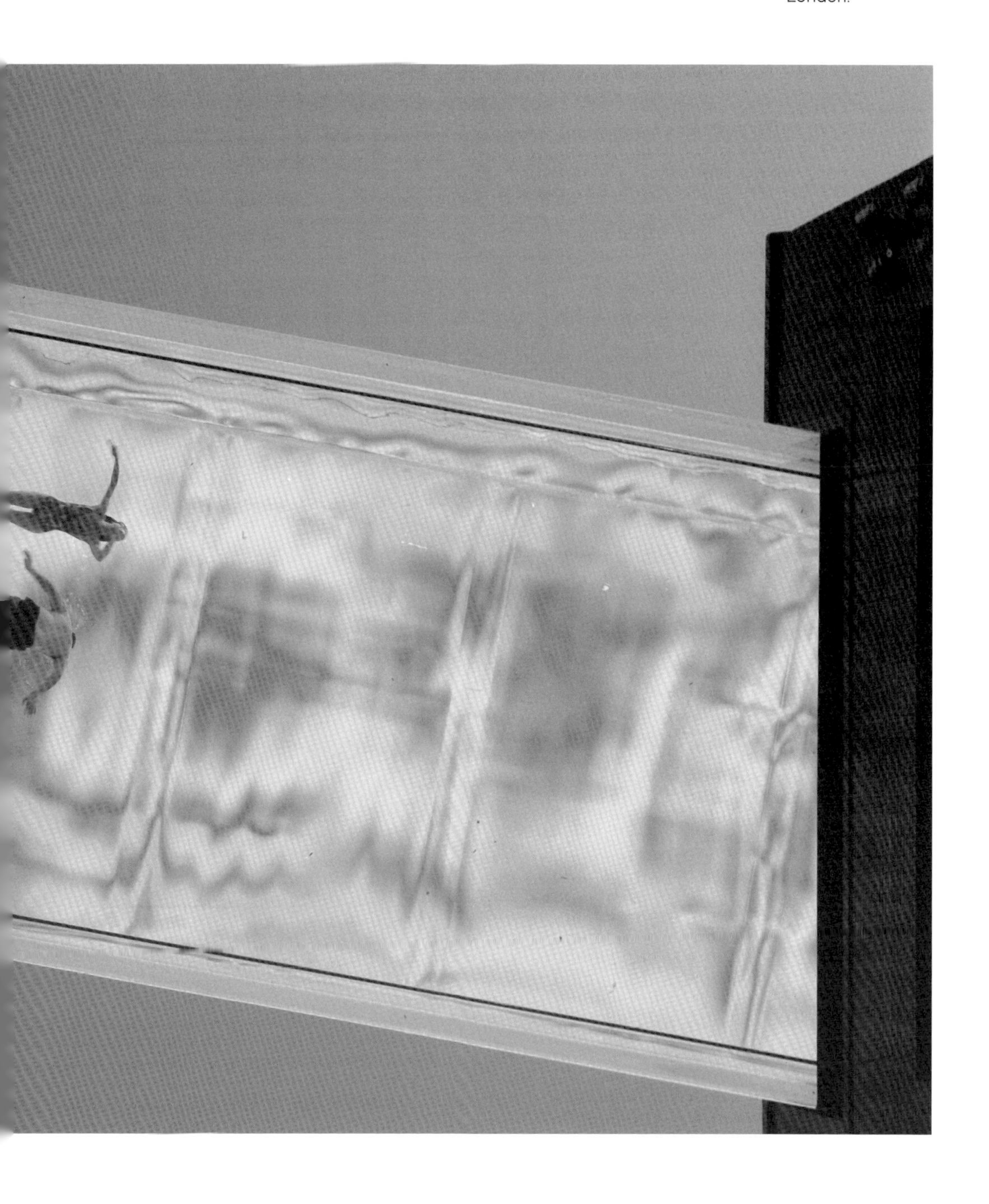

In May 2021, in the midst of the COVID-19 pandemic, a swimming pool suspended ten storeys above the ground was unveiled in London's riverside district of Embassy Gardens (fig.37). Made of transparent acrylic, the 'Sky Pool', designed by HAL Architects, connects the rooftops of two apartment blocks standing 14 metres apart. Its exclusive location was branded the 'jewel in the crown' of the Nine Elms redevelopment. In the pool, club members can enjoy the thrills of floating in a state of suspension while gazing at the U.S. Embassy building and its surroundings. The original design, complete with a parallel walkway that bridges the 'sky decks' atop the towers, epitomises a mode of value production based on the pursuit of memorable experiences. More specifically, it illustrates the emergence of high-rise built environments designed as *mise en scène* for the performances of subjects-consumers.

The Sky Pool belongs to a typology of spaces that, as shown in the book, stage the encounter with the abyss as an immersive experience. By reconfiguring the axis of verticality, this *architecture of vertigo* embodies a desire to transcend the constraints of gravity and to subjugate space to virtually unlimited control. It gives form to the illusion of boundless freedom that permeates our liquid modern societies, an ideology predicated on intense and individualised forms of enjoyment. Its point of application is an autotelic body in pursuit of ever newer pleasures that in turn become sources of perpetual anxiety. As social behaviours are modelled on the free-market principles of consumption and competition, architecture is deeply embedded in the production of spaces that reflect, and at the same time reinforce, the hegemonic neoliberal subjectivity. In Zygmunt Bauman's words: 'The struggle for *uniqueness* has now become the main engine of *mass* production and *mass* consumption.'[1]

The exclusive spatial devices that play on the sense of balance are only the tip of an iceberg which encompasses a wide realm of immersive and interactive experiences, extending from thrill tourism to the realms of art, theatre and cinema. Architecture partakes in this process by fostering visceral forms of experience: thus, urban observation decks are no longer conceived exclusively for the view from above but as stages for gravity plays that challenge the sense of balance. In this respect, the Sky Pool encapsulates the fundamental ambivalence of vertigo, oscillating between anxiety and pleasure. By denying the former while pursuing the latter, designers strive to exorcise the sense of instability that affects the contemporary urban condition.

A trend of staging visceral thrills has been thriving since the turn of the millennium. While climbers and aerialists transgress the boundaries of vertical cities, their bodily practices have increasingly been turned into mediatised spectacles. In parallel, the boom of adventure tourism has revived a time-honoured history that stretches back to the late 19th century, when gravity plays constituted the main attractions of funfairs and amusement parks. In recent decades, this phenomenon has fuelled an economy of vertigo that banks on the growth of vertical cities to evoke, and drive out, the collective fear of falling.

The design of spaces that challenge the user's balance is evidenced by observation towers that operate as playgrounds for adults. Tall structures such as Toronto's CN Tower, Auckland's Sky Tower, the Strat in Las Vegas and Macau Tower offer manifold opportunities to thrill seekers, ranging from bungee jumping to edge walking. The urban adventure industry feeds off ever more extreme experiences that vie for attention, not only in bespoke entertainment towers but also in skyscrapers located in central business districts. The case of Shanghai is remarkable in this respect: the financial citadel of Lujiazui is home to a cluster of high-rises that offer a variety of gravity plays, from 'Skywalk 100' at the World Financial Centre to the glass-bottomed edgewalk at JinMao Tower. Over and above them, Shanghai Tower boasts the tallest observation deck in the world at 562 metres from the ground, crowning one of the symbols of 21st-century China. The district is sited in the Pudong New Area, the epicentre of China's financial power whose skyline has come to rival that of Manhattan through a distinct blend of originality and imitation.[2] In fact, it was in Pudong that the first suspended glass pool was built, in 2012, cantilevering out of the 24th storey of the Holiday Inn Hotel. While Shanghai set its own model of vertical urbanism, the race for ever more original games of *ilinx* has been spreading globally.

Countless other cases can be found around the urbanised world. Notably, the waterfront development of Marina Bay in Singapore is punctuated with a string of gravity-defying features including the giant Ferris Wheel (Singapore Flyer) and the 'supertrees' that dot the Gardens by the Bay, inviting visitors to tread on suspended walkways at the feet of the imposing Sands resort. Similarly, high-rise developments in the Arab world, such as Aykon City in Dubai, boast 'vertigo-inducing attractions' that increase their attractiveness, while the cradles of the American skyscraper – Chicago and New York – are firmly in the race for the most thrilling crowd-pleaser. On the whole, these endeavours to brand architecture as a site of kinaesthetic experience are turning the built environment into a field of gravity plays. While the precipice used to evoke the dizziness of freedom underlying the modern condition, today it is sought after as a source of fleeting thrills. Hence, Kierkegaard's idea that 'freedom succumbs to dizziness' appears to have been reversed: it is dizziness itself that gives way to a seemingly boundless freedom, or more likely to its false consciousness.

And yet, the architecture of vertigo is not limited to the glamorous tourist bubbles that can be found atop skyscrapers and amusement towers. Besides those conscious attempts to challenge the user's sense of balance, there has emerged a more widespread tendency towards the design of spaces that pose severe challenges to subjects affected by visual height intolerance and balance disorders. Examples range from the glass parapets used in balconies and terraces to the transparent floors that are fitted in museums and office buildings, which transpose the aesthetic of the glass box to the horizontal plane. By reducing the materiality of the edge to its minimal terms, these features elicit feelings of elation besides creating new vistas. At the same time, they are liable to impair or distort the perceptual stability of users who are prone to spatial disorientation, a condition that tends to increase with people's age. Yet, urban environments are increasingly designed to befit young, affluent and able-bodied users: not so much the *homo ludens* envisaged by 20th-century avant-garde architects as rather a *homo consumens* eager for visceral excitement.

Vertigo has been with us for millennia, yet we are still confronting its conundrum. This book has paved the way by charting how writers, scientists, artists, architects and sundry practitioners have variously dealt with this phenomenon. Further, it has appraised how places that trigger dizzy sensations – notably those induced by heights – have become objects of manufactured desire. As verticality provides a fecund axis for the production of space, the encounter with the abyss is increasingly commodified as a memorable experience: staged in safe environments where bodily risks are fully managed and the fear of falling is exorcised. At a psychological level, this process impinges upon our fundamental capacity to desire, a dynamic activity of the unconscious which the ego can never entirely control; for desire, in the original sense of the word, indicates a loss of orientation to which we surrender, as did the ancients who lay down at night to interrogate the stars. In the words of psychoanalyst Massimo Recalcati, 'The experience of desire is [. . .] an experience of loss of mastery, of vertigo, of something that gives itself to me as "stronger" than my will.'[3]

Relinquishing the will to conquer nature at all cost, then, may help us to acknowledge our unstable position as 'beings of gravity' and to rethink our interactions with the environment. One way to do so is by considering the agency of critical and creative practices that do not deny vertigo, nor trivialise it, but recognise it as an intrinsic aspect of human life. On balance, multiple perspectives from the arts, sciences and humanities are necessary to appraise the role of architecture as a site of embodied experience. This is not to undermine the autonomy of the discipline but, on the contrary, to reassert its unique ability to tackle complex issues by engaging with a diverse body of knowledge. If the future of cities is going to be vertical, we need to broaden our responses to their dizzy spaces.

NOTES

INTRODUCTION

1 Paul Virilio, 'Gravitational Space', in Laurence Louppe (ed.), *Traces of Dance: Drawings and Notations of Choreographers*, trans. Brian Holmes and Peter Carrier (Paris: Editions Dis Voir, 1994), p.39.
2 Alex Ross, 'The Music that Casts the Spells of "Vertigo"', *The New York Times*, 6 October 1996, p.17.
3 The 1954 French novel *D'entre les morts*, by Pierre Boileau and Thomas Narcejac (*nom de plume* of Pierre Ayraud), was published in English in 1956 as *The Living and the Dead* and adapted by Alex Coppel and Samuel Taylor into the screenplay of *Vertigo*.
4 The *campanario* of Mission San Juan Bautista, reconstructed in the film studio, is also the site of Scottie's redemption in the film's dramatic dénouement.
5 Doreen Huppert, Eva Grill and Thomas Brandt, 'Down on Heights? One in Three has Visual Height Intolerance', *Journal of Neurology*, vol.260, no.2, February 2013, pp 597–604.
6 Paul Haacke, *The Vertical Imagination and the Crisis of Transatlantic Modernism* (Oxford: Oxford University Press, 2021), p.5.
7 The Council of Tall Buildings and Urban Habitat defines as 'supertall' those buildings exceeding 300 metres in height, and 'megatall' those above 600 metres.
8 Stephen Graham, *Vertical: The City from Satellites to Bunkers* (London: Verso, 2016), p.1.
9 See, for instance, 'Imaginaires de la vi(ll)e en hauteur', *Géographie et Cultures*, no.102, 2017.
10 Carey D. Balaban and Rolf G. Jacob, 'Background and History of the Interface between Anxiety and Vertigo', *Journal of Anxiety Disorders*, vol.15, nos 1–2, 2001, pp 27–51.
11 Roger Caillois, *Man, Play and Games*, trans. Meyer Barash (Urbana and Chicago, IL: University of Illinois Press, 2001).
12 Richard Steele, *The Funeral; or, Grief a-la-mode. A comedy* (London: Butters, 1701), p.6.
13 Lucy Yardley, *Vertigo and Dizziness* (London: Routledge, 1994), p.2.
14 Thomas Brandt, *Vertigo: Its Multisensory Syndromes* (London: Springer, 1991), p.233.
15 Danielle Quinodoz, *Emotional Vertigo: Between Anxiety and Pleasure* (London: Routledge, 1997).
16 Huppert, Grill and Brandt, op.cit.
17 Claude Perrin, *Le Vertige: Histoire et actualité* (Paris: Louis Pariente, 1988).
18 These include phobic postural vertigo, space-motion discomfort and chronic subjective dizziness, along with visual vertigo.
19 Zeynep Çelik Alexander, *Kinaesthetic Knowing: Aesthetics, Epistemology, Modern Design* (Chicago, IL: Chicago University Press, 2017).
20 Sarah Robinson and Juhani Pallasmaa (eds), *Mind in Architecture: Neuroscience, Embodiment, and the Future of Design* (Cambridge, MA: MIT Press, 2017).
21 Harry Francis Mallgrave, *From Object to Experience: The New Culture of Architectural Design* (London: Bloomsbury, 2018).
22 Christine Wall, *An Architecture of Parts: Architects, Building Workers and Industrialisation in Britain 1940–70* (London: Routledge, 2013).
23 George Garnham. Interview by Christine Wall, 2011. Bishopsgate Institute Archives (CPWB/3/4).
24 Daniel M. Knight, *Vertiginous Life: An Anthropology of Time and the Unforeseen* (Oxford: Berghahn, 2021).
25 Jock Young, *The Vertigo of Late Modernity* (London: Sage, 2007), p.12.

26 ibid., p.13.

27 Isabell Lorey, *State of Insecurity: Government of the Precarious* (London: Verso, 2014).

28 Bruno Latour, *Down to Earth: Politics in the New Climatic Regime* (Cambridge: Polity Press, 2018), p.1.

29 ibid., p.8.

30 ibid.

31 Jane Rendell, 'Working Between and Across: Some Psychic Dimensions of Architecture's Inter- and Transdisciplinarity', *Architecture and Culture*, vol.1, no.1, 2013, pp 128–40.

1 SENSING THE ABYSS

1 Jean-Paul Sartre, *Being and Nothingness: An Essay on Phenomenological Ontology* (1943), trans. Hazel E. Barnes (London and New York, NY: Routledge, 2003), p.53.

2 The massive stone tower was the tallest building in the world for 227 years, between 1647 and 1874, and is still the tallest structure built entirely in the Middle Ages.

3 Johann Wolfgang von Goethe, *Autobiography of Goethe: Truth and Poetry Relating to My Life*, trans. John Oxenford (Auckland, NZ: The Floating Press, 2008), p.609.

4 Johann Wolfgang von Goethe, 'On German Architecture' (1772), in Matthew Bell (ed.), *The Essential Goethe* (Princeton, NJ: Princeton University Press, 2016), pp 867–71; p.870.

5 Kenneth Calhoon, 'The Gothic Imaginary: Goethe in Strasbourg', *Deutsche Vierteljahrsschrift für Literaturwissenschaft und Geistesgeschichte*, vol.75, no.1, 2001, pp 5–14.

6 Doreen Huppert, Max Wuehr and Thomas Brandt, 'Acrophobia and Visual Height Intolerance: Advances in Epidemiology and Mechanisms', *Journal of Neurology*, vol.267, 2020, pp 231–40.

7 The *Corpus Hippocraticum* was written in the 5th century BCE, whereas the *Huangdi Neijing* dates to the 2nd–3rd centuries CE. See Thomas Brandt and Doreen Huppert, 'Fear of Heights and Visual Height Intolerance', *Current Opinion in Neurology*, vol.27, no.1, 2014, pp 111–17.

8 Matthias Bauer, Doreen Huppert and Thomas Brandt, 'Fear of Heights in Ancient China', *Journal of Neurology*, vol.259, no.10, 2012, pp 2223–5.

9 Julien Offray de La Mettrie, *Traité du vertige avec la description d'une catalepsie hystérique* (Rennes: Veuve de P.A. Garnier, 1737), p.36. Author's translation.

10 Bernard Andrieu, *Donner le vertige: Les arts immersifs* (Montreal: Liber, 2014).

11 Erasmus Darwin, *Zoonomia; or, the Laws of Organic Life* (1794), vol.1 (New York, NY: AMS Press, 1974), p.231.

12 ibid., p.233.

13 Gerald Wiest, 'The Origins of Vestibular Science', *Annals of the New York Academy of Sciences*, no.1343, April 2015, pp 1–9; p.1.

14 Carey D. Balaban and Rolf G. Jacob, 'Background and History of the Interface between Anxiety and Vertigo', *Journal of Anxiety Disorders*, vol.15, nos 1–2, 2001, pp 27–51; p.30.

15 Johann G. Spurzheim, *Observations on the Deranged Manifestations of the Mind, or Insanity*, 1st American edn (Boston: Marsh, Capen & Lyon, 1833), p.31.

16 Wiest, op.cit., p.1.

17 William R. Gowers, *A Manual of Diseases of the Nervous System*, vol.II, 3rd edn (Philadelphia: Blakiston, 1907), p.777.

18 Andrea Verga, 'Acrophobia', *American Journal of Insanity*, vol.45, no.2, 1888, pp 288–93.

19 ibid., p.290.

20 Anthony Vidler, *Warped Space: Art, Architecture, and Anxiety in Modern Culture* (Cambridge, MA: MIT Press, 2000).

21 ibid., p.26.

22 Felicity Callard, '"The Sensation of Infinite Vastness"; or, the Emergence of Agoraphobia in the Late 19th Century', *Environment and Planning D: Society and Space*, vol.24, 2006, pp 873–89.

23 Danielle Quinodoz, *Emotional Vertigo: Between Anxiety and Pleasure* (London: Routledge, 1997).

24 ibid.

25 ibid., p.137.

26 ibid., p.141.

27 Gavin J. Andrews, 'Spaces of Dizziness and Dread: Navigating Acrophobia', *Geografiska Annaler:*

Series B, Human Geography, vol.89, 2007, pp 307–17.

28 Joyce D. Davidson, *Phobic Geographies: The Phenomenology and Spatiality of Identity* (Aldershot: Ashgate, 2003), p.87.
29 Quinodoz, op.cit., p.7.
30 Søren Kierkegaard, *The Concept of Anxiety: a simple psychologically orienting deliberation on the dogmatic issue of hereditary sin* (1844), ed. and trans. Reidar Thomte with Albert B. Anderson (Princeton, NJ: Princeton University Press, 1980).
31 ibid., p.61.
32 ibid., p.159.
33 Edgar Allan Poe, 'The Imp of the Perverse' (1845), in *The Works of the Late Edgar Allan Poe*, vol.1 (New York, NY: J.S. Redfield, Clinton Hall, 1850), p.356.
34 Kester Rattenbury, *The Wessex Project: Thomas Hardy, Architect* (London: Lund Humphries, 2018).
35 Michel Foucault, 'What Is Enlightenment?', in *Ethics: Subjectivity and Truth. The Essential Works of Foucault, 1954–1984, Vol.1*, ed. Paul Rabinow, trans. Robert Hurley et al. (New York, NY: The New Press, 1997), pp 303–21; 310.
36 Sartre, op.cit.
37 ibid., p.53.
38 ibid., p.54.
39 ibid., p.55.
40 ibid., p.56.
41 Pierre Boileau and Thomas Narcejac, *Vertigo*, trans. Geoffrey Sainsbury (London: Bloomsbury, 1997), p.22. This and other references are based on a newer edition of *The Living and the Dead*, which was re-titled after Hitchcock's film.
42 W.H. Auden, *The Age of Anxiety: A Baroque Eclogue* (New York, NY: The Random House, 1947).
43 Boileau and Narcejac, op.cit., p.154.
44 Gaston Bachelard, *Earth and Reveries of Will: An Essay on the Imagination of Matter* (1948), trans. Kenneth Haltman (Dallas, TX: Dallas Institute Publications, 2002).
45 ibid., p.264.
46 ibid.
47 ibid.
48 Doreen Huppert, Eva Grill and Thomas Brandt, 'Down on Heights? One in Three has Visual Height Intolerance', *Journal of Neurology*, vol.260, no.2, February 2013, pp 599–600.
49 Bachelard, op.cit., pp 264–5.
50 ibid., p.265.
51 ibid., p.267.
52 ibid., p.266.
53 Charles A. Kane and M. Stuart Strong, 'Dizziness and Vertigo: Diagnosis and Treatment', *Medical Clinics of North America*, vol.41, no.5, September 1957, pp 1229–44; p.1233.
54 David D. DeWeese, *Dizziness: An Evaluation and Classification* (Springfield, IL: Charles C. Thomas, 1954), p.13.
55 Roland Barthes, 'The Eiffel Tower' (1964), in Susan Sontag (ed.), *A Barthes Reader* (New York, NY: Hill & Wang, 1983), pp 236–50; p.242.
56 Michel de Certeau, *The Practice of Everyday Life*, trans. Steven Rendall (Berkeley, CA: University of California Press, 1984).
57 ibid., p.92.
58 Milan Kundera, *The Unbearable Lightness of Being*, trans. Michael H. Heim (New York, NY: Harper & Row, 1985).
59 ibid., pp 59–60.
60 Jennifer L. Hames, Jessica D. Ribeiro, April R. Smith and Thomas E. Joiner, 'An Urge to Jump Affirms the Urge to Live: An Empirical Examination of the High Place Phenomenon', *Journal of Affective Disorders*, vol.136, no.3, 2012, pp 1114–20.
61 ibid., p.1120.
62 Barbara Ehrenreich, *Fear of Falling: The Inner Life of the Middle Class* (New York, NY: Pantheon Books, 1989), p.11.
63 ibid., p.15.
64 Paul Auster, book endorsement in W.G. Sebald, *Vertigo*, trans. Michael Hulse (London: Harvill Press, 1999), n.p.
65 Mark R. McCulloch, *Understanding W.G. Sebald* (Columbia, SC: University of South Carolina Press, 2003).
66 Sebald, op.cit., p.115.
67 ibid., p.116.
68 John Wylie, 'The Spectral Geographies of W.G. Sebald', *Cultural Geographies*, vol.14, no.2, April 2007, pp 171–88; p.179.

69 ibid., p.173.
70 Amy Butt, 'Vicarious Vertigo: The Emotional Experience of Height in the Science Fiction City', *Emotion, Space and Society*, vol.28, August 2018, pp 114–21.
71 Fredric Jameson, *Archaeologies of the Future: The Desire Called Utopia and Other Science Fictions* (New York, NY: Verso, 2005).

2 DIZZY VISIONS

1 Michel Setboun, *New York Vertigo: Photographs by Michel Setboun* (New York, NY: Abrams, 2008), n.p. [2].
2 Germano Celant, 'Le ragioni di Vertigo', in Germano Celant and Gianfranco Maraniello (eds), *Vertigo: Il secolo di arte off-media dal futurismo al web* (Milan: Skira, 2007), pp 3–15; p.7. Author's translation.
3 Catherine James, *Falling for Gravity: Invisible Forces in Contemporary Art* (Oxford: Peter Lang, 2018).
4 Maria Morris Hambourg and Christopher Phillips (eds), *The New Vision: Photography between the World Wars* (New York, NY: The Metropolitan Museum of Art, 1989).
5 Margarita Tupitsyn, *Aleksandr Rodchenko: The New Moscow* (Munich: Schirmer/Mosel, 1998).
6 Alexander Rodchenko, 'Downright Ignorance or a Mean Trick?', in Christopher Phillips (ed.), *Photography in the Modern Era: European Documents and Critical Writings, 1913–1940* (New York, NY: Metropolitan Museum of Art, 1989), p.246.
7 Peter Galassi, 'Rodchenko and Photography's Revolution', in Magdalena Dabrowski, Leah Dickerman and Peter Galassi (eds), *Aleksandr Rodchenko* (New York, NY: The Museum of Modern Art, 1998), p.120.
8 Anton Giulio Bragaglia, *Fotodinamismo Futurista*, 3rd edn (Rome: Nalato Editore, 1913), p.33. Author's translation.
9 Anton Giulio Bragaglia, 'Excerpts from *Futurist Photodynamism*' (1913), in Phillips (ed.), *Photography in the Modern Era*, pp 287–95; p.294.
10 Lewis Mumford, *Sticks and Stones: A Study of American Architecture and Civilization* (New York, NY: Boni & Liveright, 1924), p.169.
11 ibid., p.175.
12 Christoph Lindner, *Imagining New York City* (Oxford: Oxford University Press, 2015), p.38.
13 Mumford, op.cit., p.174.
14 Max Page, *The Creative Destruction of Manhattan, 1900–1940* (Chicago: The University of Chicago Press, 2001).
15 Thomas Stubblefield, 'The City from Afar: Urbanization and the Aerial View in Alvin Coburn's *The Octopus*', *Journal of Urban History*, vol.41, no.2, 2015, pp 340–53; p.341.
16 Kate Sampsell-Willmann, *Lewis Hine as Social Critic* (Jackson, MS: University of Mississippi, 2009).
17 Susan Meyer, 'In Anxious Celebration: Lewis Hine's Men at Work', *Prospects*, vol.17, 1992, pp 319–52.
18 David Weitzman, *Skywalkers: Mohawk Ironworkers Build the City* (New York, NY: Roaring Brook Press, 2010).
19 ibid., p.104.
20 Margaret Bourke-White, *Portrait of Myself* (New York, NY: Simon & Schuster, 1963), p.78.
21 ibid.
22 Berenice Abbott and Elizabeth McClausland, *Changing New York, Photographs by Berenice Abbott* (New York, NY: E.P. Dutton & Company, 1939), n.p. Caption to figure 28: 'Wall Street, Showing East River'.
23 David E. Nye, *American Technological Sublime* (Cambridge, MA: MIT Press, 1996), p.96.
24 ibid., p.77.
25 ibid., p.97.
26 ibid., p.106.
27 Terri Weissman, *The Realisms of Berenice Abbott: Documentary Photography and Political Action* (Berkeley, CA: University of California Press, 2011).
28 Gabriele Basilico, *Architetture, città, visioni: Riflessioni sulla fotografia*, ed. Andrea Lissoni (Milan: Bruno Mondadori, 2007).
29 Davide Deriu, 'A Dynamic Attitude of the Gaze: Gabriele Basilico's Sense of Vertical Space', *The Journal of Architecture*, vol.24, no.8, 2019, pp 1096–1117.
30 Gabriele Basilico, quoted on the *Verticale* exhibition website (accessed 7 October 2018), http://www.photoandcontemporary.com/event.aspx?ev=1137, author's translation.

31 Gabriele Basilico, *Vertiginous Moscow: Stalin's City Today*, ed. Umberto Zanetti and Alessandro De Magistris (London: Thames & Hudson, 2009).
32 Alessandro De Magistris, 'Axis Mundi: A Vertical Moscow in Stalin's Shadow', in Basilico, *Vertiginous Moscow*, p.7.
33 Katherine Zubovich, *Moscow Monumental: Soviet Skyscrapers and Urban Life in Stalin's Capital* (Princeton, NJ: Princeton University Press, 2020).
34 Karl Schlögel, *Moscow* (London: Reaktion, 2004), p.23.
35 Gabriele Basilico, 'Photography Programme. Lesson Ten: Vertiginous Moscow', *Abitare*, no.496, 2009, p.25.
36 ibid.
37 Elisabeth Essaïan, *Moscou*, special issue of *Archiscopie* (Paris: Cité de l'architecture et du patrimoine, 2009), p.37.
38 Basilico, 'Photography Programme', p.27.
39 Romain Jacquet-Lagreze, *Vertical Horizons* (Hong Kong: Asia One Publishing, 2012).
40 Adam Frampton, Jonathan D. Solomon and Clara Wong, *Cities Without Ground: A Hong Kong Guidebook* (Point Reyes Station, CA: ORO Editions, 2012).
41 *The New Normal* exhibition, UCCA Center for Contemporary Art, Beijing, 2017.
42 Margaret Hillenbrand, 'The Cliffhangers: Suicide Shows and the Aesthetics of Protest in China', *Cultural Politics*, vol.16, no.2, 2020, pp 147–70; p.150.
43 Hito Steyerl, 'In Free Fall: A Thought Experiment on Vertical Perspective', *e-flux*, no.24, April 2011 (accessed 30 January 2022), https://www.e-flux.com/journal/24/67860/in-free-fall-a-thought-experiment-on-vertical-perspective/.
44 Davide Deriu, 'The Art of Vertigo: On Catherine Yass' Architectural Visions', in *Falling Away – Catherine Yass at Ambika P3*, exh.cat., ed. Davide Deriu and Michael Mazière (London: University of Westminster, 2021), pp 3–21.
45 Michael Newman, 'A Fold in Time: Catherine Yass's *Descent*', in Álvaro Rodríguez Fominaya (ed.), *Catherine Yass: Filmografía/Filmography* (Las Palmas: Centro Atlántico de Arte Moderno – CAAM, 2005), pp 9–55; p.23.
46 Gaston Bachelard, *Earth and Reveries of Will: An Essay on the Imagination of Matter* (1948), trans. Kenneth Haltman (Dallas TX: Dallas Institute Publications, 2002), p.263.
47 Álvaro Rodríguez Fominaya (ed.), '*Flight* into Kinetics: A Curator's Notes', in *Catherine Yass: Filmografía/ Filmography*, pp 57–71; p.59.
48 Adrian Forty, *Concrete and Culture: A Material History* (London: Reaktion, 2012).
49 Mark Godfrey, 'A Conversation with Catherine Yass', in Fominaya (ed.), *Catherine Yass: Filmografía/ Filmography*, pp 91–117; p.113.
50 Owen Hatherley, 'The Government of London', *New Left Review*, no.122, March/ April 2020 (accessed 13 April 2022), https://newleftreview.org/issues/ii122/articles/owen-hatherley-the-government-of-london.
51 Ruth Anderwald and Leonhard Grond, 'Dizziness – A Resource?', in Ruth Anderwald, Karoline Feyertag and Leonhard Grond (eds), *Dizziness – A Resource* (Berlin: Sternberg Press, 2019), pp 22–53; p.24.

3 WIRE WALKING IN THE CITY

1 Philippe Petit, *To Reach the Clouds: My High-Wire Walk Between the Twin Towers* (London: Faber & Faber, 2002), p.218.
2 Johan Huizinga, *Homo Ludens: A Study of the Play-Element in Culture* (New York, NY: Roy Publishers, 1950).
3 Roger Caillois, *Man, Play and Games*, trans. Meyer Barash (Urbana and Chicago, IL: University of Illinois Press, 2001), p.23.
4 ibid., p.31.
5 ibid., p.137.
6 Erith Jaffe-Berg, *Commedia dell'Arte and the Mediterranean: Charting Journeys and Mapping 'Others'* (London: Routledge, 2016), p.100.
7 Cristóbal Amunátegui, 'Circles, Circuits, Cycles', *AA Files*, vol.71, 2015, pp 75–89.
8 Jean Starobinski, *Portrait de l'artiste en saltimbanque* (Geneva: Skira, 1970). Author's translations from the Italian edition: *Ritratto dell'artista come saltimbanco* (Torino: Bollati Boringhieri, 1984).

9 Starobinski, *Ritratto*, p.149.

10 Paul Ginisty, *Mémoires d'une danseuse de corde: Madame Saqui, 1786–1866* (Paris: Eugène Fasquelle, 1907), p.90. Author's translation.

11 Percy Bysshe Shelley, 'Mont Blanc: Lines Written in the Vale of Chamouni', in Mary W. Shelley and Percy B. Shelley, *History of a six weeks' tour through a part of France, Switzerland, Germany and Holland: with letters descriptive of a sail round the Lake of Geneva, and of the glaciers of Chamouni* (London: T. Hookham and C. and J. Ollier, 1817), p.177.

12 Immanuel Kant, *Critique of Judgment* (1790), trans. Werner S. Pluhar (Indianapolis, IN and Cambridge, MA: Hackett, 1987), p.115.

13 ibid., p.120.

14 Edmund Burke, *A Philosophical Inquiry into the Origin of Our Ideas of the Sublime and Beautiful* (London: R. and J. Dodsley, 1757), pp 13–14.

15 Garrett Soden, *Falling: How Our Greatest Fear Became Our Greatest Thrill* (New York, NY: W.W. Norton & Co, 2003), p. 74.

16 Barbara Penner, 'Niagara: It Has It All', *Places Journal* (online), September 2009, https://doi.org/10.22269/090924.

17 George Linnaeus Banks, *Blondin: His Life and Performances* (London: Routledge, Warne and Routledge, 1862), p.71.

18 Charles Mackay (ed.), 'Sensation Spectacles', in *The London Review and weekly journal of politics, literature, art, and society*, vol.2, no.48, 1 June 1861, p.632.

19 Steven Miller, 'The Coup: Behind the Scenes of the Act with Philippe Petit', *Differences: A Journal of Feminist Cultural Studies*, vol.28, no.2, 2017, pp 116–33; p.119.

20 Friedrich Nietzsche, *Thus Spoke Zarathustra: A Book for All and None* (1883), trans. Adrian Del Caro (Cambridge: Cambridge University Press, 2006), p.4.

21 Steven Connor, 'Man Is a Rope', in *Catherine Yass: High Wire* (London: Artangel, 2008), n.p.

22 Iza de Cérigny, 'La Spelterini', *L'Univers illustré*, no.967, 4 October 1873, p. 638.

23 Soden, op.cit., p.133.

24 Yuliya Komska, 'On the Wire above the Ruins: Funambulism in Postwar Germany', *Cabinet*, 4 March 2021 (accessed 16 May 2022), https://www.cabinetmagazine.org/kiosk/komska_yuliya_4_march_2021.php.

25 Soden, op.cit., p.137.

26 ibid., p.133.

27 Oli Mould, *Urban Subversion and the Creative City* (Abingdon: Routledge, 2015), p.xii.

28 Susan Stewart, *On Longing: Narratives of the Miniature, the Gigantic, the Souvenir, the Collection* (Durham, NC: Duke University Press, 1984).

29 See, for instance, Gwyneth Shanks, 'The Politico-Aesthetics of Groundlessness and Philippe Petit's High-Wire Walk', *Performance Matters*, vol.2, no.2, 2016, pp 43–62.

30 Minoru Yamasaki, *A Life in Architecture* (New York and Tokyo: Weatherhill, 1979), p.112.

31 Kurt Wurmli, 'Theater in the Sky: Philippe Petit's Unique Art of Theatrical Highwire Performance', *Journal of American Culture*, vol.20, no.1, 1997, pp 117–23.

32 Philippe Petit, *On the High Wire* (New York, NY: Random House, 1985).

33 Paul Auster, 'On the High Wire', in *Collected Prose* (London: Faber & Faber, 2003), p.302.

34 The story was also adapted by American artist Mordicai Gerstein to a children's book, *The Man Who Walked Between the Towers* (New York, NY: Roaring Brook, 2003), which was later turned into an animated film.

35 Petit, *To Reach the Clouds*.

36 This idea is also reflected in subsequent books written by Petit, such as *L'Art du Pickpocket* (Arles: Actes Sud, 2006), and *Creativity: The Perfect Crime* (New York, NY: Riverhead Books, 2014).

37 Philippe Petit, 'The Laura Flanders Show', *GritTV*, 14 December 2010.

38 Georg Simmel, 'Bridge and Door' (1909), *Theory, Culture & Society*, vol.11, no.1, 1994, pp 5–10; p.6.

39 ibid.

40 Petit, *To Reach the Clouds*, p. 67.

41 ibid.

42 ibid., p.17.

43 ibid., p.18.

44 ibid., p.19.

45 ibid., pp 175–8.

46 ibid., p.179 (italics in original).

47 Colum McCann, *Let the Great World Spin* (London: Bloomsbury, 2009), p.164.

48 Miller, op.cit., p.128.
49 Jim LeBlanc, 'The Acrophobe and the Funambulist: Existential and Cinematic Perspectives on the Phenomenology of Extreme Vertical Space', *Emotion, Space and Society*, vol.4, no.1, February 2011, pp 1–7.
50 Thomas Brandt, *Vertigo: Its Multisensory Syndromes* (London: Springer, 1991), p.245.
51 Petit, *On the High Wire*, p.109.
52 Caillois, op.cit., p.138.
53 Danielle Quinodoz, *Emotional Vertigo: Between Anxiety and Pleasure*, trans. Arnold Pomerans (London: Routledge, 1997), p.171.
54 Auster, op.cit., p.301.
55 For a critique of *Man on Wire* as a manifestation of American 'victory culture', see Chris Vanderwees, 'A Tightrope at the Twin Towers', in Robert Fanuzzi and Michael Wolfe (eds), *Recovering 9/11 in New York* (Newcastle: Cambridge Scholars, 2014), pp 228–47.
56 Chloe Johnston, 'On Not Falling', *Performance Research: A Journal of the Performing Arts*, vol.18, no.4, 2013, pp 30–35; p.34.
57 See Gwyneth Shanks, 'The Politico-Aesthetics of Groundlessness and Philippe Petit's High-Wire Walk', *Performance Matters*, no.2, 2016, pp 43–62.
58 Richard Brody, '"The Walk" Falls Short of Artistry', *The New Yorker*, 30 September 2015, https://www.newyorker.com/culture/richard-brody/the-walk-falls-short-of-artistry.
59 Douglas Kellner, *Media Spectacle* (London: Routledge, 2003).
60 Igor Marjanović and Katerina Rüedi, *Bertrand Goldberg's Urban Vision* (New York, NY: Princeton Architectural Press, 2010), pp 146–8.
61 Byung-Chul Han, *The Transparent Society*, trans. Erik Butler (Stanford, CA: Stanford Briefs, 2015).
62 Miller, op.cit., p.121.
63 Catherine James, *Falling for Gravity: Invisible Forces in Contemporary Art* (Oxford: Peter Lang, 2018), p.27.
64 Connor, op.cit., n.p.

4 URBAN ASCENTS

1 Michel Serres, *Variations on the Body*, trans. Randolph Burks (Minneapolis, MN: Univocal Publishing, 2011), p.8.
2 Jim Ring, *How the English Made the Alps* (London: Faber & Faber, 2000).
3 Ronald Clark, *The Victorian Mountaineers* (London: B.T. Batsford, 1953), p.15.
4 Danielle Quinodoz, *Emotional Vertigo: Between Anxiety and Pleasure* (London: Routledge, 1997), pp 152 ff.
5 Geoffrey Winthrop Young, *The Roof-Climber's Guide to Trinity. Containing a practical description of all routes* (Cambridge: W.P. Spalding, 1899), n.p.
6 Geoffrey Winthrop Young, *Wall and Roof Climbing* (Eton: Spottiswoode & Co., 1905), p.53.
7 Whipplesnaith [Noël H. Symington], *The Night Climbers of Cambridge* (1937) (Cambridge: Oleander Press, 2007).
8 ibid., p.10.
9 ibid., p.181.
10 Johan Huizinga, *Homo Ludens: A Study of the Play-Element in Culture* (1938) (New York, NY: Roy Publishers, 1950), p.10.
11 ibid., p.13.
12 Jacob Smith, *The Thrill Makers: Celebrity, Masculinity and Stunt Performance* (Berkeley, CA: University of California Press, 2012), p.21.
13 Steven Jacobs, 'Slapstick Homes: Architecture in Slapstick Cinema and the *Avant-Garde*', *The Journal of Architecture*, vol.23, no.2, 2018, pp 225–48.
14 George H. Douglas, *Skyscrapers: A Social History of the Very Tall Building in America* (Jefferson, NC and London: McFarland & Co., 1996).
15 Jacobs, op.cit., p.227.
16 *King Kong* (dir. Merian C. Cooper and Ernest B. Schoedsack, USA, 1933).
17 Maria Manuel Lisboa, *The End of the World: Apocalypse and its Aftermath in Western Culture* (Cambridge: Open Book Publishers, 2011).
18 Douglas, op.cit., pp 214 ff.
19 *A Spire: The Story of the First Climb of Sydney Tower* (dir. Chris Hilton and Glenn Singleman, Australia, 1988).
20 Meaghan Morris, 'Great Moments in Social Climbing: King Kong and the Human Fly', in Beatriz Colomina (ed.), *Sexuality and Space* (New York, NY: Princeton Architectural Press, 1992), pp 1–51; p.31.
21 Quinodoz, op.cit., pp 152 ff.
22 ibid., p.171.

23 Serres, op.cit., p.129.
24 ibid., p.132.
25 Alain Robert, *With Bare Hands: The Story of the Human Spider*, 2nd edn (Dunboyne: Maverick House, 2008).
26 ibid., p.57. See also Lauren Collins, 'The Vertical Tourist: Alain Robert's Obsession with Skyscrapers', *The New Yorker*, 13 April 2009, https://www.newyorker.com/magazine/2009/04/20/the-vertical-tourist.
27 Gérard Hoël, 'Foreword', *With Bare Hands*, p.8.
28 Robert, op.cit., p.30.
29 Jason Bainbridge, '"I am New York" – Spider-Man, New York City, and the Marvel Universe', in Jörn Ahrens and Arno Meteling (eds), *Comics and the City: Urban Space in Print, Picture and Sequence* (London: Bloomsbury, 2010), pp 163–79.
30 Bernard Andrieu, *Donner le vertige: Les arts immersifs* (Montreal: Liber, 2014).
31 ibid., p.41.
32 Iain Borden, *Skateboarding, Space and the City: Architecture and the Body* (Oxford: Berg, 2001), p.1.
33 Quentin Stevens, *The Ludic City: Exploring the Potential of Public Spaces* (London: Routledge, 2007), p.144.
34 ibid., p.41.
35 Bradley L. Garrett, *Explore Everything: Place-Hacking the City* (London: Verso, 2013).
36 ibid., p.89.
37 Katherine Rundell, 'Diary: Night Climbing', *London Review of Books* (online), vol.37, no.8, 23 April 2015, https://www.lrb.co.uk/the-paper/v37/n08/katherine-rundell/diary.
38 Ashlee Humphreys, *Social Media: Enduring Principles* (Oxford: Oxford University Press, 2016). See also Bernie Hogan, 'The Presentation of Self in the Age of Social Media: Distinguishing Performances and Exhibitions Online', *Bulletin of Science, Technology & Society*, vol.30, no.6, 2010, pp 377–86.
39 Davide Deriu, '"Don't Look Down!" – A Short History of Rooftopping Photography', *The Journal of Architecture*, vol.21, no.7, 2016, pp 1033–61.
40 Philip Nobel, 'Introduction', in *The Future of the Skyscraper* (New York, NY: Metropolis Books, 2015), p.10.
41 Bradley L. Garrett, Alexander Moss and Scott Cadman, *London Rising: Illicit Photos from the City's Heights* (Munich and London: Prestel Verlag, 2016).
42 Bradley L. Garrett, 'Corporate Heights', in *London Rising*, pp 119–75; p.123.
43 ibid.
44 Bradley L. Garrett and Alexander Moss, 'Introduction', in *London Rising*, p.9.
45 Andrea Mubi Brighenti and Andrea Pavoni, 'Climbing the City: Inhabiting Verticality Outside of Comfort Bubbles', *Journal of Urbanism: International Research on Placemaking and Urban Sustainability*, vol.11, no.1, 2017, pp 63–80; p.74.

5 THRILLS OF GRAVITY

1 Danielle Quinodoz, *Emotional Vertigo: Between Anxiety and Pleasure* (London: Routledge, 1997), p.101.
2 Michel Serres, *Variations on the Body*, trans. Randolph Burks (Minneapolis, MN: Univocal Publishing, 2011), p.118.
3 Rebekka Ladewig, *Schwindel: Eine Epistemologie der Orientierung* (Tübingen: Mohr Siebeck, 2016).
4 Robert Cartmell, *The Incredible Scream Machine: A History of the Roller Coaster* (Fairview Park, OH: Amusement Park Books, 1987).
5 Garrett Soden, *Falling: How Our Greatest Fear Became Our Greatest Thrill* (New York, NY: W.W. Norton & Co, 2003), p.37.
6 Dean MacCannell, *The Tourist: A New Theory of the Leisure Class* (1976) (Berkeley, CA: University of California Press, 1999).
7 Josephine Kane, *The Architecture of Pleasure: British Amusement Parks 1900–1939* (Farnham: Ashgate, 2013).
8 ibid., pp 19–20.
9 ibid., pp 28–32.
10 Benjamin C. Truman, *History of the World's Fair, Being a Complete and Authentic Description of the Columbian Exposition* (New York, NY: E. B. Treat, 1893), p.619.
11 Kane, op.cit.
12 Georg Simmel, 'The Metropolis and Mental Life' (1903), in G. Bridge and S. Watson (eds), *The*

Blackwell City Reader (Oxford: Wiley-Blackwell, 2002), pp 11–19; p.12.

13 Marshall Berman, *All That Is Solid Melts Into Air: The Experience of Modernity* (London and New York, NY: Verso, 1983), p.16.

14 Anthony Sutcliffe, *Metropolis: 1890–1940* (London: Mansell, 1984).

15 Steven Jacobs, Eva Hielscher and Anthony Kinik (eds), *The City Symphony Phenomenon: Cinema, Art, and Urban Modernity Between the Wars* (London: Routledge, 2019).

16 Sabine Hake, *Topographies of Class: Modern Architecture and Mass Society in Weimar Berlin* (Ann Arbor, MI: The University of Michigan Press, 2008), p.250.

17 Lynd Ward quoted in David A. Beronä, 'Introduction to the Dover Edition', in Lynd Ward, *Vertigo: A Novel in Woodcuts* (1937) (Mineola, NY: Dover Publications, 2009), pp v–ix; p.vi.

18 Adnan Morshed, 'The Aesthetics of Ascension in Norman Bel Geddes's Futurama', *Journal of the Society of Architectural Historians*, vol.63, no.1, 2004, pp 74–99.

19 Adnan Morshed, *Impossible Heights: Skyscrapers, Flight, and the Master Builder* (Minneapolis, MN: University of Minnesota Press, 2015), pp 5–6.

20 ibid., p.154.

21 John B. Manbeck, *Brooklyn: Historically Speaking* (Charleston, SC: The History Press, 2008).

22 Johan Huizinga, *Homo Ludens: A Study of the Play-Element in Culture* (New York, NY: Roy Publishers, 1950), p.1.

23 Roger Caillois, *Man, Play and Games*, trans. Meyer Barash (Urbana and Chicago, IL: University of Illinois Press, 2001), p.23.

24 ibid., p.25.

25 ibid., p.24.

26 Jacques Lacan, *The Seminar of Jacques Lacan, Book X: Anxiety, 1962–1963*, ed. Jacques-Alain Miller, trans. Adrian Price (Cambridge: Polity, 2014).

27 Michael Balint, *Thrills and Regressions* (London: Maresfield Library, 1959), p.19.

28 ibid., p.23.

29 ibid.

30 ibid., p.31.

31 Donald W. Winnicott, 'Ego Distortion in Terms of True and False Self' (1960), in *The Maturational Processes and the Facilitating Environment* (Madison, CT: International Universities Press, 1987), pp 140–52.

32 Quinodoz, op.cit.

33 John R. Salassa and David A. Zapala, 'Love and Fear of Heights: The Pathophysiology and Psychology of Height Imbalance', *Wilderness & Environmental Medicine*, vol.20, no.4, 2009, pp 378–82.

34 ibid.

35 Zygmunt Bauman, 'From Pilgrim to Tourist, or a Short History of Identity', in Paul du Gay and Stuart Hall (eds), *Questions of Cultural Identity* (London: SAGE, 1996), pp 18–36; p.32.

36 Soden, op.cit., 1–5.

37 David Attenborough, *Quest in Paradise* (London: Lutterworth Press, 1960). See also David F. Attenborough, 'The Land-diving Ceremony in Pentecost, New Hebrides', *Philosophical Transactions of the Royal Society B*, vol.251, no.772, 1966, pp 503–4.

38 Soden, op.cit., pp 1–5.

39 Joseph Pine II and James H. Gilmore, *The Experience Economy: Work Is Theatre & Every Business a Stage* (Boston, MA: Harvard Business School Press, 1999), p.35.

40 ibid., p.31.

41 ibid., p.59.

42 MacCannell, op.cit., p.21.

43 Bauman, 'From Pilgrim to Tourist', p.29.

44 William Davies, *The Happiness Industry: How the Government and Big Business Sold Us Well-Being* (London: Verso, 2015).

45 Zygmunt Bauman, *Liquid Modernity* (Cambridge: Polity Press, 2000), p.92.

46 ibid., p.91.

47 Byung-Chul Han, *The Agony of Eros*, trans. Erik Butler (Cambridge, MA: MIT Press, 2017).

48 Zygmunt Bauman, *Consuming Life* (Cambridge: Polity Press, 2007), p.78.

49 Mark Windsor, 'Art of Interaction: A Theoretical Examination of Carsten Höller's Test Site', *Tate Papers*, no.15, Spring 2011 (accessed 3 April 2022), https://www.tate.org.uk/research/tate-papers/15/art-of-interaction-a-theoretical-examination-of-carsten-holler-test-site.

50 Dorothea von Hantelmann, 'I', in Jessica Morgan (ed.), *Carsten Höller: Test Site* (London: Tate, 2006), pp 19–38; pp 21–22.
51 General Public Agency, 'Slides in the Public Realm', in Morgan (ed.), op.cit., pp [illegible].
52 Carsten Höller interviewed by Derek Blasberg in 'Carsten Höller: A Slide in London', *Gagosian Quarterly*, 8 July 2016 (accessed 3 April 2022), https://gagosian.com/quarterly/2016/07/08/carsten-hollers-arcelormittal-orbit-slide/.
53 Caillois, op.cit., p.44.
54 Cristóbal Amunátegui, 'Circles, Circuits, Cycles', *AA Files*, vol.71, 2015, pp 75–89.
55 Elizabeth Wilhide, *The Millennium Dome* (London: Harper Collins, 1999).
56 Paul Verhaege, *What About Me? The Struggle for Identity in a Market-Based Society* (London: Scribe Publications, 2014), p.249.
57 Brian Lonsway, *Making Leisure Work: Architecture and the Experience Economy* (London: Routledge, 2009), p.19.
58 Andrew Smith, 'Vertical City Tourism: Heightened Aesthetic and Kinaesthetic Experiences', in Andrew Smith and Anne Graham (eds), *Destination London: The Expansion of the Visitor Economy* (London: University of Westminster Press, 2019).
59 Zygmunt Bauman, *Liquid Life* (Cambridge: Polity Press, 2005), p.91.
60 Johan Huizinga, *In the Shadow of Tomorrow* (New York, NY: W.W. Norton & Company, 1936), p.177.

6 LOSING THE GROUND

1 Jacques Herzog, 'Foreword', in Rowan Moore (ed.), *Vertigo: The Strange New World of the Contemporary City* (London: Lawrence King Publishing, 1999), pp 6–7; p.6.
2 Stephen Eskilson, *The Age of Glass: A Cultural History of Glass in Modern and Contemporary Architecture* (London: Bloomsbury, 2018), p.89.
3 Adrian Forty, *Words and Buildings: A Vocabulary of Modern Architecture* (London: Thames & Hudson, 2000), p.286.
4 ibid.
5 Annette Fierro, *The Glass State: The Technology of the Spectacle, Paris, 1981–1998* (Cambridge, MA: MIT Press, 2003), pp viii–ix.
6 Reyner Banham, *Megastructure: Urban Futures of the Recent Past* (London: Thames & Hudson, 1976), p.207.
7 Selim O. Khan-Magomedov, *Georgii Krutikov: The Flying City and Beyond*, trans. Christina Lodder (Barcelona: Tenov Books, 2015).
8 Paul Dobraszczyk, *Future Cities: Architecture and the Imagination* (London: Reaktion, 2019).
9 Sigfried Giedion, *Building in France, Building in Iron, Building in Ferroconcrete* (1928), trans. J. Duncan Berry (Santa Monica, CA: Getty Centre for the History of Art and the Humanities, 1995), p.142.
10 ibid., p.169.
11 Hilde Heynen, *Architecture and Modernity: A Critique* (Cambridge, MA: MIT Press, 1999).
12 Giedion, op.cit., p.143.
13 ibid., p.102.
14 Le Corbusier, *The City of Tomorrow and Its Planning*, trans. Frederick Etchells (Cambridge, MA: MIT Press, 1971), p.186. Originally published in 1925 as *Urbanisme*.
15 Herbert Bayer, Walter Gropius and Ise Gropius (eds), *Bauhaus, 1919–1928* (New York: The Museum of Modern Art, 1938). See also Jeannine Fiedler, *Photography at the Bauhaus* (Cambridge, MA: MIT Press, 1990).
16 Giedion, op.cit., p.147.
17 Sigfried Giedion, *Space, Time and Architecture: The Growth of a New Tradition* (Cambridge, MA: Harvard University Press, 1941). Jorge Otero-Pailos, *Architecture's Historical Turn: Phenomenology and the Rise of the Postmodern* (Minneapolis, MN: University of Minnesota Press, 2010).
18 Sigfried Giedion, 'The Need for a New Monumentality', in Paul Zucker (ed.), *New Architecture and City Planning* (New York, NY: Philosophical Library, 1944), pp 549–68; pp 559–61.
19 Douglas Tallack, 'Siegfried Giedion, Modernism and American Material Culture', *Journal of American Studies*, vol.28, no.2, 1994, pp 149–67.
20 Sigfried Giedion, Fernand Léger and Josep Lluís Sert, 'Nine Points on Monumentality' (1943), in

Sigfried Giedion, *Architecture, You and Me: The Diary of a Development* (Cambridge, MA: Harvard University Press, 1958), pp 48–51; p.50.

21 Sigfried Giedion, *Mechanization Takes Command: A Contribution to Anonymous History* (New York, NY: Oxford University Press, 1948), p.720.

22 Adrian Forty, 'Festival Politics', in Mary Banham and Bevis Hillier (eds), *A Tonic to the Nation: The Festival of Britain 1951* (London: Thames & Hudson, 1976), pp 26–38.

23 Rika Devos and Mil De Kooning (eds), *L'architecture moderne à l'Expo 58* (Antwerp: Dexia/Fonds Mercator, 2006).

24 João Cunha Borges and Teresa Marat-Mendes, 'Walking on Streets-in-the-Sky: Structures for Democratic Cities', *Journal of Aesthetics & Culture*, vol.11, no.1, 2019, n.p.

25 Ian McCallum, 'Syntax: The Contribution of the Curtain Wall to a New Vernacular', *Architectural Review*, vol.121, no.724, 1957, pp 299–336. See also David Yeomans, 'The Pre-history of the Curtain Wall', *Construction History*, vol.14, 1998, pp 59–82.

26 Phyllis Lambert, *Building Seagram* (New Haven, CT and London: Yale University Press, 2013).

27 Kiel Moe, *Unless: The Seagram Building Construction Ecology* (Barcelona: Actar, 2021).

28 Phyllis Lambert, email correspondence with the author, 13 February 2020.

29 ibid.

30 Banham, op.cit., p.207.

31 Rodrigo Pérez de Arce, *City of Play: An Architectural and Urban History of Recreation and Leisure* (London: Bloomsbury, 2018), p.220.

32 Simon Sadler, *The Situationist City* (Cambridge, MA: MIT Press, 1998).

33 Pérez de Arce, op.cit., p.227.

34 Pamela Johnston (ed.), *The Function of the Oblique: The Architecture of Claude Parent and Paul Virilio 1963–1969* (London: Architectural Association, 1996).

35 Claude Parent, *Vivre à l'oblique* (1970) (Paris: Nouvelles editions Jean-Michel Place, 2012), p.5. This and following quotes translated by the author.

36 ibid., p.33.

37 Fredric Jameson, 'The Cultural Logic of Late Capitalism', *New Left Review*, no.146, 1984, pp 53–92; p.60.

38 ibid., p.80.

39 ibid., p.62.

40 Fredric Jameson, *Postmodernism, or The Cultural Logic of Late Capitalism* (Durham, NC: Duke University Press, 1991), p.117.

41 ibid., p.43.

42 ibid.

43 ibid., p.44.

44 ibid.

45 Charles Rice, *Interior Urbanism: Architecture, John Portman and Downtown America* (London: Bloomsbury, 2016), p.8.

46 Rodney R. Adler, *Vertical Transportation for Buildings* (New York, NY: Elsevier, 1970), p.184.

47 Peter A. Hall, 'Designing Non-Space: The Evolution of the Elevator Interior', in Alisa Goetz (ed.), *Up, Down, Across: Elevators, Escalators, and Moving Sidewalks* (London and New York, NY: Merrell, 2003), pp 59–77; p.73.

48 Adler, op.cit., p.184.

49 Tom Dyckhoff, *The Age of Spectacle: Adventures in Architecture and the 21st-Century City* (New York, NY: Random House, 2017), p.5.

50 Rowan Moore, 'Introduction', *Vertigo: The Strange New World of the Contemporary City* (London: Lawrence King, 1999), pp 8–59; p.10.

51 ibid.

52 Guy Debord, *Society of the Spectacle* (1967), trans. Fredy Perlman and John Supak (Detroit, MI: Black & Red, 1983), p.10.

53 Moore, op.cit., p.12.

54 Herzog, op.cit., p.6.

55 Mark Dorrian, 'The Aerial Image: Vertigo, Transparency and Miniaturisation', *Parallax*, vol.15, no.4, 2009, pp 83–93; p.86.

56 ibid., p.90.

57 ibid., p.91.

58 Bruno Latour, *Down to Earth: Politics in the New Climatic Regime* (Cambridge: Polity Press, 2018), p.8.

59 Shiloh Krupar and Stefan Al, 'Notes on the Society of the Brand', in C. Greig Crysler, Stephen Cairns and Hilde Heynen (eds), *The SAGE Handbook of Architectural Theory* (London: SAGE, 2012), pp 247–63.

60 Brian Lonsway, *Making Leisure Work: Architecture and the Experience Economy* (London: Routledge, 2009), p.1.

61 Anna Klingmann, *Brandscapes: Architecture in the Experience Economy* (Cambridge, MA: MIT Press, 2007).

62 Jan Specht, *Architectural Tourism: Building for Urban Travel Destinations* (New York, NY: Springer, 2014), p.96.

63 Benjamin Lee and Edward LiPuma, 'Cultures of Circulation: The Imaginations of Modernity', *Public Culture*, vol.14, no.1, 2002, pp 191–213.

64 Joan Ockman, 'Culture of Circulation', lecture delivered at the *Neoliberalism and Neobaroque* symposium, Architectural Association, London, 25 November 2016.

65 Manuel Castells, 'Space of Places, Space of Flows', in William Braham and Jonathan Hale (eds), *Rethinking Technology: A Reader in Architectural Theory* (London: Routledge, 2007), pp 440–56; p.448.

66 *Gehry's Vertigo* (dir. Ila Bêka and Louise Lemoine, Spain, 2013).

67 Ila Bêka and Louise Lemoine, *Gehry's Vertigo* (BêkaPartners Publishers, 2013), p.62.

68 Ila Bêka, 'Behind the Image', interview with Marie Bruneau and Bertrand Genier, in Bêka and Lemoine, op.cit., p.xxii.

7 ARCHITECTURES OF VERTIGO

1 Roald Dahl, *Charlie and the Glass Elevator* (New York, NY: Alfred A. Knopf, 1972), p.7.

2 Lee E. Gray, *From Ascending Rooms to Express Elevators: A History of the Passenger Elevator in the 19th Century* (Mobile, AL: Elevator World, 2002).

3 Le Corbusier, *The Radiant City: Elements of a Doctrine of Urbanism to be Used as the Basis of Our Machine-Age Civilization* (1935), trans. Derek Coltman, Pamela Knight and Eleanor Levieux (London: Faber & Faber, 1967), p.38.

4 Clay Lancaster, 'The Philadelphia Centennial Towers', *Journal of the Society of Architectural Historians*, vol.19, no.1, March 1960, pp 11–15.

5 Émile Augier, *Souvenir de mon ascension à la Tour Eiffel* (Paris: L. Warnier, 1889), p.37. Author's translation.

6 Eugène-Melchior de Vogüé, *Remarques sur l'Exposition du centenaire* (Paris: E. Plon, Norrit et Cie., 1889), p.26.

7 Meir Wigoder, 'The "Solar Eye" of Vision: Emergence of the Skyscraper-Viewer in the Discourse on Heights in New York City, 1890–1920', *Journal of the Society of Architectural Historians*, vol.61, no.2, June 2002, pp 152–69; p.159.

8 Catherine James, 'Vertigo: Redeeming the Fall', *Performance Research: A Journal of the Performing Arts*, vol.18, no.4, 2013, pp 91–7.

9 George H. Douglas, *Skyscrapers: A Social History of the Very Tall Building in America* (Jefferson, NC and London: McFarland & Co., 1996), pp 169–74.

10 Minoru Yamasaki, *A Life in Architecture* (New York, NY and Tokyo: Weatherhill, 1979), p.117.

11 James Glanz and Eric Lipton, *City in the Sky: The Rise and Fall of the World Trade Center* (New York, NY: Times Books/Henry Holt & Company, 2003), p.109. See also: Dale Allen Gyure, *Minoru Yamasaki: Humanist Architecture for a Modernist World* (New Haven, CT: Yale University Press, 2018), p.174.

12 Yamasaki, op.cit., p.117.

13 *All the Vermeers in New York* (dir. Jon Jost, USA, 1990).

14 Kathleen M. Kirby, *Indifferent Boundaries: Spatial Concepts of Human Subjectivity* (New York, NY and London: The Guilford Press, 1996), p.96. Ellipsis in original.

15 Lucy Yardley, *Vertigo and Dizziness* (London: Routledge, 1994), pp 8–9.

16 Kirby, op.cit., pp 98–99.

17 ibid., p.101.

18 B. Alexandra Szerlip, *The Man Who Designed the Future: Norman Bel Geddes and the Invention of Twentieth-Century America* (New York, NY: Melville House, 2017).

19 Gavin J. Andrews, 'Spaces of Dizziness and Dread: Navigating Acrophobia', *Geografiska Annaler: Series B, Human Geography*, vol.89, 2007, pp 307–17.

20 Doreen Huppert, Eva Grill and Thomas Brandt, 'Down on Heights? One in Three has Visual Height Intolerance', *Journal of Neurology*, vol.260, no.2, February 2013, p.597.

21 ibid. See also Thomas Brandt and Doreen Huppert, 'Fear of Heights and Visual Height Intolerance', *Current Opinion in Neurology*, vol.27, no.1, 2014, pp 111–17.

22 Botond Bognar, *Hiroshi Hara: The Floating World of his Architecture* (Hoboken, NJ: John Wiley & Sons, 2001).
23 ibid., p.120.
24 Steven A. Mansbach, 'An Earthwork of Surprise: The 18th-Century Ha-Ha', *Art Journal*, vol.42, no.3, Autumn, 1982, pp 217–21.
25 Jason Pomeroy, *The Skycourt and Skygarden: Greening the Urban Habitat* (London: Routledge, 2013).
26 Yuri Hadi, Tim Heath and Philip Oldfield, 'Gardens in the Sky: Emotional Experiences in the Communal Spaces at Height in the Pinnacle@Duxton, Singapore', *Emotion, Space and Society*, vol.28, August 2018, pp 104–13.
27 Davide Deriu, 'Skywalking in the City: Glass Platforms and the Architecture of Vertigo', *Emotions, Space and Society*, vol.28, August 2018, pp 94–103.
28 Jos Gamble, *Shanghai in Transition: Changing Perspectives and Social Contours of a Chinese Metropolis* (London: Routledge, 2003).
29 Li Shiqiao, *Understanding the Chinese City* (London: SAGE Publications, 2014), p.92.
30 Nicole Porter, *Landscape and Branding: The Promotion and Production of Place* (London: Routledge, 2015), p.207.
31 Comments to Marcus Fairs, 'Kew Tree Top Walkway by Marks Barfield Architects', *Dezeen*, 27 May 2008 (accessed 8 April 2022), https://www.dezeen.com/2008/05/27/kew-tree-top-walkway-by-marks-barfield-architects/.
32 ibid.
33 Michael Gresty, 'Spatial Disorientation in Architecture', unpublished paper delivered to the *Vertigo in the City* symposium, University of Westminster, London, 29 May 2015.
34 Bernard Tschumi, *Architecture and Disjunction* (Cambridge, MA: MIT Press, 1996), p.22.
35 Philippe Trétiack, 'Our Project Takes the Building into Unexplored Territory' (interview with Alain Moatti), *L'architecture d'aujourd'hui*, special issue, AA Projects: Tour Eiffel, 2014, pp 18–23.
36 Alain Moatti, interviewed in *L'experience du vide* (dir. Ila Bêka and Louise Lemoine, France, DVD, 2014).
37 Peter Adey, *Levitation: The Science, Myth and Magic of Suspension* (London: Reaktion, 2017).
38 Paul Auster, *Mr Vertigo* (London: Faber & Faber, 1994).
39 Dennis R. Judd, 'Constructing the Tourist Bubble', in Dennis R. Judd and Susan S. Fainstein (eds), *The Tourist City* (New Haven, CT: Yale University Press, 1999), pp 35–53.
40 Eleanor J. Gibson and Richard D. Walk, 'The "Visual Cliff"', *Scientific American*, vol.202, no.4, 1960, pp 64–71; p.65.
41 'Edge: Into the Sky', official website (accessed 4 March 2021), https://www.edgenyc.com.
42 Joseph Pine II and James H. Gilmore, *The Experience Economy: Work is Theatre & Every Business a Stage* (Boston, MA: Harvard Business School Press, 1999), p.59.
43 Jonathan Hilburg, 'Hudson Yards and its *Vessel* Open to the Public', *The Architect's Newspaper*, 15 March 2019 (accessed 4 March 2021), https://www.archpaper.com/2019/03/hudson-yards-vessel-open/.
44 Henriette Steiner and Kristin Veel, *Tower to Tower: Gigantism in Architecture and Digital Culture* (Cambridge, MA: MIT Press, 2020), pp 107–8.
45 Roland Barthes, 'The Eiffel Tower' (1964), in Susan Sontag (ed.), *A Barthes Reader* (New York, NY: Hill & Wang, 1983), p.250.
46 Douglas Spencer, *The Architecture of Neoliberalism: How Contemporary Architecture Became an Instrument of Control and Compliance* (London: Bloomsbury, 2016), p.1.

EPILOGUE

1 Zygmunt Bauman, *Liquid Life* (Cambridge: Polity Press, 2005), p.24.
2 Jeroen de Kloet and Lena Scheen, 'Pudong: The *Shanzhai* Global City', *European Journal of Cultural Studies*, vol.16, no.6, 2013, pp 692–709.
3 Massimo Recalcati, *Ritratti del desiderio* (Milan: Raffaello Cortina, 2012), p.27. Author's translation.

SELECTED BIBLIOGRAPHY

Abbott, Berenice and McClausland, Elizabeth, *Changing New York, Photographs by Berenice Abbott*, E.P. Dutton & Company, New York, NY, 1939

Adey, Peter, *Levitation: The Science, Myth and Magic of Suspension*, Reaktion, London, 2017

Anderwald, Ruth, Feyertag, Karoline, and Grond, Leonhard (eds), *Dizziness – A Resource*, Sternberg Press, Berlin, 2019

Andrieu, Bernard, *Donner le vertige: Les arts immersifs*, Liber, Montreal, 2014

Attenborough, David, *Quest in Paradise*, Lutterworth Press, London, 1960

Auster, Paul, *Mr Vertigo*, Faber & Faber, London, 1994

Bachelard, Gaston, *Earth and Reveries of Will: An Essay on the Imagination of Matter* (1948), trans. Kenneth Haltman, Dallas Institute Publications, Dallas, TX, 2002

Balint, Michael, *Thrills and Regressions*, Maresfield Library, London, 1959

Banham, Reyner, *Megastructure: Urban Futures of the Recent Past*, Thames & Hudson, London, 1976

Basilico, Gabriele, *Vertiginous Moscow: Stalin's City Today*, ed. Umberto Zanetti and Alessandro De Magistris, Thames & Hudson, London, 2009

Bauman, Zygmunt, *Liquid Modernity*, Polity Press, Cambridge, 2000

Bauman, Zygmunt, *Liquid Life*, Polity Press, Cambridge, 2005

Berman, Marshall, *All That Is Solid Melts Into Air: The Experience of Modernity*, Verso, London and New York, NY, 1983

Borden, Iain, *Skateboarding, Space and the City: Architecture and the Body*, Berg, Oxford, 2001

Brandt, Thomas, *Vertigo: Its Multisensory Syndromes*, Springer, London, 1991

Caillois, Roger, *Man, Play and Games* (1958), trans. Meyer Barash, University of Illinois Press, Urbana and Chicago, IL, 2001

Celant, Germano and Maraniello, Gianfranco (eds), *Vertigo: Il secolo di arte off-media dal futurismo al web*, Skira, Milan, 2007

Çelik Alexander, Zeynep, *Kinaesthetic Knowing: Aesthetics, Epistemology, Modern Design*, Chicago University Press, Chicago, IL, 2017

Certeau, Michel de, *The Practice of Everyday Life*, trans. Steven Rendall, University of California Press, Berkeley, CA, 1984

Crysler, C. Greig, Cairns, Stephen and Heynen, Hilde (eds), *The SAGE Handbook of Architectural Theory*, SAGE, London, 2012

Darwin, Erasmus, *Zoonomia; or, the Laws of Organic Life* (1794), AMS Press, New York, NY, 1974

Davidson, Joyce D., *Phobic Geographies: The Phenomenology and Spatiality of Identity*, Ashgate, Aldershot, 2003

Debord, Guy, *The Society of the Spectacle* (1967), trans. Fredy Perlman and John Supak, Black & Red, Detroit, MI, 1983

Dobraszczyk, Paul, *Future Cities: Architecture and the Imagination*, Reaktion, London, 2019

Douglas, George H., *Skyscrapers: A Social History of the Very Tall Building in America*, McFarland & Co., London and Jefferson, NC, 1996

Ehrenreich, Barbara, *Fear of Falling: The Inner Life of the Middle Class*, Pantheon Books, New York, NY, 1989

Eskilson, Stephen, *The Age of Glass: A Cultural History of Glass in Modern and Contemporary Architecture*, Bloomsbury, London, 2018

Forty, Adrian, *Words and Buildings: A Vocabulary of Modern Architecture*, Thames & Hudson, London, 2000

Foucault, Michel, *Ethics: Subjectivity and Truth. The Essential Works of Foucault, 1954–1984, Vol.1*, ed. Paul Rabinow, trans. Robert Hurley et al., The New Press, New York, NY, 1997

Garrett, Bradley L., *Explore Everything. Place-Hacking the City*, Verso, London, 2013

Giedion, Sigfried, *Architecture, You and Me: The Diary of a Development*, Harvard University Press, Cambridge, MA, 1958

Giedion, Sigfried, *Building in France, Building in Iron, Building in Ferroconcrete* (1928), trans. J. Duncan Berry, Getty Centre for the History of Art and the Humanities, Santa Monica, CA, 1995

Goethe, Johann W. von, *Autobiography of Goethe: Truth and Poetry Relating to My Life* (1848), trans. John Oxenford, The Floating Press, Auckland, 2008

Goetz, Alisa (ed.), *Up, Down, Across: Elevators, Escalators, and Moving Sidewalks*, Merrell, London and New York, NY, 2003

Gowers, William R., *A Manual of Diseases of the Nervous System*, 3rd edn, Blakiston, Philadelphia, PA, 1907

Graham, Stephen, *Vertical: The City from Satellites to Bunkers*, Verso, London, 2016

Haacke, Paul, *The Vertical Imagination and the Crisis of Transatlantic Modernism*, Oxford University Press, Oxford, 2021

Hambourg, Maria M. and Phillips, Christopher (eds), *The New Vision: Photography between the World Wars*, The Metropolitan Museum of Art, New York, NY, 1989

Han, Byung-Chul, *The Transparent Society*, trans. Erik Butler, Stanford Briefs, Stanford, CA, 2015

Heynen, Hilde, *Architecture and Modernity: A Critique*, MIT Press, Cambridge, MA, 1999

Huizinga, Johan, *Homo Ludens: A Study of the Play-Element in Culture* (1938), Roy Publishers, New York, NY, 1950

James, Catherine, *Falling for Gravity: Invisible Forces in Contemporary Art*, Peter Lang, Oxford, 2018

Jameson, Fredric, *Postmodernism, or The Cultural Logic of Late Capitalism*, Duke University Press, Durham, NC, 1991

Judd, Dennis R. and Fainstein, Susan S. (eds), *The Tourist City*, Yale University Press, New Haven, CT, 1999

Kane, Josephine, *The Architecture of Pleasure: British Amusement Parks 1900–1939*, Ashgate, Farnham, 2013

Kant, Immanuel, *Critique of Judgment* (1790), trans. Werner S. Pluhar, Hackett, Indianapolis, IN and Cambridge, 1987

Kellner, Douglas, *Media Spectacle*, Routledge, London, 2003

Kierkegaard, Søren, *The Concept of Anxiety: a simple psychologically orienting deliberation on the dogmatic issue of hereditary sin* (1844), ed. and trans. Reidar Thomte with Albert B. Anderson, Princeton University Press, Princeton, NJ, 1980

Kirby, Kathleen M., *Indifferent Boundaries: Spatial Concepts of Human Subjectivity*, The Guilford Press, New York, NY and London, 1996

Klingmann, Anna, *Brandscapes: Architecture in the Experience Economy*, MIT Press, Cambridge, MA, 2007

Kundera, Milan, *The Unbearable Lightness of Being*, trans. Michael H. Heim, Harper & Row, New York, NY, 1985

Lacan, Jacques, *The Seminar of Jacques Lacan, Book X: Anxiety, 1962–1963*, ed. Jacques-Alain Miller, trans. Adrian Price, Polity, Cambridge, 2014

La Mettrie, Julien O. de, *Traité du vertige avec la description d'une catalepsie hystérique*, Veuve de P.A. Garnier, Rennes, 1737

Latour, Bruno, *Down to Earth: Politics in the New Climatic Regime*, Polity Press, Cambridge, 2018

Lindner, Christoph, *Imagining New York City*, Oxford University Press, Oxford, 2015

Lonsway, Brian, *Making Leisure Work: Architecture and the Experience Economy*, Routledge, London, 2009

McCann, Colum, *Let the Great World Spin*, Bloomsbury, London, 2009

MacCannell, Dean, *The Tourist: A New Theory of the Leisure Class* (1976), University of California Press, Berkeley, CA, 1999

Mallgrave, Harry F., *From Object to Experience: The New Culture of Architectural Design*, Bloomsbury, London, 2018

Moore, Rowan (ed.), *Vertigo: The Strange New World of the Contemporary City*, Lawrence King, London, 1999

Morshed, Adnan, *Impossible Heights: Skyscrapers, Flight, and the Master Builder*, University of Minnesota Press, Minneapolis, MN, 2015

Mould, Oli, *Urban Subversion and the Creative City*, Routledge, London, 2015

Mumford, Lewis, *Sticks and Stones: A Study of American Architecture and Civilization*, Boni & Liveright, New York, NY, 1924

Nobel, Philip (ed.), *The Future of the Skyscraper*, Metropolis Books, New York, NY, 2015.

Nye, David E., *American Technological Sublime*, MIT Press, Cambridge, MA, 1996

Otero-Pailos, Jorge, *Architecture's Historical Turn: Phenomenology and the Rise of the Postmodern*, University of Minnesota Press, Minneapolis, MN, 2010

Page, Max, *The Creative Destruction of Manhattan, 1900–1940*, The University of Chicago Press, Chicago, IL, 2001

Parent, Claude, *Vivre à l'oblique* (1970), Nouvelles editions Jean-Michel Place, Paris, 2012

Pérez de Arce, Rodrigo, *City of Play: An Architectural and Urban History of Recreation and Leisure*, London, Bloomsbury, 2018

Perrin, Claude, *Le Vertige: Histoire et actualité*, Louis Pariente, Paris, 1988

Petit, Philippe, *To Reach the Clouds: My High-Wire Walk Between the Twin Towers*, Faber & Faber, London, 2002

Pine II, Joseph and Gilmore, James H., *The Experience Economy: Work is Theatre & Every Business a Stage*, Harvard Business School Press, Boston, MA, 1999

Porter, Nicole, *Landscape and Branding: The Promotion and Production of Place*, Routledge, London, 2015

Quinodoz, Danielle, *Emotional Vertigo: Between Anxiety and Pleasure*, trans. Arnold Pomerans, Routledge, London, 1997

Rattenbury, Kester, *The Wessex Project: Thomas Hardy, Architect*, Lund Humphries, London, 2018

Recalcati, Massimo, *Ritratti del desiderio*, Raffaello Cortina, Milan, 2012

Rice, Charles, *Interior Urbanism: Architecture, John Portman and Downtown America*, Bloomsbury, London, 2016

Ring, Jim, *How the English Made the Alps*, Faber & Faber, London, 2000

Robert, Alain, *With Bare Hands: The Story of the Human Spider*, 2nd edn, Maverick House, Dunboyne, 2008

Sartre, Jean-Paul, *Being and Nothingness: An Essay on Phenomenological Ontology* (1943), trans. Hazel E. Barnes, Routledge, London and New York, NY, 2003

Sebald, W.G., *Vertigo*, trans. Michael Hulse, Harvill Press, London, 1999

Serres, Michel, *Variations on the Body*, trans. Randolph Burks, Univocal Publishing, Minneapolis, MN, 2011

Shiqiao, Li, *Understanding the Chinese City*, SAGE Publications, London, 2014

Smith, Jacob, *The Thrill Makers: Celebrity, Masculinity and Stunt Performance*, University of California Press, Berkeley, CA, 2012

Soden, Garrett, *Falling: How Our Greatest Fear Became Our Greatest Thrill*, W.W. Norton & Co, New York, NY, 2003

Sontag, Susan (ed.), *A Barthes Reader*, Hill & Wang, New York, NY, 1983

Spencer, Douglas, *The Architecture of Neoliberalism: How Contemporary Architecture Became an Instrument of Control and Compliance*, Bloomsbury, London, 2016

Starobinski, Jean, *Portrait de l'artiste en saltimbanque*, Skira, Geneva, 1970

Steiner, Henriette and Veel, Kristin, *Tower to Tower: Gigantism in Architecture and Digital Culture*, MIT Press, Cambridge, MA, 2020

Stevens, Quentin, *The Ludic City: Exploring the Potential of Public Spaces*, Routledge, London, 2007

Tschumi, Bernard, *Architecture and Disjunction*, MIT Press, Cambridge, MA, 1996

Verhaege, Paul, *What About Me? The Struggle for Identity in a Market-Based Society*, Scribe Publications, London, 2014

Vidler, Anthony, *Warped Space: Art, Architecture, and Anxiety in Modern Culture*, MIT Press, Cambridge, MA, 2000

Wall, Christine, *An Architecture of Parts: Architects, Building Workers and Industrialisation in Britain 1940–70*, Routledge, London, 2013

Ward, Lynd, *Vertigo: A Novel in Woodcuts* (1937), Dover Publications, Mineola, NY, 2009

Weitzman, David, *Skywalkers: Mohawk Ironworkers Build the City*, Roaring Brook Press, New York, NY, 2010

Whipplesnaith [Noël H. Symington], *The Night Climbers of Cambridge* (1937), Oleander Press, Cambridge, 2007

Yamasaki, Minoru, *A Life in Architecture*, Weatherhill, New York, NY and Tokyo, 1979

Yardley, Lucy, *Vertigo and Dizziness*, Routledge, London, 1994

Young, Geoffrey Winthrop, *The Roof-Climber's Guide to Trinity. Containing a practical description of all routes*, W.P. Spalding, Cambridge, 1899

Young, Jock, *The Vertigo of Late Modernity*, Sage, London, 2007

INDEX

Note: *italic* page numbers indicate integrated black and white figures. Colour plates are designated as *pl.*

PICTURE CREDITS

FIGURES

1 Courtesy of the Library of Congress; 2 Photo by E.O. Beaman, courtesy of the Library of Congress; 3 Courtesy of Rijksmuseum; 4 Courtesy of Preus Museum; 5 Courtesy of the Miriam and Ira D. Wallach Division of Art, Prints and Photographs: Photography Collection, the New York Public Library; 6 Courtesy of Archivio Gabriele Basilico; 7 © Catherine Yass; 8 © Catherine Yass; 9 © The Trustees of the British Museum; 10 Courtesy of the Jerome Robbins Dance Division, the New York Public Library; 11 Courtesy of the Miriam and Ira D. Wallach Division of Art, Prints and Photographs: Photography Collection, the New York Public Library; 12 Courtesy of the Bibliothèque nationale de France; 13 Courtesy of the Bibliothèque nationale de France; 14 © Catherine Yass; 15 Masheter Movie Archive/Alamy; 16 Courtesy of Chris Hilton; 17 Photo by Weber, courtesy of the Library of Congress; 18 Courtesy of the Library of Congress; 19 © Robin Ward Savage; 20 Courtesy of the Library of Congress; 21 Courtesy of AJ Hackett International; 22 The Royal Society Publishing; 23 Photo by Davide Deriu; 24 Photo by Wouter Hagens, public domain image sourced from Wikimedia Commons; 25 Courtesy of the Canadian Centre for Architecture; 26 Photo by Bernard William Lee, public domain image sourced from Wikimedia Commons; 27 Courtesy of University of Westminster Library; 28 © Ezra Stoller/Esto; 29 Photo by Gilles Ehrmann, courtesy of Claude Parent Archives; 30 Photo by Davide Deriu; 31 Photo by Neurdein brothers (detail), courtesy of the Bibliothèque nationale de France; 32 Courtesy of the Library of Congress; 33 Photo by Balthazar Korab, courtesy of the Library of Congress; 34 Photo by Davide Deriu; 35 © SETE/Michel Denanc; 36 Photo by Mitch Hodiono from Unsplashs; 37 Photo by Cmglee, public domain image sourced from Wikimedia Commons

PLATES

1 © Navid Baraty; 2 © André Lichtenberg; 3 Courtesy of Archivio Gabriele Basilico; 4 © Chen Chenchen; 5 © Dimitri Venkov; 6 © Jean-Louis Blondeau/Polaris; 7 Photo by Brian Kersey/Alamy; 8 Photo by David Freeman; 9 Courtesy of the Swiss National Library; 10 Guy Bell/Alamy Live News; 11 Photo by Benoit Tessier, courtesy of Reuters/Alamy; 12 © Bradley Garrett; 13 © Tom Ryaboi; 14 Public domain image sourced from Wikimedia Commons; 15 Courtesy of Wire and Sky + Nathan Turner; 16 © Charles Rice; 17 Photo by Davide Deriu; 18 © Nigel Young/Foster + Partners; 19 © Ila Bêka and Louise Lemoine; 20 Photo by Lars Plougmann, public domain image sourced from Wikimedia Commons; 21 Photo by Pedro Szekely, public domain image sourced from Wikimedia Commons; 22 © CHIA Ming Chien; 23 Photo by eye35/Alamy; 24 Photo by Davide Deriu; 25 © Skydeck Chicago/Willis Tower; 26 © 360 Chicago; 27 Photo by Elvis Yang from Pexels; 28 Courtesy of One World Observatory